THE FILMS OF RICHARD LESTER

CROOM HELM STUDIES ON FILM, TELEVISION
AND THE MEDIA
General Editor: Dr Anthony Aldgate, The Open University

The Films of Richard Lester
Neil Sinyard

THE FILMS OF
RICHARD LESTER

NEIL SINYARD

CROOM HELM
London & Sydney

© 1985 Neil Sinyard
Croom Helm Ltd, Provident House, Burrell Row,
Beckenham, Kent BR3 1AT
Croom Helm Australia Pty Ltd, First Floor, 139 King Street,
Sydney, NSW 2001, Australia

British Library Cataloguing in Publication Data

Sinyard, Neil
  The Films of Richard Lester
  1. Lester, Richard
  I. Title
  791.43'0233'0924   PN1998.A3L479
  ISBN 0-7099-3347-9

Printed and bound in Great Britain

CONTENTS

Preface   vii

1. LEARNING THE CRAFT   1
   The Running, Jumping & Standing Still Film (1959); *It's Trad, Dad* (1962); *The Mouse on the Moon* (1963)

2. SWINGIN' SIXTIES   18
   A Hard Day's Night (1964); *The Knack* (1965); *Help!* (1965)

3. COMEDY TONIGHT, TRAGEDY TOMORROW   39
   A Funny Thing Happened on the Way to the Forum (1966)

4. TRILOGY OF DISILLUSIONMENT   48
   How I Won the War (1967); *Petulia* (1968); *The Bed-Sitting Room* (1969)

5. ALL FOR ONE AND EVERY MAN FOR HIMSELF   76
   The Three Musketeers (1973); *The Four Musketeers* (1974)

6. HOLDING THE COUNTRY TO RANSOM   91
   Juggernaut (1974)

7. FAME AND MISFORTUNE   106
   Royal Flash (1975); *Robin and Marian* (1976); *Butch and Sundance: The Early Days* (1978)

8. MIXED BATHING   138
   The Ritz (1976)

9. ROMANCE AND REVOLUTION   143
   Cuba (1979)

10. MEN AND SUPERMEN   154
    Superman II (1981); *Superman III* (1983)

Filmography   164

Index   170

PREFACE

The films of Richard Lester have something for everyone. He has made musicals, farces, historical romances, adventures both ancient and modern, political thrillers, war films and a western. His budgets have ranged from seventy pounds (*The Running, Jumping & Standing Still Film*) to approximately 25 million dollars (*Superman II*). Some of his films (like *A Hard Day's Night* or *The Three Musketeers*) have been received as amongst the most instantly accessible and popular of modern films, whilst others (like *How I Won the War*, or *Cuba*) have a forbidding, eccentric obliqueness whose expressive originality only becomes apparent with the passage of time. Films such as *The Knack*, *Petulia* and *Juggernaut* have an intense immediacy that seems to catch on the wing the transient spirit of a particular period and place, and establish Lester as one of the cinema's sharpest chroniclers of contemporary society. Yet he is also one of the cinema's most adventurous time-travellers, exploring, for example, Ancient Rome in *A Funny Thing Happened on the Way to the Forum*, England in the Middle-Ages in *Robin and Marian*, the France of Louis XIII in the *Musketeers* films, and the American West of the nineteenth century in *Butch and Sundance: The Early Days*. The sheer variety of style and tone in Lester — from Dumas to Doomsday, from farce to tragedy — is one of the major attractions of his work.

At the heart of this diverse body of work lies an intriguing paradox. Lester is an entertainer, a comedian, a man with a capacity, as Jules Feiffer once put it, for 'making a film your friend'. Yet he has also made some of the darkest, most densely intellectual films of the mainstream contemporary cinema. He wants to divert an audience but he also wants to provoke them and make them work. He makes films for instant consumption, intimating that he regards them as disposable objects, but he packs them with such a busy surface and soundtrack as to defy assimilation on a single viewing. Although often approached as the products of a knockabout farceur with modest satirical aspirations, Lester's films are occasionally scathingly misanthropic, where compassion stands momentarily aghast at human callousness. Throughout his career so far, he has juggled judiciously with different potentialities within himself as a film-maker and within the cinema as an industry, for the most part successfully reconciling popularity with profundity and box-office with self-expression.

Born in Philadelphia in 1932, Lester was an intellectually preco-cious child who entered university at the age of fifteen and grad-uated with a degree in clinical psychology four years later. He quickly landed a job at a local TV station and rose rapidly to the position of television director, giving up such lucrative security for a trip abroad, during which he made a scanty living from writing, tuning pianos and busking. ('I used to play guitar in Spanish cafés and would put three pesetas in a cap at the start of my performance and, at the end, I'd look down and there'd be only two left.') At a point of near-starvation and when he needed a place where English was the native language, he arrived in England in May 1955, with three years' television experience behind him, just at the time when commercial television was opening. He had no difficulty in finding work and he quickly made contact with people such as Peter Sellers, Alun Owen and Spike Milligan, who were to play an important role in the early stages of his film career.

The career has been running, jumping and only occasionally standing still ever since. The most difficult period was the time between 1968 and 1973, after the failure of *The Bed-Sitting Room* and before *The Three Musketeers* rescued his career from the dol-drums. Ostensibly, this period represents a break of continuity, the contemporary comedies and musicals that dominated the output in the sixties being displaced by the historical romances of the seven-ties. For some it represents a decisive *qualitative* break, with (according to taste) the modish early work being displaced by a con-templative maturity or, alternatively, the audacious vitality of the sixties giving way to conventional commercialism. Lester denies that there was a significant stylistic shift, but offers a straightforward explanation for the change of pace and material. 'Films reflect their times, it's as simple as that,' he says.

> The films of the early sixties were responding to a feeling that anything could be achieved and that there was a new opportunity for the structure of life in England. The seventies was a period of

negativism and disenchantment, so naturally the response was to do period and historical films. There are references to our times but it's indirect as opposed to being on the surface.

For all the superficial differences between the two decades, Lester has preserved a remarkable consistency of outlook throughout his films. A distinctive social vision has been conveyed through a probing intelligence and a remarkably flexible and versatile technique. Two quotations seem to me particularly applicable to fundamental areas of his work. The first is that exchange in Brecht's play, *Galileo Galilei*, where one of the disillusioned disciples says to Galileo, 'Unhappy is the land that has no heroes,' to which Galileo replies: 'Unhappy is the land that *needs* a hero.' Lester's films are fascinating analyses of societies that are either without heroes, or place intolerable burdens on the heroes they espouse, or worship people who are patently unworthy of their esteem. The second is Lester's own comment, 'Comedy films are desperately serious to me.' It is not simply a statement of the hard work and thought required for successfully putting over a comedy routine, but a declaration that comedy is Lester's instrument for making a serious statement that could not be made so effectively in any other way. I might add that, if there is one quotation that underpins the book, it is James Monaco's contention in *American Film Now* (Plume 1979) that Richard Lester is 'the world's most underrated director'. I hope that this book will go some way towards rectifying this underestimation.

For help and encouragement at various stages of the writing, I would like to thank the following people: Tony Aldgate, David Castell, Melanie Crook, Dave Hutchison, Scott Murray, David Shipman, Adrian Turner and Pete Walsh. As always, at all stages of the book, my wife Lesley, who has given me support and stimulation of incalculable value. My final thanks go to Richard Lester: for his kindness in granting me lengthy interviews with him (all unattributed quotations in the book are from these); for his generosity in providing stills for the book; and, above all, for his films, which have given me as much pleasure as those of any director of his generation.

Neil Sinyard

Chapter ONE

LEARNING THE CRAFT

The Running, Jumping & Standing Still Film

The Running, Jumping & Standing Still Film was made on a couple
of Sundays at a cost of £70, using (and essentially testing) a 16 mm
camera that had been bought by Peter Sellers. It was made solely for
the amusement of the participants, with Lester writing the music, a
friend writing the titles, and Bruce Lacey 'borrowing' the props
from Granada Television (where he worked at that time). However,
Sellers showed the short to the film critic of the *Daily Express*, on
whose recommendation it was submitted to and exhibited at the
Edinburgh Film Festival. It subsequently won a prize at the San
Francisco Festival and was eventually nominated for an Academy
Award, to date Lester's only Oscar nomination. It has been running
and jumping ever since. Rarely has a squib shown such powers of
endurance.

The manner of its execution and exhibition was eccentric, and
eccentricity is its theme. At the time the humour of mad Englishness
was being celebrated with great popularity by the Goons on the
radio and, to a lesser extent, by N.F. Simpson in the theatre (the
Monty Python team were particularly to continue this tradition of
cheerful illogicality and pugnacious zaniness). Basically the film is
about the English Sunday, and a look at what hobbies people take
up to entertain themselves on the cheap. It not only observes this: it
is this itself. It is a perfect marriage of form and content.

The cross-section offered of the leisure and recreation studies of
the English is suitably bizarre. Mrs Mopp is seen vigorously scrub-
bing a field. An outdoor enthusiast (Spike Milligan) sets up camp,
whilst an athlete (David Lodge) jogs and does exercises. A long-
sighted violinist reads his score through a telescope and then cycles
across to the music stand to turn the pages. An amateur photographer (Mario Fabrizi) develops his film instantly by submerging it
in a pond, whilst a painter (Richard Lester) is guided in his artistic

1

endeavours by the numbers drawn on his model's face. A game-keeper (Peter Sellers) is fleetingly glimpsed wearing a frogman's snorkel and flippers, and he is to encounter a man who has put a gramophone record on the nearest flat surface and then raced round and round it with a needle to reproduce the sound. Most ambitiously, Britain's first astronaut (Graham Stark) is spearheading his country's maiden space-launch in a precarious kite that is being pulled by enthusiastic volunteers at the end of a long length of rope. These motley madmen are observed by a man (Leo McKern) through a field glass who, having punched the grounded astronaut, retires to his caravan, sprays his throat with his door knob, and settles into his bed.

All of these enthusiastic amateurs seem to be solitaries. Even the painter and the astronaut are using other people for their own purposes rather than with any intention of sharing their pleasures. Their faces are set and unsmiling and the film observes in similarly dead-pan fashion the incongruous seriousness of the British at play. Nevertheless, although solitaries, these people keep disturbing or falling over each other, as if the world is so full of such weird antagonists that there is not room enough for each to develop his own diversion without collision.

Lester makes enterprising play with these intersections of idiosyncrasy. In one typical gag, myriad meanings of the word 'shot' collide in one image: that shot of the shot-putter's shot being shot down by the over zealous gamekeeper. The most extended joke of collision comes near the end when Graham Stark sidles forward from the distance into close-up at the behest of a beckoning finger foreground left of the frame, only to be thumped from the opposite side by a boxing glove. It anticipates a similar gag in *The Knack*, when a surveyor's directions to his partner become confused with his courteous instructions to Rita Tushingham on how to find the YWCA, with the result that his partner, in the deep background of the shot, obediently disappears down a man-hole. Both jokes offer a light but potent little parable on the bruising fate that might await those who too trustingly allow themselves to be directed by others.

There are a number of other pointers to Lester's future. The irreverent use of the Union Jack (it is draped around Graham Stark's ill-fated flying machine) prefigures similar such usages in, for example, *It's Trad, Dad* and *Royal Flash*. It is Lester's way of signalling an ironic perspective of England's position on the world stage. Her attempted entry into the space age in *The Running*,

Jumping & Standing Still Film is an act of mad chauvinism, the flag an incongruous and deluded symbol of national greatness, the kite as substitute satellite a signifier of Britain's actual status now in comparison with a superpower like America. Lester is to return to the theme of the little state with big ideas in his space-race comedy, *The Mouse on the Moon*. The image of failed flight touches and amuses Lester much more than any successful soaring — that is, *delusions* of grandeur attract the dramatist in him much more than grandeur itself. This is something to bear in mind in relation to *Superman II*, and Lester's interest in Superman when vulnerable and grounded and displaying human confusion rather than super-human powers.

In general atmosphere, the short is probably closest to *The Bed-Sitting Room* of Lester's subsequent films. There is the vacant setting and the same intermittent elements of disquiet, with odd little outbursts of violence — a duel, a fight — as various English obsessives nervously cross each other's paths. The character of the humour also anticipates the later film: subdued surrealism, formally controlled and calm, and with an interest in following minute behavioural quirks rather than a strict plot.

The main allusions to Lester's later career are perhaps less to do with specific detail than with overall ambience. The short is word-less and plotless, and this discloses a number of things which are to become more apparent about Lester as his career develops: his enduring respect for the routines and visual inventiveness of silent comedy, his disdain for linear narrative and his fondness for the absurd. Also it is a short with absolutely no waste. Every shot exposed is in the finished film. Even then he was proclaiming his aversion to excess footage, and his capacity to work with quick efficiency.

The film has been likened to Jean Vigo and early Luis Buñuel and credited with replacing 'Titfield type nostalgia by an indefinable quality of rage, at betrayal by the smug inadequacy of one's cultural patrimony'.[1] Such approaches seem rather ponderous attempts to turn a trifle into a three-course meal. Although there are hints of the darker undercurrents that Lester will explore in later comedies, the short is essentially a nonchalant *divertissement*, with Lester's cool jazzy score accentuating the light tone, as does the cheerful call of the cuckoo over the soundtrack to convey the mental state of the characters. (A similar call is to accompany Spike Milligan in one of his appearances in *The Three Musketeers*.)

'It was all mates in a field,' says Lester. It is a remark which evokes that celebrated moment of release for the Beatles in *A Hard Day's Night* when they banish their feelings of claustrophobia by indulging in crazy games in a field, whilst 'Can't Buy Me Love' bounces ecstatically over the soundtrack. It is a moment when they can temporarily forget about being superstars and just be ordinary lads spontaneously enjoying themselves. *The Running, Jumping & Standing Still Film* is an anticipation of that spirit, and a reminder of the fun that filming can be before you get into the world of stars, big budgets, distribution deals and special effects. It is a long way from that to the multi-million dollar productions of *Superman II and III.* But the spirit of delight, first displayed on that field, has never deserted Lester's filming.

It's Trad, Dad

'After the success of *The Running, Jumping & Standing Still Film* and the Academy Award nomination,' Lester recalled, 'I went roaring around, saying "I'm a film director" to a lot of people, and they would look at the short and say: "It's very funny — if we ever want a full-length version of that, we'll call you". Well, to this day, nobody's called me for *that*.'

However, he was called by producer Milton Subotsky about a project called *It's Trad, Dad*. Subotsky had seen the short and a 30-minute pilot Lester had made called *Have Jazz, Will Travel*, which was a mixture of documentary techniques and modern jazz. Having a tradition of giving first-time directors a chance, Subotsky thought Lester would be a good director for his new film. When Lester was first given the complete script (about the attempts of two teenagers to attract a Dixieland band to their staid New Town) it was so thin that Lester thought it was merely a synopsis. The *raison d'être* of the film is to fit in 26 musical numbers in the space of about an hour and a quarter. The film was shot in three weeks at a cost of £50,000, with Lester also travelling to New York at his own expense to shoot a 'Twist' sequence (the dancing rage of the time) that would be an added novelty to the final film. He was, he says, 'moderately free' to choose his own performers, though, 'to my utter shame, I rejected George Melly, because he never sang in tune. Not that the others did, but George was even more noticeable.'

In order to have a sufficient amount of footage for a feature-length film with a minimal plot on a three-week schedule, Lester opted for shooting with multiple cameras, a technique he still uses. The shooting strategy consisted of having three cameras filming each musical number three times, giving the director a variety of visual and editing possibilities; and of having an adaptable honey-comb-shaped set which was economical enough to be accommodated on one sound stage and flexible enough to provide different and appropriate backdrops for each performance. The film's visual imagination took critics somewhat by surprise. Alexander Walker was struck by the disproportionate inspiration to be found in what sounded like an unpromising assignment;[2] John Cutts delighted in the experience of seeing it 'surrounded by personalities basking in the light of their own image with obvious adoration';[3] Philip French was to describe it as 'extraordinarily inventive', one of the most imaginative British movies of the decade.[4] In *The Times*, David Robinson referred to 'Lester's immoderate interest in technical tricks — speeded up action, multiple exposures, eccentric angles, tricky masking and so on,' but had to admit that 'it is all done with such frank enjoyment and at such a determined pace that criticism is disarmed'.[5] Criticism was not often to be so 'disarmed' at Lester's work, and the director has commented somewhat ruefully that 'I've had the best reviews out of *It's Trad, Dad* that I've ever gotten'.[6]

With a cast that includes Craig Douglas, Helen Shapiro, Acker Bilk, Chubby Checker and Gene Vincent, the film nowadays looks more of a period piece than *Robin and Marian*. But it must be remembered that the British pop musical of the early sixties was instrumental in giving an important impetus to the careers of such fine directors as Lester, John Boorman, Sidney Furie and Peter Yates. The datedness of *It's Trad, Dad* is part of its appeal as well as the price Lester willingly pays for an indelible record of a specific time, place and event.

The film is not only a period piece, however, having, within its own modestly defined limits, enduring qualities. There are three particular areas which warrant closer study: the filming of the musical numbers; the vitality of the film's visual humour; and less overt, but clearly signalled, its cynical observation of the pop music business, and its astute perception of aspects of the generation gap and of modern Britain. 'I prefer the social attitudes of the young people to the disapproval of their parents,' Lester was quoted as saying at the time. 'If you deal with a subject then you have to take sides somewhere so I've chosen the side which I have the most sympathy for'.[7] In this, the film can be compared with another modest and distinguished film of the same period, Clive Donner's *Some People* (1962), and also with the tenor of all Lester's early films, which are all vigorously on the side of youth.

If the main purpose of the film is to cram in as many musical numbers as possible by as many popular performers as feasible, Lester is to be commended for the way the musical virtuosity of some of the performers is allied to a corresponding technical virtuosity of direction, photography and editing. He might have been forgiven for an essentially static presentation of the numbers, but the musical sequences are wittily and exhilaratingly put together. The Brooke Brothers sing 'Double Trouble' surrounded by pictures of themselves which are edited into even greater prominence when the film cuts in a manner matching the rhythmic flourish of the music. It is a nifty elaboration of the self-adoration lurking in both song and delivery, the style providing an appropriate support for a performance that oozes glutinous narcissism. Alternatively, Gene McDaniels' rendering of the Burt Bacharach song, 'Another Tear Falls' is much moodier, shot in shadow, smokey, with slow dissolves which correspond to the performer's rendering of sorrow and inner disintegration. Del Shannon's 'She Never Talked About Me' is filmed in emphatic close-up as befits the song's blatantly egotistical theme, whilst John Leyton's 'Lonely City' is introduced by a shot of the singer seen through a circular window like a disc. The romantic lyric is undercut by Leyton's casual smoking between vocals, so that a sense of boredom seeps into the recording experience. It is a tiny shaft of disenchantment — a quick glimpse of the *routine* of stardom — that is to infiltrate the film quite strikingly on subsequent occasions.

Lester particularly enjoys himself on those numbers which afford opportunities for instrumental wizardry. He himself was at that time an accomplished musician, having written the score for *The Running, Jumping & Standing Still Film* and music for commercials, including a score for an advertisement for Aero chocolate directed by Joseph Losey. (He was originally asked to write the score for Losey's *The Criminal* until circumstances prevented him from doing this and the assignment was taken over by John Dankworth.) The film is full of details of the instruments and close-ups of nimble fingers that become mini-tributes to musical prowess, moments which encapsulate the professional's sheer enjoyment of music-making. There is also recognition of some of its hazards, like the wry smile shared between the jazz musicians as one of Acker Bilk's men fluffs a difficult note. Terry Lightfoot and his band perform 'Tavern in the Town', the screen sectionalised for visual variety and virtuosity; the Temperance Seven play and perform 'Let's Have A Dream', with vocalist Paul McDowell delivering the song in English before giving a version in French, unhelpfully accompanied by French subtitles.

Acker Bilk's big number is 'Frankie and Johnny'. This is accompanied by an inset of stills that illustrate the plot of the song, with a judge transporting Frankie to jail riding a camel with a Union Jack on its back. The performance is decorated with differently angled close-ups of the apparatus of the Bilk mystique (the cigarette, the bowler, the bottle of cider). Visual interest is sustained through negative shots and by placing wire mesh in front of the camera, giving the impression, as Philip French noted, 'either of newsphotos or Lichtenstein prints'.[8] The film ends in a blaze of trad triumph, with Otillie Patterson belting out 'Down By the Riverside' ('ain't gonna study war no more,' she sings — an early hint of a key Lester preoccupation) and 'When the Saints Go Marching In', with editing and music marching often to the same rhythm. The overall vivacity and the unconventional, youthful style are clearly laying the ground for the association with the Beatles and the excellence of *A Hard Day's Night* and *Help!* There is a lightness of touch, a feeling of a director on top of, and not encumbered by, his technical toys.

As well as the inventiveness of the musical presentation, the film is equally enlivened by the quirky humour of *The Running, Jumping & Standing Still Film*. All the more remarkable, of course, because the actual crowding of the narrative with musical performance does not permit much room for incidental humour of character or behaviour. Nevertheless, there are some nice touches which deflate certain hallowed British institutions. The Town Hall Committee ('men dedicated to the principles of democratic action') are first seen dealing out playing cards as if they were agendas. During the proceedings the secretary's earphone, which has seemed on first sight to be a hearing aid, is actually connected to her transistor radio playing pop music and the Mayor petulantly swipes it with his gavel (which we have seen him using earlier as a nutcracker). All this is in contrast to the external dignity of these people, in which an appropriately adjusted flag on the Mayor's Rolls Royce indicates when he is in residence. The BBC is represented as an institution in which the most prominent visual object is a model elephant stuck in a door;

where a bored announcer (played by Frank Thornton, who actually *is* the BBC in *The Bed-Sitting Room*) listens to the Test Match on his radio; and where the Music Department has live musicians sprawled out on shelves and waiting for their call. There is a nice scene too in the New Town's café, where the manager butters bread to the tempo of Kenny Ball, and where, as part of the Mayor's plan to make the town seem 'nice and dignified', a gardener comes round to tidy up the café's potted plant and to snip and spray 'Flit' fly spray on a lettuce sandwich.

The other main source of the humour comes from the playful relationship Lester sets up between himself, the material and the film audience. Given the opportunistic premise of the film, he makes a positive virtue out of its *naïveté*, not by attempting to disguise it, but by frankly acknowledging and then playing with it. So captions are used: the primitive material is given some charm by being presented in the form of a comic. A narrator begins, 'Once upon a time . . .' in that deadly charming vein recognisable from the 'Look at Life' shorts, but the irony of this tone is soon discernible. We are told that the setting is a staid New Town which must remain nameless — and Lester obliges with a shot of a 'You Are Now Entering' sign with the name of the town missing. 'He's bound to have an idea, otherwise there's no picture,' says the narrator calmly about his hero; and when the hero and heroine need to get to the TV centre from their town, the narrator obligingly arranges for the backdrop to be changed. 'These are the recording studios,' says the narrator about the BBC, 'barred to all except highly skilled technical staff' — and in come the hero and heroine with the tea trolley. This kind of incongruity and contrast is clearly not very deep, but it is intriguing that Lester, even at this stage, is not interested in trying to create the illusion of a narrative event. He is much more concerned that an audience steps out of the event rather than into it, thinks rather than empathises and enjoys a game with cinematic conventions. The hero addresses the camera directly on more than one occasion and with particular feeling when he is obstructed yet again from entering the recording studio by an officious doorman (Hugh Lloyd). Turning to the camera, Craig Douglas says, 'Can't you do something about this character?', and obligingly, a hand produces a custard pie and thrusts it straight into the doorman's face.

In a way, what has so far been said might give the impression of a film offering a sprightly but rather unvaried jokiness. This would conform to an image often projected of Lester in his early films, and

beyond — that of a facile freneticism, what Manny Farber characterised as 'the day of the Lesteroid'.[9] Leslie Halliwell talks of 'style
going way over the top'[10] and the impression of zany superficiality is
expanded by Roy Armes. 'Façade is a key word in any summing up
of Lester's achievement,' he says,

> the bright glossy surface, the quirky visual gimmicks, the card-
> board cut-out characters endlessly swapping jokes, the cigarette
> commercial imagery and colour supplement decor . . . an act of
> conscious manipulation by a man used to the need to pep up the
> surface of his work to make it more immediately enjoyable.[11]

This criticism is very misleading and is no more true of *It's Trad,
Dad* than it is true of subsequent works like *Help!* or *The Knack*,
which have a serious undertone beneath their crackling surfaces.

One way this more melancholic side of *It's Trad, Dad* is signalled
is through the content of some of the songs. There is, for example, a
cumulative motif of tears — in the songs of Craig Douglas, Helen
Shapiro, Del Shannon and Gene McDaniels — which highlights the
theme of emotional disillusionment and an over-sensitive self
regard. The film sidesteps convention by not suggesting any fame or
fortune awaiting the two ambitious teenagers who have initiated the
action. They perform vigorously at the concert, but their local talent
is not discovered and popularised by the disc jockeys, and the narrator concludes somewhat sourly that 'they lived happily ever after
. . . at least 'til after the finale'. If the film's appeal is transient (in
the sense that it was made very much for its time), one should also
insist that transience is very much a major theme. Some prominence
is given in the final dance to a girl's frenzied trampling on a news-
paper, which makes its own comment on the flimsiness of fame and
the rapidity with which superstars become yesterday's headlines.
The theme is reinforced by the end titles being presented in the form
of newsprint photographs — paper, after all, tears easier than
celluloid.

Like a number of Lester's early films, the film is about the generation gap. The stuffiness of a stubborn older generation is represented by the Mayor's pictures of Albert and Victoria in his room
and by his malicious crushing of pop records in a press, checked only
by the rescue of a record by Lawrence Welk. This image of elderly
obstructiveness is reinforced by the police decision to set up a road
block to check the invasion of the performing artists — the desire of

the authoritarian elders to block the wishes of the young here given physical form. More incisively observed is the way in which the elders accede to the demands of the young when they see how it can be exploited for their own purposes. The Mayor is very quickly seduced by the attention given to him by the media as a liberal supporter of youth, and realises how this flattering image of him not only supports his vanity but can be used to improve his political standing. It is an early indication of something that was to become very topical in Britain: the power of the media, and particularly the new medium of television, to make or break political careers. This is the age of the satirical British television programme *TW3* (which so discomforted some politicians) and the dawning age of self-proclaimed television superstar Harold Wilson, who just happened also to be Prime Minister (Wilson's media self-consciousness was wickedly caricatured by Kevin Billington in his 1970 film *The Rise and Rise of Michael Rimmer*). If the film's verve anticipates swinging Britain and the Lester of *A Hard Day's Night*, its cynicism gives a hint of the exploitation of the youth movement that was to destroy this image in the late sixties and lead to the Lester of *How I Won the War* and *Petulia*.

The same kind of bite is seen in the presentation of the three disc jockeys, who were the three key purveyors of popular music in Britain at that particular time — Alan Freeman, David Jacobs and Pete Murray (neither at the time nor since a notably progressive trio). The initial response of all of them to the request for help of the teenagers is distinctly dusty. Alan Freeman wants nothing to do with them, but he will sign his autograph — his vanity is moved, if not his generosity. David Jacobs is preoccupied with his role at the 'Clique Club' (an evocative name for a BBC establishment). Pete Murray will not meet them until they practically disrupt his show. If this seems to be reading a lot into what might be a simple plot device, such doubts are surely silenced by the pointed presentation of them in the scene where they do agree to help. The scene takes place in front of a make-up mirror in a dressing room, and the associations of posturing narcissism and presenting a façade are fully appropriate to the conversation which follows. As befits the use of the mirror, the conversation is essentially about themselves and their own images ('You wear this?' says Freeman in disbelief at Murray's tie). 'Not bad publicity for us,' says Jacobs, supporting the idea of a concert. It is one of Lester's most concentrated scenes on one of his favourite comic themes — vanity. The self-preening of the DJs

('Disc jockeys? What do you want with them?' Acker Bilk has asked, as if they were some sort of alien species) connects directly with the self-adoration of the pop performers and the growing vanity of the TV director who, having announced 'I am the director of this programme', starts adjusting his tie and straightening his hair. Part of the reason why the wide-eyed idealism of Craig Douglas and Helen Shapiro does not become gushing and coy in the film is that the context in which it is placed is so contrastingly consumed with self-interest and self-absorption.

A final aspect of the film's critical sense is its evocation of the New Town itself. Much of this can be attributed to limited resources, but the stark stylisation does seem to be making a point of its own. The shops are strictly utilitarian, having no character, simply labelled as 'News', 'Travel', 'Discs', 'Bank' and 'Restaurant'. This might be a continuation of the film's comic-strip style. It is also a somewhat chilling image of the facelessness of modern Britain. Unmistakeably, Britain is a key theme of the film.

Ostensibly, the film's mood is bright and cheerful, and a celebration of the vivacity of the young. It is a film which seems to be ushering in a fresh breeze of youth and idealism, as the two teenagers achieve their concert and brighten up their dull surroundings. When the road blocks are broken and the performers start appearing, the arrival of the jazz band is signalled significantly by a rousing performance of 'Keep the Red Flag Flying'. It might be a prophetic blast, to usher in the 'progressive' Wilson Government and the trouncing of 13 years of Conservatism.

But *It's Trad, Dad* is no more to be judged simply on its surface attractions than any other Lester film. The film's sub-text is more cautionary: a perceptive premonition of how youthful idealism can be exploited for selfish ends by cynical elders pretending to endorse a new spirit. It is a sharp critique of a society where even its rebellions are converted to consumerism. In the slick conversion of the Mayor and the shady motivations of the DJs lie the seeds of doubt about the genuineness of the British Revolution that are to overtake Lester in the late sixties when he sees the dream collapsing in cynicism, selfishness and violence.

The Mouse on the Moon

When the Duchy of Grand Fenwick's wine crop fails and financial

ruin seems imminent, Prime Minister Mountjoy (Ron Moody) proposes they ask the Americans for a loan for rocket research. He
really wants the money for his indoor plumbing, but the devious
Americans agree, reckoning that such a magnanimous gesture will
be a master-stroke of international diplomacy. The Russians react
by sending an actual rocket to Grand Fenwick. In the meantime, the
Duchy's own Professor of Science (David Kossoff) has discovered
that the volatile local wine which has caused the problem would
effectively fuel a launch to the moon, a discovery which instantly
outpaces the space research of the superpowers.

Lester was offered the job of directing *The Mouse on the Moon*
on the recommendation of Peter Sellers, so it is ironical that, when
the film came out, the principal source of complaint was the absence
of Peter Sellers. The film was designed as a sequel to the very successful Sellers film, *The Mouse That Roared*, directed by Jack
Arnold in 1959, in which Grand Fenwick had declared war on the
United States with the intention of immediately losing and gaining
all the advantages and financial aid traditionally offered to the
vanquished. The new film — the first of several sequels in which
Lester has been involved — was designed to duplicate the subdued
satire on English eccentricity and American diplomacy that had
proved such a winning formula.

Lester had little room for manoeuvre on areas of casting and
writing. He recalls that he worked for about a week with Michael
Pertwee re-writing the script, and that the 'wine vat jokes and everything with George Chisholm in it are mine'. His ingenuity was
mostly tested in eliciting a delightfully dithering performance from
Margaret Rutherford as Queen Gloriana XIII in two days, when it
was found that she was uninsurable (her doctor had said she was too
old to be working so hard and she had become so outraged at such
impudence that her blood pressure had soared). Lester's solution
was to shoot all her lines in close-up, he and the producer putting up
their salary to cover the insurance for those two days' shooting: once
they had that in the can, if Miss Rutherford was unable to carry on
filming, they could use a double. Happily, as it turned out, this was
not necessary. Thus a bemused Miss Rutherford was sat down on a
chair and asked to speak her lines, first to one side, then to the other,
whilst different backgrounds were wheeled behind her. As Lester
said: 'And all the while she's thinking, "I've suddenly discovered
the *Nouvelle Vague* way of film-making — and I'm not sure I like
it".'

Funnily enough, this separation of the performance from its context does not jar, because the Queen herself seems in a different world from her subjects anyway, her isolation further increased by the wooziness caused by her frequent imbibing of the local wine. She dozes through the Trooping of the Colour; ritually refers to 'My husband and I' (overlooking the fact that he is dead); and never quite seems to know whether she is opening a pig-breeders' convention or launching a battle-ship. The rocket, given to the Grand Fenwickians by the Russians for 'space research', remains 'that nasty great tin thing' to the Queen. When a flying tea-pot soars spectacularly into her royal bedroom, buoyed by the local wine, she responds to it unconcernedly as the most natural thing in the world. Whatever the trials of shooting, it is a nicely conceived and executed comic cameo, and not the only one in the film.

Lester was also restricted by having to use sets left over from a previous Cornel Wilde film at Pinewood (*Lancelot and Guinevere*). However, as he has subsequently proved, he has a sharp eye for what can actually be manipulated to his purposes. The film does not look lavish, but makes a virtue out of its cramped conditions. Grand Fenwick becomes a little like Swift's Lilliput. Ceremonies like the Trooping of the Colour look comically incongruous when done on such a miniature scale, so that the flag-bearer has to stoop to get his flag under the archway of Grand Fenwick. Yet the very absurdity of it makes a comment on small countries acting big. It is hard not to think of Grand Fenwick as (to borrow Raymond Durgnat's phrase) the 'Spirit of Great Britain',[12] acting out an anachronistic pomp in a post-imperial age. Grand Fenwick was founded by an Englishman, is 'the smallest and least progressive country in the world', and, it is said, 'clings loyally to her British traditions'.

The satire is particularly elaborated through one of the most inventive aspects of the film: Ron Moody's performance of Prime Minister Mountjoy. Whether cheating at croquet or justifying his tactic of extracting money from the Americans under false pretences ('The American tax-payer has *always* been deceived: it is his birthright'), Mountjoy is the liveliest character in the film. Moody plays him as a sprightly cross between Machiavelli and Harold Macmillan. The Macmillan parallels are energetically pursued. Mountjoy goes on the Duchy's own portable television station to proclaim to his people that he has 'led you into a situation where you have never had it so bad'. His crisis of confidence seems to chime in neatly with that of the 1962 Conservative government. 'They don't call me

Mountwonder anymore,' he muses, abstractedly catching a tomato thrown through his window by a demonstrator ('This week tomatoes — next week bombs'). Like Macmillan, Mountjoy even has a son whom he is grooming for a political career but who seems to be turning out quite disappointingly. 'He had all the makings of a great politician,' he muses. 'As a child he was fantastically sly and dishonest'. With the PM's job being a hereditary position and with madness being no obstacle to political advancement (a picture of an alarming Mountjoy ancestor stares wild-eyed from the wall), Mountjoy seems to symbolise the disreputable but inexorable continuity of the British Establishment.

It was an Establishment that Lester at this time felt was in its death-throes. The message is not put over as strongly as Lester would like in this film, but there are glimmerings of it, in the film's satire of the vaulting ambition and duplicity of the modern political state; in the presentation of members of the Establishment who are seen as either tired or corrupt; and in the characterisation of the young who are at least adventurous (like Mountjoy's son who wants to be an astronaut) and idealistic (like the Opposition leader's daughter, who protests at the inefficient and dishonest running of the country's affairs). Unfortunately, the romance between Bernard Cribbins's bashful hero and June Ritchie's pert heroine seems tentative and routine. The beatnik scene, with Cribbins dancing to Grand Fenwick's Victorian idea of a juke-box, is rather embarrassing. The anti-Establishment ideas are therefore projected less through the alternative energy of the young, as in *It's Trad, Dad* and later in *A Hard Day's Night* and *The Knack*, but through a satire on the cynicism and incompetence of the old. This does not completely work.

Reviewing the film at the time, a number of critics summoned up the spirit of Ealing. This is not surprising: writer Michael Pertwee had worked on a number of Ealing films; and Frankie Howerd's cameo and even Terry Thomas's flimsy camouflage as a spy recall a couple of comic highlights from the Ealing classic, *The Ladykillers* (1955). But the comfortable Ealing-esque humour of the script and the sharper more critical personality of the director do not go together. There is a neat little anti-authoritarian tract lurking in there somewhere but it is subsumed by the affectionate presentation of British quaintness and quirkiness. There are, for example, two amiable jokes about the renowned British tea-break. One interrupts a count-down ('we'll begin again after three'). The other occurs during a so-called Emergency Top Secret meeting at the Foreign Office, that is punctuated by the noisy interruption of a cleaning lady; by a discussion on whether the biscuit cupboard is locked; and by inordinate praise for an aged secretary, Smithers ('Excellent chap, that — a man to watch') because he has had the foresight to provide tea on a Saturday afternoon. British Intelligence is represented by Terry Thomas, which is an insult to British Intelligence but clearly a good-natured one. This is not displeasing and is sometimes funny but its tepid conservatism is alien to Lester's progressive sympathies. His other films are more sceptical of the older generation and the ties of tradition.

The humour about the British spreads more generally to a sardonic look at the theme of nationalism, as the Duchy of Grand Fenwick finds itself a pawn in an elaborate diplomatic game between the Americans and the Russians. The lunacy of the space race is indicated through a strict paralleling of the American and Russian scenes, with identical dialogue, similar rocket experts from Germany, and even a simultaneous split-screen launching. 'All super-powers are the same' is the implication. When the countries' representatives gather in Grand Fenwick, the film's off-beat attitude to nationalism is indicated by the variety of tunes which greet the dignitaries. The themes are all nearly, but not quite, national anthems: 'Rule Britannia' for the British; 'Song of the Volga Boatman' for the Russians; 'Columbia, the Gem of the Ocean' for the Americans. It is one of the many felicitous touches in Ron Grainer's witty score. The strategy of the film is to cut the super-powers down to size, through exposing the limitations of an over-complex technology (in contrast, the controls of the Grand Fenwick rocket are old-fashioned beer-pump handles) but also to show the absurdity of nationalistic obsession. Even the British newsreader, reporting the successful American space launch, has to insist at great length that it might not have been possible without the precision of a *British* wrist-watch worn by one of the astronauts.

The film has some attractive ideas, but it could have done with more incisive plotting. Lester was to make a more penetrating comment on the space race and the precariousness of détente in one scene of *Superman II*. The film is flawed by a modesty and sentimentality which Lester's approach can moderate but can never remove. Nevertheless, he packs the frame as much as possible with an accumulation of crazy detail. There are characteristic bits of comic business: hat collides with head as Mountjoy is reunited with son (a favourite Lester flourish which also appears in *Royal Flash*); a pigeon refuses to play messenger (a variation on the joke is to appear in *A Funny Thing Happened on the Way to the Forum*). Mario Fabrizi has an exuberant comic turn as Mountjoy's servant, equally sycophantic whether trimming his master's toe-nails, selecting his ties, or pouring his cold bath water from a silver salver. The Lester touch is also evident in details of music, design and colour. There are a number of scenes involving tiny musical ensembles (notably the GF brass band conducted with fervent melodrama by Clive Dunn) which invariably occur affectionately in his films. Comic details of design emerge in the sub-Edwardian interior of the Fenwickian rocket, which has hot-water bottles on the wall and sausages hanging from the ceiling, and also in small details of Fenwickian incompetence, such as the shot of the hen-coop where one notices that the label 'Thomas' has been corrected to 'Thomasina'. The use of colour adds a definite zip to the pro-ceedings, as when the Government and Opposition are visually contrasted by the black morning suits of the former standing out against the brown tweeds of the latter, or when Professor and astronaut step out of their rocket and are instantly assailed by multi-coloured garbage which has been dolefully pursuing them through space.

A parallel between the terminology of space and the terminology of plumbing is exhaustively elaborated. The British spy mistakes the word 'cistern' for 'system', and reads lunar rather than lavatorial implications into the sign: Blast Proof Evacuation Centre. When the Professor explains the principles of his rocket to the British Ambas-sador and talks of 'regenerating air by catalytic dissociation', the Ambassador promptly replies: 'How very unpleasant for you'. These jokes are actually thematically relevant — after all, the film is about the space race as money down the drain. It is also about how low nations are prepared to sink in order to have an advantage over each other. The film ends on a note of friction, with an argument about who landed first (not the only Lester film to end with an argument), and a parody of the RAF motto: 'Per Harmonium Ad Lunum'. This is translated as 'Together — Moonwise' i.e. toge-therness, on America's terms.

One can understand why Lester might be a little embarrassed by *The Mouse on the Moon*. But he has done a professional job. What is more, it introduced him to the producer Walter Shenson who, on the basis of Lester's work here, offered him the chance of directing the first Beatles picture. As a result, Lester's career was to soar as unexpectedly as the Fenwickian rocket.

Notes

1. See George Melly's *Revolt into Style* (Penguin, 1970) and Raymond Durgnat's *A Mirror for England* (Praeger, 1971).

2. *Evening Standard*, 29 March 1962.

3. *Films and Filming*, May 1962.

4. *Movie*, No. 14, Autumn 1965.

5. 29 March 1962.

6. Interview with Joseph Gelmis, *The Film Director as Superstar* (Doubleday & Co., 1970)

7. A radio interview, quoted in *Movie*, No. 14, Autumn 1965.

8. *Movie*, No. 14, Autumn 1965.

9. Manny Farber, *Negative Space* (Studio Vista, 1971).

10. *Halliwell's Filmgoers Companion*, 6th edn (Granada Publishing, 1979).

11. Roy Armes, *A Critical History of the British Cinema* (Secker & Warburg, 1978).

12. *Films and Filming* review, June 1963.

Chapter TWO

SWINGIN' SIXTIES

The Youth Trilogy

Richard Lester's films have a peculiar relationship with time. On the one hand, they can seem very much tied to the period in which they were made and so have a built-in obsolescence. As Lester said in a radio interview in the mid-sixties: 'I don't really have any desire for any of my films to go into time capsules. And I expect *A Hard Day's Night*, which I haven't seen for a year, to be absolutely dreadful now. Because it was of that period of the pop explosion'.[1] However, the films catch that moment in time with such intensity that they become a lasting document on the era, contributing to its mythology whilst simultaneously submitting it to an ironical critical scrutiny. These remarks are especially applicable to the three films that Lester made between 1964 and 1965 and what I would loosely call his Youth Trilogy — *A Hard Day's Night, The Knack* and *Help!* They should be discussed as a trilogy because together they comprise a response to a single phenomenon — that of 'Swingin' Britain' in the mid 1960s. If audiences now wished to remind themselves of what the spirit and the atmosphere of that time were — its exuberance, its vulnerable idealism — they could do no better than re-view these three films.

At the beginning of the decade, the literary critic and sociologist, Raymond Williams, had characterised Britain as a country still confused about democracy and the economy, and still not having come to terms with itself as a consumer society. According to Williams, Britain was still in the grip of an inertia that was partly to do with the exclusion of people from decisions which affected their lives, and still hopelessly muddled about class as it moved through a stage of transition from 'a social stratification based on birth to one based on money and actual position'.[2] However, with the collapse of confidence in its political peers as a result of events as diverse as Suez and the Profumo scandal, and with the corresponding cultural

attack that could be felt from voices as different as the new drama of
Osborne and Pinter to the satirical iconoclasm of *TW3*, the kind of
malaise that Williams had so cogently defined seemed at last to be
breaking down. Inertia and gentility were being displaced by energy
and social movement. A fading political order (Lord Home's Conservative government) was giving way to an ostensibly dynamic
alternative (the Labour government of Harold Wilson, with its talk
of technocratic revolution and its first hundred days of power which
would transform the face of British society). Even sexual attitudes
were being liberalised. As Philip Larkin expressed it poetically:

Sexual intercourse
Began in 1963,
Between the end of the Chatterley ban
And the Beatles' first LP.

Lester's 'trilogy' came in on the wave of that mood, expressing
the cockiness and confidence of a new generation that was no longer
intimidated by class and no longer awed by society's symbols of
authority and power. The three films are an indelible part of a
period in which London momentarily belonged to the young, and in
which England seemed momentarily the centre of the universe.
'There was an enormous sense of optimism that I felt in England
from 1962–3 on until 1967, which is when it started to go wrong, it
seems to me,' Lester told me. 'During that time, the films had a
sense of a response to a feeling that anything could be achieved, that
the class structure was breaking down, that there was a new opportunity for education and a new opportunity for the structure of life
in England.' The films elevated Lester from a position of compara-
tive obscurity to one of considerable fame and influence. They also
had the negative effect of casting a shadow over his subsequent critical reputation quite as pervasive and damaging as that of *Citizen
Kane* over the reputation and achievements of Orson Welles. (If this
comparison seems somewhat grandiose, it should be recalled that
Andrew Sarris was moved to describe *A Hard Day's Night* as the
'*Citizen Kane* of the juke-box musical').[3]
    The 'trilogy' must be seen as more than a fortuitously topical and
ephemeral response to a specific historical moment. The cinematic
qualities of the three films are solid and durable. Neither before nor
since have pop personalities in a musical been better served by their
director than the Beatles by Lester in *A Hard Day's Night* and *Help!*

The Knack remains not simply a joyous comedy about the contemporary sexual revolution, but a timelessly witty contrast of the morality of different generations. The films have a wholly individual sense of rhythm and quickness in the editing which bears out Lester's view that 'a director's editing style is based absolutely on his own metabolism'. They also have an original combination of anarchy and discipline, which gives ostensibly improvisational, formless material a solidity of structure and tone. They delight in the ambiguities and richness of language. In all three films the star is essentially the camera, a reflection of an era in which style might be said to have held precedence over substance, but also for Lester a characteristic modernist preoccupation with the manner as well as the matter of what is said. (One thinks of Ezra Pound's: 'I judge a poet's sincerity by his technique'.)

When the 'trilogy' first appeared, it was something of a commonplace to attribute the style and attitude of the films to the influence of the *Nouvelle Vague*. This was, and is, nonsense. It is true that Lester's 'trilogy' shared with Truffaut and Godard an emphasis on young people and real locations; an irreverent attitude to traditional tenets of narrative construction; and a delight in technical display (freeze-frames, jump-cuts, elaborate titles). *The Knack* could be compared to Truffaut's *Les Quatres Cents Coups* (1959) and *Jules et Jim* (1961) in its exuberant demonstration of the potentialities of the camera, and to Godard's *Une Femme Mariée* (1964) in its stylistic and thematic observations on consumerist society. But it could equally be likened to Losey's *The Servant* (1963) in its sense of relationships as a struggle for power; in its expressive use of games and mirrors; and in its response to decor which impedes, forms and reflects the characters, suggesting their temperament, narcissism and territorial instincts. It could equally be compared with Polanski's *Repulsion* (1965), in its observation of a quirky seething London from the point of view of an outsider, its air of sexual threat and black-and-white vision of oppressive males and passive females. One could even include Lester's 'trilogy' in a context which would embrace the anguished world of the poet-novelist Sylvia Plath. Unlike the trilogy, her works (most notably her famous poem, 'Daddy' in her posthumous collection, *Ariel*)[4] employ horror-film imagery to convey the impression of a mind at the end of its tether. But Plath's poems and Lester's 'trilogy' are comparable in that both achievements are a quintessentially sixties' response to what they see as a worn-out and discredited older generation, with its crippling legacy of World War Two, Cold War hostilities, militarism and the Bomb. To talk of Lester's 'trilogy' in terms of '*Nouvelle Vague* tricksiness' is not only simplistic: it neglects innumerable cultural crosscurrents that were much closer to home.

The fact is that the cultural impulses and influences acting upon Lester — which made his interaction with the Beatles and the 'swingin' London' scene such an explosive and momentous one — were extraordinarily complex and various. In attempting to summarise Lester's qualifications for immersing himself so successfully in the 'pop style', George Melly listed his particular qualities as follows: 'a sophisticated innocence, a brilliant technique, an encyclopedic knowledge of twentieth-century avant-garde experiment and a shameless magpie-like eclecticism'.[5] I would endorse those and add a few others of equal importance. Lester was a director in tune with the advanced modernist tendencies of early sixties cinema, which enabled the 'trilogy' to transcend the usual drabness of pop films and be taken seriously by the intelligentsia. Like more obviously serious contemporary British directors such as Lindsay Anderson, Tony Richardson and John Schlesinger, he was eager to make use of the vitality of contemporary British drama, which influenced Lester's collaboration with Alun Owen and Charles Wood and gave the films an unusual verbal freshness and resonance. Lester was also knowledgeable about Modern Art and the films brilliantly reflect this, having the multiple perspectives of Cubism as well as something of the iconography (its visual zaniness) and ideology (its sense of social revolt) of Surrealism. There was a sense of a young director pushing the expressiveness of film to the limits, of crowding images and soundtrack to bursting point. 'I believe in a complex structure in film-making,' Lester was saying around this time. 'I like films that stretch me to the utmost and I like to stretch film, as I know it, to the utmost; to pack as much into it as possible on as many different levels as possible so that any ten people in an audience are seeing ten different films'.[6]

Allied to Lester's intellectual sophistication was an equally valuable popular sensibility. Lester had gained experience in the ITV boom, had practised and learned his trade through his work on commercials, but had not lost his sense of the ironies of exploitation. So the films had the instant impact of pop but they used this impact wittily and ironically rather than superficially and sensationally. They employed the techniques of the television commercial: 'that jump-cut from wish to fulfilment,' as Ronald Bryden evocatively put it.[7] But they employed them in contexts that were either funny and distancing (as in the commercial break in *Help!*) or in a way that clearly revealed the fantasy behind the reality (as in the opening of *The Knack*, whose imagery is drawn from the commercial packaging of sex appeal and is not the situation itself but an extreme subjective fantasy triggered by sexual envy). The critic David Sylvester at this time made a distinction between what he termed 'coke culture' (something that was popular, immediate, transient) and 'wine culture' (something that was aesthetic, mature, lasting).[8] Part of the appeal of Lester's 'trilogy' at the time was that it had something for both palates.

Above all, Lester brought to these films what I would call a 'temperamental authenticity' which was quite distinct from any pop film-maker before him. It was not simply that he liked pop and that he was musically literate, which partially accounts both for the enthusiastic presentation of the musical numbers and the rhythmic dexterity of their filming. It was not only that he was a young film-maker of 32, which contrasted strikingly with the Hollywood directors who were making youth pictures at the time and whose average age, as calculated by the critic Robin Bean, was 65.6 years old.[9] It was basically that Lester was sympathetic with the young. He allied himself with the forces of progressiveness against the forces of stagnation, favoured vitality and sexuality against the grey values of the Establishment, and a living art against a dead art. The friction sparked between the man, the material and the moment produced an aesthetic verve that took its form from the feeling. The trilogy is Lester's Utopian vision of modern Britain. As we shall see, it is a Utopia with cracks.

A Hard Day's Night

During an exchange of letters over the London opening of *Superman II*, Lester commented to me: 'I'm very glad you managed to see it surrounded by children. I saw it at the premier and was deafened by the rattling jewelry.' The humour is characteristic. So is the ghost it conjures up: that of the Beatles' epoch-making Royal Variety performance in November 1963 and John Lennon's quip to the audience during his introduction to 'Twist and Shout' — that those in the cheaper seats could respond by clapping their hands and those in the more expensive ones by rattling their jewelry.

Lester's life and career have been deeply marked by his film asso-ciations with the Beatles. He once said: 'In thirty years' time no matter what films I make or what service I do for the community, when I die the placards will read "Beatles director in death drama".'[10] Lester had been cast for the film by producer Walter Shenson, partly because of the facility he had already displayed in shooting musical numbers (*It's Trad, Dad*); partly because of their successful working experience on *The Mouse on the Moon*; and partly because the Goon-like surrealist humour of *The Running, Jumping & Standing Still Film* particularly appealed to the Beatles. Indeed, the evocative title of the film, *A Hard Day's Night* — a phrase that Ringo had drunkenly uttered one night and which Shenson seized on as ideal for the film — has something of the surreal flavour that is characteristic of Lester's work. (If the title seems surreal, the title song, written by Lennon and McCartney, had a gritty down-to-earth quality that cleverly matched another dimen-sion of the film, and was hailed by the poet Thom Gunn as a major breakthrough in pop realism: 'Where, by comparison, in a Frank Sinatra ballad is there any suggestion that he works for a living?')

The boys suggested Alun Owen as writer because he was talented and from Liverpool. He could with feeling write the kind of devasta-ting insult that Ringo flings at a policemen during the film: 'South-erner!' As it happened, Owen had worked before with Lester on a short-lived, ad-lib comedy show in the early days of ITV called 'The Dick Lester Show'. ('Short-lived' is something of a euphemism, it lasted one programme.) The Beatles thought the presence of Owen as writer would help avoid the usual clichés of the pop musical — weak romance, the 'talent show' and the kind of phoney excuses for musical interventions that John Lennon sends up deli-ciously in this film in his preamble to one of the numbers: 'Hey, kids, I've got an idea. Why don't we do the show right here!' The film was to be rooted in regionalism and realism. From this premise, it was decided at an early stage that the Beatles should play them-selves and that the film should adopt a reportage style of 'A day in the life of . . .'

This decision had a number of implications. Because the film had a semi-documentary concept, it allowed for a certain roughness and spontaneity of style, something very much to Lester's taste. Where most rock musicals had seemed ponderous and plodding in their visuals, *A Hard Day's Night* had the raw immediacy of ciné-verité. The film has a flexible but compact form that is loose enough for small cadenzas of character and comedy but taut enough to sustain attention. The first third leads to the moment of release in the field; the second third builds up the pressure on Ringo, to the point where he plays truant; and the last part is the convulsive final concert. (Lester has often talked of the value of having a tight time-structure on a film, which provides a tension of its own: he was not to work again within a similar structure until *Juggernaut*.) But the film never entirely loses the sense of a camera's casually following the boys on a typical day, responding to their fluctuating moods. The film is actually at its weakest when it tries to insert 'plot', notably in the uninteresting machinations of Paul McCartney's grandfather, unsympathetically played by Wilfred Brambell.

The 'day in the life of . . .' structure had implications not only for the film's style but also its material. In following the Beatles, Alun Owen was most struck by the amount of pushing and jostling they had to endure as a consequence of their adulation by the media. For Lester, the remark that stuck in his mind was John Lennon's reply to his question about how he'd liked Stockholm: 'It was a plane, a car, a hotel room and a sandwich'. Both Lester and Owen were impressed by the Beatles as a social phenomenon, whose assertive natural talent seemed to break down decades of working-class intimidation by accent, class and breeding (their encounter with the *Financial Times* reader on the train quickly establishes that: he is the class enemy but his pretension can be wittily deflated). But they were even more struck by the claustrophobia of their lives, the necessity of disguise to avoid being mobbed, the feeling of being imprisoned by their own fame. 'They were revolutionaries in a goldfish bowl,' said Lester,[11] and it is this that the film chooses to explore: not the characters of the Beatles (they are presented throughout as likeable innocents, whereas John Lennon said about their life at this time that it resembled *Fellini's Satyricon*)[12] but their situation of power without freedom. It is the finest example in Lester's work of something that is to occupy him a great deal in the future: the fate of superheroes, those idols whom a society chooses to worship (Flashman in *Royal Flash*, Robin Hood in *Robin and Marian*, Superman in *Superman II*), who find that their status is more curse than blessing, forcing them into a role which prevents them from leading a normal life. The theme of power without freedom is also to be elaborated on a much larger social scale in Lester's masterwork, *Petulia*.

Lester's films — and this is particularly true of the 'youth

trilogy', *How I Won the War* and *The Bed-Sitting Room* — are
sometimes best approached not as conventional narratives but more
as essays on a theme. The theme in *A Hard Day's Night* is
Beatlemania: its effect on young and old, on the media and on the
Beatles themselves. The phenomenon itself is most stunningly real-
ised in the final concert, the camera craning behind the Beatles and
zooming towards the audience in a virtuoso display that forges an
overwhelming emotional unity between performers and audience.
Stepping back one pace, the film also looks at the response of an
earlier generation to Beatlemania, and its observation here is cooler
and more cynical. Kenneth Haigh appears as a professional trend-
follower looking to identify and exploit the teenage market, thrown
by the mysterious youth language of George Harrison, and with a
rather disquieting contempt for the culture on which he fattens
himself.

In the brilliant press conference sequence, the media's tendency to
feed off the fame of the Beatles is even more marked. Whilst the
boys cannot get hold of any food and drink at this reception supposedly held in their honour, the press gorge themselves so zealously
that they do not even notice when the Beatles leave. This sequence is
now famous for the quick-witted verbal felicities of the Beatles. To
the question, 'How did you find America?', John Lennon answers,
'Turn left at Greenland'; to the question, 'What would you call that
hair-style you're wearing?', George Harrison replies, 'Arthur'. The
Beatles' skill at the satirical put-down was probably the thing that
caused so many critics of the time to think of the Marx Brothers,
though the connection was not often seen (as it should have been) in
terms of linguistic dexterity. More importantly, though, the
sequence represents a confrontation between the values of the 1950s
and those of the 1960s. The different social level of the press from
that of the Beatles is implied by their voices, their condescending
manner, their obsession with appearance: they stand for a class and
a period that have for the moment had their day. The Beatles' verbal
victories over them represent a (temporary) social victory as well.
The boys are looking forward in confidence, not looking back in
anger.

The greatest sequence in the film is the 'Can't Buy Me Love' romp
in the field. It is memorable for the sheer bounce of the number and
the way camera and performance combine to create a definitive
short ballet of youthful high spirits. But one should pay tribute
not simply to the sequence itself but to its whole preparation and

context. Before it, the Beatles have been pursued, pestered and pawed. They have been seen in train, car, hotel room, club, with hardly any fresh air. The sequence structurally represents a massive exhalation of breath which, to some extent, explains its feeling of release. It is prefaced by the boys' spotting a door marked 'Fire Escape', and as the camera's quick panning movement to the door lingers for a split-second on the word 'Escape', the opportunity for freedom is grasped and the boys burst out joyously into the open. It is as if the word itself has subconsciously generated that surge of energy. The ending of the sequence is also interesting. A burly middle-aged man appears, rather like the policeman at the end of Gene Kelly's 'Singin' in the Rain' routine and similarly representing the image of elderly authority calling a halt to an ecstasy of liberation. 'I suppose you know this is private property,' he says curtly — the voice of conformity and acquisition. The irony is that the status of the Beatles as *public* property is the thing that has driven them into this field. In the full context of Lester's sixties' films, it is an ominous moment.

Nevertheless, Lester keeps the tone of the film light and effervescent. There are numerous quick sight gags that keep the humour ticking over: the manager (Norman Rossington) fighting a losing battle with a milk carton and later momentarily convincing himself that John Lennon has disappeared down a plug-hole; a hapless magician (Derek Nimmo) who is covered with feathers and has to change the number of his disappearing doves from ten to nine when McCartney's grandfather heartily slaps him on the arm. A particularly endearing sequence has Ringo on his own, trying and failing to play, first, darts (his three arrows land, respectively, in a cheese sandwich, a pint of bitter and a parrot cage) and then Sir Walter Raleigh (his politely draped raincoat over a muddy path for the benefit of a young lady is to land her in a man-hole). The film is intelligent enough to show the limitations of being a Beatle, but determined nevertheless to sustain its optimism and high spirits.

If Beatlemania as a force is convincingly celebrated in *A Hard Day's Night*, one of the reasons is that the Beatles play themselves so well, whereas the other actors (excepting Victor Spinetti's brilliant cameo as a mohair-sweatered paranoid director) play their characters rather uneasily. It might make for an uncomfortable break in the style but the positive thing is that it makes the Beatles and what they represent seem that much more genuine and authentic than the slightly artificial context that surrounds them. In a way this authenticity is achieved through artifice. Alun Owen's skilfully contrives a script of sharp one-liners for the Beatles, so that their acting inexperience is not over-exposed: Lester's camera virtuosity *implies* a musical virtuosity that, at that time, was slightly flattering to them as musicians, if not as composers. But presenting the Beatles in the best possible light is not simply a strategy of the film, but its meaning. Everything in the film seeks to persuade you of their attractiveness as a focus of youth assertion, as Rebels without a Care. Rather than the *Citizen Kane* of the juke-box musical, I would call *Hard Day's Night* its *Battleship Potemkin*. The message is in the montage and the music, and the message is one of social revolution.

The Knack

In an oft-quoted remark, Lester has said that the difference between *A Hard Day's Night* and his following film, *The Knack* is that, whereas the former film was about four people who could communicate without speaking, the latter is about four people who speak to each other without ever communicating.[13] Awarded the Golden Palm at Cannes in 1965 (the first British film to be so honoured since Carol Reed's *The Third Man* in 1949), *The Knack* is at once a happening that takes place on the streets of London and an exuberant fantasia on the theme of youth and age.

The basic situation of Ann Jellicoe's original play is left intact. The sleek sexuality of Tolen (Ray Brooks) who has the knack of attracting girls, is contrasted with the frustrated longings of his landlord Colin (Michael Crawford) who does not have this knack. A new tenant, a lively Irishman by the name of Tom (Donal Donnelly), is less bothered about having or not having the knack than about painting rooms white. The household is completed by the arrival of Nancy (Rita Tushingham), searching for the London branch of the YWCA and upon whom Tolen agrees to demonstrate his infallible seduction technique whilst Colin takes notes.

The contrast in character is reinforced visually. Colin is a tea-drinking buffoon in a grey room whom Lester can use for broad slapstick counterpoint (Colin's tendency throughout to get wet or stuck on things is a naughty metaphor for the character's unhappy sexual frustration and fantasising). Tolen is a black seducer in a dark room, whose sun glasses, slim tie and leather gloves contribute to his cultivated aura of sexual mystery and menace. Tom's penchant for white creates a spatial and spiritual void for himself, though his constant talk of animals finds an echo in the predatory instincts of the characters and it leads to the disturbing 'lion-taming' game in which Tolen's cult of dominance is given full rein.[14] By making this visual contrast so stark, Lester has a lot of visual opportunities with which to play. For example, by staging Tolen's stalking of Nancy in the white room, Lester ensures that the character's dark presence dominates and Colin's pale protests are almost invisible.

In Ann Jellicoe's play, Tolen's sexuality is specifically linked to Fascism. His fetishes about cleanliness and power represent an image of virility and supremacy that is threatening but can be fatally attractive.[15] 'Girls don't get raped unless they want it,' he says smugly. In fact, the second half of the play is ingeniously to invert this. Nancy initially finds Tolen both fearful and fascinating, an ambivalence that culminates in a confused tirade at him ('Don't you come near me, d'you hear? Just you don't come near me — come near me, d'you hear? Come near me!') and a fainting fit. But her subsequent fantasy that she has been raped by Tolen completely checks his rake's progress, since the whole edifice of his sexuality is founded on the assumption that women find him irresistible. From that point, Nancy is in control, taking over Tolen's room and bursting the tyres on his bike. In so doing, she deflates his ego to the extent that, in the film, he starts having the same fantasy of rejection at the end, aggravated by Colin's romance with Nancy, that Colin was having at the beginning when tormented by visions of Tolen's sexual success.

Lester's tactic in adapting the play with Charles Wood was basically to explode it rather than stretch it, and then try and put the pieces back together in a new and original form. The play's complex verbal rhythms, its sense of the 'action truth' that takes place behind the conversational evasions and cross-purposes of the characters are skilfully reproduced in the film.[16] The lion-taming sequence and Nancy's outburst (filmed with an alternation of reverse and forward zooms that is a brilliant visual analogue for the attraction/repulsion tension of the speech) are from the original. But many speeches are redistributed and transposed; the character of Tom is differently integrated; and the characters of Nancy and Tolen are fundamentally reconceived. Nancy's search for the YWCA is seen more quizically in the film than in the play, her real search seeming for romantic fulfilment as defined in the magazine *Honey* which she clutches as she arrives in London. (When Tolen tries to take the magazine from her, implicitly threatening her romantic illusions, she strikes him across the face.) Tolen is seen in completely different terms from the play — more a crypto-capitalist than a crypto-Fascist. He promises and exudes satisfaction in the voice and the imagery of contemporary consumerism (Green Shield stamps for sexual favours, an assembly-line of available, beautiful girls). This point is reinforced by the use of certain fringe characters who seem a bizarre extension of Tolen's values: like the dim husband whose wife poses for him in a photo-booth, which is depersonalised, coin-in-the-slot sexual stimulation at its most mundane; and the smooth salesman in the dress shop whose seductive patter is his way of getting women out of their clothes for his own commercial ends. 'Tolen' even sounds like a brand name. His boast is that he gives the customers what they want and they come back for more. It is the 'cool' alternative to romantic love, stressing satisfaction more than feeling, and it is to be vanquished when Nancy ultimately chooses the more conventionally romantic Colin. By the end, Tolen has become as conservative as the 'Greek chorus' of middle-aged figures who stalk through the film and comment reprovingly on the action.

This 'Greek chorus' is Lester's most significant addition to the play. What he did was to hide a camera and photograph people watching the filming: afterwards he and Charles Wood wrote lines to fit the faces. Lester feels that one of the virtues of the device was to give the piece a specific place and time: otherwise it might simply seem a fantasy for four people. In addition to giving a context for the action though, it provides a dialectic. The 'new spirit' of the four principals is set against a grumpy older generation whose criticism seems actually to stem from a recognition of their own lack of vitality. Conservative moans such as 'There's no National Heritage anymore, it's all on the National Health' alternate with laboured ponderings such as, 'I think a bed's place is definitely in the home.' 'I *blame* . . .' is a recurrent refrain from them. Disapproval turns unwittingly into outrageous innuendo, as a girl on a motorcycle elicits such responses as 'she'll regret she didn't wear a safety device', 'I feel for her chest,' and 'I've seen many a foreign part.' In comparison with the movement of the youngsters, the stiffness of the elders' joints has hardened into a blandness of outlook. Nancy offers the observation 'Rape!' to a middle-aged housewife on her doorstep who replies placidly 'Not today, thank you' and closes the door. The older generation surrounds the film with an old-style morality that the vivacity of the characters in the centre implicitly shatters: rather in the manner of the film's approach to the play, it explodes it from within. 'It's interesting and pleasing that a number of reactionary middle-aged people have been outraged by *The Knack*,'[17] said Lester, whose audacious armoury of Freudian symbolism (some of the most suggestive opening doors and windows of any film) is mischievously allied with a visual inexplicitness that permits only one kiss in the entire film. The *double entendres* have a wicked combination of outrageousness and innocence. 'I'm being picked up, aren't I?' Nancy says to Tom and Colin when she is sitting on a bed and being lifted down some steps. It is sexually suggestive but also literally true — the very combination that would outrage and yet enthral the passionless and the prurient.

Lester's addition of the running commentary not only highlights the themes of the alternative morality and the generation gap; it defines the material as quintessentially British. The commentary is a remarkable insight into the way the British have a tendency to internalise dissent: none of the criticism is addressed directly to the young people. The other effect of the commentary is to surround the film with a perpetual grumble. If anything defines the British as a nation, it is that we are a people who love to grumble. In his 1941 essay, 'The Lion and the Unicorn', George Orwell defined England as 'a family with the wrong members in control', which Richard Hoggart has said is an epigram peculiarly typical of Orwell and of the English: 'it assumes that we are a family, and it grumbles about the way the family is being run'.[18] For English families to grumble is not only a national trait: it is their birthright.

As a screwball sex comedy, *The Knack* has stood the test of time rather better than other such period pieces as *Billy Liar, Tom Jones, Georgy Girl* or *What's New Pussycat?* There are a number of reasons for this. One is the visual inventiveness of the humour: like the beautifully constructed joke where Nancy feigns pregnancy as a desperate solution to the perennial problem of crossing a busy London road; or the scene where she, Colin and Tom transport a double-bedstead through the London traffic, and the bed, in the hands of these young fantasists, becomes a vehicle of adventure and romance — by turn, a chariot, a trampoline, a raft. Also, *The Knack* stands up well because, for all its eccentric eclectism, it has quite a tight structure. Compositionally similar close-ups of two people mark crucial points in the narrative: Tolen's Mephistophelian offer to share his women with Colin; Tom's thoughtful suggestion to Colin that 'we're all more or less sexual failures'; Tolen's insolent enquiry about Tom's homosexuality, to which Tom smartly responds: 'I'm not — thanks all the same.' Rhyming visual motifs draw together disparate moments which reflect and comment on each other. A freeze frame of Nancy when Tolen declares that 'women should be dominated' is echoed much later in the film when he takes Nancy to the park prior to his 'dominance' being demonstrated and then irrevocably undermined. Tolen's insistent 'look at me' to Nancy during his seduction of her is suddenly recalled in one of Colin's final scenes with Nancy, reminding us perhaps of the fate that Nancy has avoided but also the danger of a latent Tolen in all men through sexual stereotyping and indoctrination.

Indoctrination is actually a key theme in the film. It is present in the dismally identical old-fashioned values of the elders; through Tolen's lessons to Colin on sexual success, in which Colin takes notes; to the scenes in school where the children tonelessly chant and repeat the formulae of their teachers/elders. Colin is pulled up short by this trait towards the end: when Nancy is tormenting him with accusations of rape, her comment, 'Little did his pupils think . . .' is echoed and chanted in Colin's mind by the children at school. The phrase itself — 'little did his pupils *think* . . .' is a pointed one. One must assume that Colin's development away from Tolen's influence to his own individual manhood might allow him as a teacher to encourage individuality a little more in the children under his charge. One brilliant visual joke in the film does suggest a capacity in Colin for this kind of developing self-awareness. Looking out of the school window in disgust to see a group of old men lining the playground to watch the girls play netball, he suddenly seems to see himself amongst their number. It suggests the danger of Colin's identifying with the prurience of the older generation, as Tolen has done by the end of the film. It suggests the danger of Colin's sexual dissatisfaction becoming warped into the febrile frustrations of a 'dirty old man'. (Oddly enough, Colin as the outsider tenant-cum-landlord, with voyeuristic sexual hang-ups, does initially resemble Michael Powell's disturbed hero in the 1959 *Peeping Tom*.) But the fact that Colin can see this himself — and the timing of the shot is sure enough to be funny and to make the point — is a reassurance that this will not happen.

In George Melly's phrase, *The Knack* 'anatomised the whole approach of a generation to morality'.[19] It welcomes a new sexual frankness but it cannot endorse the cold-blooded hedonism of a

Tolen. It commends the vitality of the young whilst criticising the
adolescence of some of their obsessions. It satirises the soft romantic illusions of Colin and Nancy (their blissful walk at the end is
accompanied by a most feeble firework display) but prefers them to
the envious disillusionment of their elders. *The Knack* captures a
mood more than tells a story. The syncopated cinematic syntax
grows less out of the characters and their situation than the rhythm
of the city and the spirit of the age, which seems to be irresistibly
young and alive. But how long could it last? There is a moment in
the film when a chef is cracking an egg as Nancy asks him for the
YWCA — and the egg jumps back into its shell. That image might
be an omen of sixties' youth, sixties' Britain and, for that matter,
sixties' British cinema — a sudden explosion followed by a timid
retreat.

Help!

'Wilkie Collins's *The Moonstone* as drawn by Jasper Johns,'[20] is
Lester's capsule commentary on *Help!* The description catches the
essence of the film's narrative and style. Collins's novel is about the
retrieval of a precious stone: *Help!* is about the retrieval of a precious ring which, in this case, is lodged immovably on Ringo's
finger. Also like *The Moonstone*, the plot of *Help!* involves a strong
Indian sub-theme. In Collins's novel, the stone carries a fatal curse;
in the Beatles' film, the ring is necessary for an ancient Indian
sacrificial rite. But in *Help!*, the plot of pursuit, which involves the
Army, Scotland Yard, foreign assassins and brain-drain scientists,
is rendered in the style of a frantic pop collage. Outlandish characters collide in wild colour contrasts, and captions and animation
(such as the musical notes which bounce happily on the telegraph
wires during the 'Ticket to Ride' number) propel both plot and
performance. The style is comparable to that of a film made roughly
at the same time, Joseph Losey's *Modesty Blaise* (1965). But where
Losey used comic-strip to comment on what he saw as the superficial
values and irresponsible violence of 'a particularly empty and hid-
eous era of our century',[21] Lester uses it to infuse his film with comic
zest and to contain a kaleidoscopic vision of a modern Britain still in
the grip of an Imperialist past. If the style of the film, in Lester's
view, aligns Wilkie Collins and Jasper Johns, its content shows
James Bond unexpectedly making the acquaintance of Gunga Din.

The contrast to *A Hard Day's Night* is immediately apparent. The writer is Charles Wood rather than Alun Owen, which means the displacement of naturalism by a more bizarre imagination that takes much of its imagery from Empire and the military. In *Help!* narrative and fantasy take the place of the former film's journalistic realism. The cameraman is David Watkin rather than Gilbert Taylor (whom Alexander Walker reported as being so discomforted by the hysteria of Beatlemania while shooting *Hard Day's Night* that he wished not to do the second film)[22] and the film is in colour rather than black and white. Colour gives an extra frisson to Lester's filming of the musical numbers in *Help!* 'You're Gonna Lose That Girl' is strikingly edited in individual close-ups of faces shot through blue, pink and purple filters. The Alpine setting for 'Ticket to Ride' makes the number a stunning tableau of black and white — a colour game perhaps with musical notes and piano keys — whilst Paul's number in the Bahamas, 'Another Girl', is shot in warm shades of yellow, blue and pink.

If the Beatles were the driving force of *A Hard Day's Night*, they are driven themselves in *Help!*, which makes them, as John Lennon grumpily remarked, seem 'guest stars in their own film'. *A Hard Day's Night* breathes a sense of innocence, whereas *Help!* is in some ways about the end of innocence. One need only think of the title song — 'one of the only really true songs I ever wrote,' said Lennon[23] — with its poignant lyrics: 'When I was young/And so much younger than today . . . Now these days are gone . . .' Two old ladies watch them disappear into their four 'separate' terraced houses and purr, 'They're still the same as they was before they was.' But their 'homes' are revealed as an open-plan single interior of communal living. It is the last word in witty colour-supplement comfort, but a potentially alienating setting for boys who started out as working-class heroes.

The film's formal and visual extravagances are certainly more extreme than anything in *A Hard Day's Night*. But the reason for that has something to do with Lester's difficult brief for the film. His assignment was to make a sort of biographical film about the Beatles, which could not discuss their working life (because that had been done in *A Hard Day's Night*) nor their leisure (because manager Brian Epstein did not want any allusions to the Beatles' smoking, drinking or behaviour with girls) nor include any romantic interest. Lester's eventual solution was to make them innocent bystanders in an extraordinary plot which afforded the opportunity for more exotic locations than in the first film. For the purposes of the plot, he also chose to present each of them rather in the manner of the Marx Brothers through one predominant characteristic, humorously extended. Thus George becomes mean, Paul cocky, John sardonic and Ringo lovable. The Beatles were none too pleased, although George Dunning's brilliant animated feature *The Yellow Submarine* (1967) was to develop the characterisation along very similar lines.

In fact, for all the Beatles objections to the film's distortions, *Help!* looks an uncommonly prophetic film in some ways. The disguises they adopt at the airport when they are escaping to the Bahamas might have looked grotesque and unlikely at the time, but in five years, some of the Beatles are actually going to look like that. The title song 'Help!' is filmed in black and white with sudden flashes of colour when the Indian villain, Clang (Leo McKern), throws brightly coloured darts at Ringo's image on the screen. Colour on black and white might indicate the way the Eastern 'plot' is to be superimposed on the 'reality' of the Beatles' lives. But it also unexpectedly prophesies the way the influence of the East was to impose itself on the Beatles in the near future, as shown in Lennon's meditation and George Harrison's music (like, for example, the 'Within You, Without You' track on the *Sergeant Pepper* album).

Rather like the snare-drum in the opening movement of Nielsen's Fifth Symphony, the plot of *Help!* seems an attempt to bring the musical performance to a halt. Leo McKern's splendidly villainous Clang pops his head out of a manhole whilst the boys are serenading Eleanor Bron's Ahme to the tune of 'You've Got to Hide Your Love Away'. The performances on Salisbury Plain of 'I Need You' and 'The Night Before' (with exhilarating helicopter shots and use of pull-focus and reverse zooms) are brought to a halt by a farcical pitched battle which, as Tim Pulleine has perceptively remarked, intriguingly anticipates the combination of chaos, comedy and confusion of the last battle in *Cuba*.[24] Unlike *A Hard Day's Night* which is building to that final concert, in *Help!* the authentic voice of the Beatles is finding it difficult to make itself heard — which is the point. Britain's contemporary cultural phenomenon keeps coming into collision with an evocative array of allusions to Britain's national heritage. The ghosts of Britain past, present and future flicker through the fabric of the film.

The past is implied by the narrative's zany recollection of the kind of Oriental villainy that British heroes were always nipping in the bud for the preservation of Empire. It is also invoked by George Harrison's recollection of Scott and Titus Oates when he is suggesting to Ringo that maybe he ought to sacrifice his finger. 'That bloke with Scott,' says George, 'I always admired the way he went out into the snow for his mates.' The present is invoked by certain unchanging icons of British tradition (Scotland Yard, Buckingham Palace); by reference to personalities who symbolise modern Britain (from the Queen to James Bond); and by the inclusion of characters who provide a topical commentary on the state of the nation. For example, the two brain-drain scientists (sprightly characterisations by Victor Spinetti and Roy Kinnear) are forever complaining about inadequate resources and superior German technology. The characters might impede the thriller plot, but they have a lot to contribute to the broader British theme, notably the failure of the Government's promised technological miracle that was to transform the country's future.

Is there any unity to all this? Is there any unity to a film which can embrace a sacrificial ring, an evocation of Empire, a reference to Scott of the Antarctic, a debate about the inferiority of British to German science, and the tribulations of Britain's foremost pop phenomenon? The answer is yes, and the unity is thematic. Almost every scene is based around the idea of sacrifice and loss: what Britain has lost; what the Beatles have sacrificed. Even a scene where a tiger is subdued by Beethoven's Ninth is thematically relevant — German culture working where English has failed. The link between Empire and pop fame is forged in that single line of the police chief to the Beatles: 'You won't last, you know.' In a way, that is the theme of the film, and it stretches through references to Britain's colonial past and the Beatles themselves to the whole atmosphere of 'Swingin' London' and the 'youth revolution'. Small wonder now that the fragmented frenzy of *Help!* looks a vulnerable comic shield against other qualities that are also there under the surface — melancholy and anarchy.

In the year of *Help!*, the identification between Beatles and Empire was officially confirmed when the boys were controversially awarded an MBE. This was not a gesture that affirmed that a social revolution had taken place, but one which demonstrated how the initial revolt was being institutionalised. It signalled not so much a change of attitude as a self-conscious token from a government wanting to be regarded as 'with it'. By the mid 1960s, 'Swingin'

London' and the 'youth revolution' were effectively finished. A reaction was bound to set in, as the Wilson Government lost credibility and the social and political convulsions of the late sixties made the initial confidence of the decade seem strident and misplaced. By the end of the decade, the whole sixties ethos was spawning shrill, reactionary but influential pieces like Christopher Booker's book, *The Neophiliacs* which was to make a sinister as well as chronological link between the emergence of the Beatles as national heroes and 'the Great Freeze of 1962/3, the deaths of Hugh Gaitskell and President Kennedy, the Profumo affair, the fall of Harold Macmillan and the Great Train Robbery'.[25] If Lester had used the Beatles as an emblem of British joyousness and flair in the early years of the decade, Lester's cameraman on *A Funny Thing Happened on the Way to the Forum* and *Petulia*, Nicolas Roeg, was to use Mick Jagger for his satanic overtones when the decade ended. Roeg's *Performance* (co-directed with Donald Cammell) is a powerful statement of the breakdown of Britain in the late sixties. It is a critique of the self-destructiveness of liberation, and the alternative culture that leads to madness: liberation becomes licence, and independence becomes indiscipline. But it is also a searing indictment of the corruption and betrayal of the mid-sixties idealism, where affluence and power were wrested from the hands of the young and put back into the hands of the political gangsters.

In May 1982, Prime Minister Margaret Thatcher and Education Secretary Rhodes Boyson were blaming this sixties' 'revolution' as the root cause of present-day rising crime and social irresponsibility. The Employment Secretary, Norman Tebbitt, audaciously claimed the period's booming birthrate — by implication, one of the by-products of its 'permissiveness' — as a main cause of the present appalling level of youth unemployment. We have come a long way from *A Hard Day's Night*. In that film, John Lennon could sing 'If I Fell' as a sardonic, consolatory song to a crestfallen Ringo whose drums have been interfered with. In Alan Parker's film, *Shoot the Moon* (1982), Diane Keaton sings 'If I Fell' almost as a dirge, bringing out all the underlying tension and pain of the lyric — which no one at the time saw — and, as her sixties' marriage collapses in the eighties, making it a Requiem for the whole sixties period.

Said Richard Lester: 'That sense of optimism, when it turned out to be a false dawn, produced the despair and anger that inevitably exploded in the late sixties. There was an overkill in terms of the optimism and an over-reaction in terms of the pessimism.' Some directors (for example, Arthur Penn) seem never to have recovered from the sixties. Lester has, but the rite of passage was to be a tormented one, and to produce the extraordinary trilogy of disillusionment — *How I Won the War, Petulia* and *The Bed-Sitting Room* — in which the idealism of the early part of the decade has turned rancid and angry.

'The same bastards are in control,' said John Lennon at the end of the decade. 'The same people are runnin' everything, it's exactly the same. They hyped the kids and the generation'.[26] Some of the darker songs of the late sixties Beatles had flickering allusions to Lester's movies. 'A Day in the Life' on the *Sergeant Pepper* album has a reference to 'filling the Albert Hall' that recalls Tolen's nightmare fantasy in *The Knack*. The same song has Lennon singing 'The English army had just won the war', which evokes Lester's devastating anti-war film, *How I Won the War*. It was the Vietnam war, and Britain's support for American policy in Vietnam, which ultimately led to Lennon's handing back of his MBE. Within five years of *Help!*, the Beatles had disbanded. To borrow two lines from a Roy Fisher poem:

They stopped singing because
They remembered why they had started.[27]

Notes

1. Quoted in *Movie*, No. 14, Autumn 1965.
2. Raymond Williams, 'Britain in the 1960s', *The Long Revolution* (Chatto & Windus, 1961).
3. '*A Hard Day's Night*', *Village Voice*, 27 August 1964.
4. Sylvia Plath, *Ariel* (Faber & Faber, 1963).
5. George Melly, *Revolt into Style* (Penguin, 1971).
6. Interview with Nina Hibbin, *Morning Star*, 12 December 1967.
7. *Observer Colour Supplement*, 7 August 1966.
8. Quoted in Melly, *Revolt into Style*.
9. Robin Bean, 'Keeping Up With the Beatles', *Films and Filming*, February 1964.
10. See the interview in J. Philip di Franco (ed.), *A Hard Day's Night: A Pictorial Record of the Movie* (Penguin, 1978).
11. Interview with Lester in Joseph Gelmis (ed.), *The Film Director as Superstar* (Doubleday & Co, 1970).
12. Jann Wenner (ed.), *Lennon Remembers* (Penguin, 1972).
13. See, for example, Lester's letter to *Sight and Sound*, Autumn 1966.
14. The confluence of animal imagery and the theme of male dominance is prominent in two other contemporary works: Alfred Hitchcock's 1964 film, *Marnie*, and

Harold Pinter's 1965 play, *The Homecoming* (which, in structure, dialogue and characterisation, has a number of similarities to *The Knack*).

15. This is another connection between *The Knack* and Sylvia Plath's *Ariel*, notably the assertion by the disturbed female protagonist in Plath's 'Daddy' that: 'Every woman adores a Fascist/The boot in the face, the brute/Brute heart of a brute like you'.

16. In John Russell Taylor's *Anger and After* (Methuen, 1962), Ann Jellicoe's views on dramatic expression are quoted: 'I try to get at them [the audience] through their eyes, by providing visual action; I try to get at them through their ears, for instance by noises and rhythm . . . The theatre is a medium which works upon people's imagination and emotion — not merely their intellect . . . I write this way because the image that everybody has of the rational, intellectual and intelligent man — I don't believe it's true. I think people are driven by their emotions and by their fears and insecurities.' Lester's film is a visual, sensory extension of this.

17. *Film*, Spring 1967.
18. Richard Hoggart, *Speaking to Each Other*, Vol. 2, (Chatto & Windus, 1970).
19. Melly, *Revolt into Style*.
20. Quoted in *Movie*, No. 14, 1965.
21. See James Leahy's *The Cinema of Joseph Losey* (Zwemmer, 1967).
22. See Walker's *Hollywood England* (Michael Joseph, 1974). 'I really disapproved of the effect they [the Beatles] were having when I witnessed the hysteria our multiple cameras recorded,' said Taylor about his experience of photographing *A Hard Day's Night*.
23. Wenner (ed.), *Lennon Remembers*.
24. *The Movie*, No. 75, June 1981.
25. Christopher Booker, *The Neophiliacs* (Collins, 1969).
26. Wenner (ed.), *Lennon Remembers*.
27. Roy Fisher, 'Why They Stopped Singing', *Collected Poems* (Fulcrum Press, 1969).

Chapter THREE

COMEDY TONIGHT, TRAGEDY TOMORROW

A Funny Thing Happened on the Way to the Forum

For Richard Lester, *A Funny Thing Happened on the Way to the Forum* might be subtitled: the trauma that was Rome. It is the odd man out of his sixties' films, the only one which is not set in modern times (perhaps anticipating the historical concerns of his films of the following decade). He signed to do it at a time when he was making the first Beatles film, obviously unaware that his career was to take off so spectacularly. By the time he came to prepare it, it is likely that it was no longer the project he would have chosen out of preference at that stage of his career. By the time he had finished it, there were no doubts about his feelings on that.

Covering the film for the *Saturday Review*, the critic Hollis Alpert speculated innocently: 'Perhaps Lester was allowed too much freedom'.[1] Lester would regard this observation as a joke in poor taste. For example, he had only limited control over the casting, the main parts having already been assigned and the director's choice being confined to the inclusion in supporting roles of actors who were to become Lester stalwarts, such as Michael Hordern, Roy Kinnear and Leon Greene. (A similar situation was to happen in *Juggernaut* in terms of casting, but Lester was to have a much freer hand in the development of the script.) The casting problems were augmented by the fact that, when filming began, it became clear that Buster Keaton was seriously ill and was not really up to the physical demands of his role (it was subsequently to prove his last film). Also Phil Silvers was having personal problems on such a scale as seriously to impair his ability to remember lines. To cover both these contingencies, Lester had to respond with a style considerably less fluid than he really desired. 'One only uses a cut because the take doesn't work,'[2] Lester has said, having had a similar problem in *Help*! when Ringo had developed a twitch every six seconds.

Lester's main difficulty, though, was not with the film's cast but with its producer, Melvin Frank,[3] who had originally been assigned to direct. Frank was a Hollywood veteran used to the ways of the studio system in its heyday, in which the producer was ultimate arbiter and the director more a sort of hired hand. The *auteur* theory had not yet leaked through to Mr Frank. Lester, on the other hand, was used to sympathetic producers in Britain like Walter Shenson and Oscar Lewenstein who had shouldered the administrative burdens but who, in general, had left the major creative decisions to the director. The different conception of their professional roles led to numerous conflicts. The arguments ranged from whether Phil Silvers should be allowed to wear glasses (Frank said yes, as this was part of his popular persona; Lester said no, because it was a blatant anachronism) to whether the film should include a ballet on the theme of 'Flags of all Nations' (Frank sent a memo to this effect which Lester has preserved to this day as a memento of one of filmland's most incredible articles).

The major disagreement, though, was not on minor detail but on fundamental approach. Frank wanted a straightforward preservation of a bawdy, popular, artificial stage comedy. Lester wanted a work that was entertaining but nevertheless said something about the cruelties and injustice of the society it examined. Frank's touchstone was Broadway, Lester's was Ancient Rome — and the road between them was wide. 'I became very interested in the sordid quality of Rome and started reading Carcopino and examining life and behaviour in Rome from a historical point of view,' said Lester,

> and so built the set, filled it with vegetables and fruit and left them to rot for two weeks so that all the flies and wasps got into it. I brought peasants down from the hills and little villages in the centre of Spain and made them live in the sets. We gave them each a particular job, sharpening knives, making pottery . . . We just left them to do a specific job for the whole film. I liked all that and was getting involved in it; it had nothing to do with all these Broadway Jewish jokes.[4]

With the help of his cameraman, Nicolas Roeg, Lester rewrote a great deal of the screenplay, particularly the scenes involving Michael Crawford and the planning of the musical numbers. Lester managed to insert personal flashes of wit, such as the horse in the steam bath, and the Christians being teed up for the gladiator who is practising his swing. But unlike his previous films, which had allowed for a degree of discovery and improvisation beyond what was written on the page, clearly there was a limit to what he could do with *Funny Thing* without exploding the original altogether, since the whole mechanism was dependent on the thorough subordination of character to plot. The producer not only disagreed with Lester's injection of harsh reality; he locked up in a vault some of the extra footage Lester had shot so that the director could not get at it.

It is small wonder, then, that Lester's memory of the film is that of a continuous battle. Lester's nimble cutting is sometimes at odds with a vehicle that relies on calculated verbal humour and a slow-burning farce where three doors need to be simultaneously visible. Nevertheless he does his best to treat the period with respect and resist anachronistic jokes (though Pseudolus's enquiry about the wine, 'Was One a good year?' was apparently as sacred as the last line of *The Front Page* and had to be included). It is a film with abundant pleasures, not the least of these being the way the musical numbers have been liberated from their theatrical origins and reconceived with considerable cinematic finesse. Although some of the original numbers have been cut, Lester retained those songs he felt were necessary for the narrative and characterisation.

Pseudolus (Zero Mostel) delivers the first song, 'Comedy Tonight', introducing the three houses that are to play an important part in the story. These are the house of Senex (Michael Hordern), whose son Hero (Michael Crawford) has Pseudolus as his slave; the house of Erronius (Buster Keaton), who is absent in search of his lost son and daughter; and the house of Lycus (Phil Silvers), who runs concubines as a commercial concern. The plot revolves around Pseudolus's attempt to gain freedom by providing Hero with the girl of his dreams, Philia, whom he has spotted in Lycus's house. But the opening song essentially sets the scene. It establishes the context (a 'less fashionable suburb of Rome'); introduces the main characters (a wonderful first shot of Keaton, balefully staring across at the Seven Hills in his search for his children); and sets up a complicity between Pseudolus and the audience through the former's direct address to the camera.

Thereafter the songs both decorate and further the narrative. 'I'm Lovely' is a song shared by Hero and Philia, filmed in a series of mock-romantic dissolves across attractive green and yellow glades and punctuated by farcical collisions with trees that indicate Lester's concern, even in the songs, to satirise character and maintain the comic momentum. However, Philia has been pledged to another, whom she first mistakes for Senex. His delight at this produces one of the highlights of the film — 'Everybody Ought to Have a Maid' — a quartet energetically led by Senex and supported by Pseudolus, Lycus, and Senex's slave Hysterium, with a degree of enthusiasm that varies according to their social status. There is a wonderful shot of their tiny figures prancing up and down on a vast Roman viaduct — all being compelled to dance to the master's tune. But there is an even more potent effect when they sing the song against a background in which dowdy domestic drudges are seen doing soul-destroying jobs. The rhyming of 'menial' with 'congenial' suddenly takes on a different tone. So also does Senex's insistence on the virtue of having a maid not for 'cleaning up' but for 'leaning *down*', a line which Michael Hordern invests with a memorably withered salaciousness. This tension between foreground and background — the contradiction between the sentiments of the song and the imagery which accompanies it — is perhaps the most powerful adumbration of the main theme of the film: that *nobody* ought to have a maid, or slave.

If Philia assumes she has been pledged to the timorous Senex, her genuine claimant is the much more fearsome Miles Gloriosus (Leon Greene), who has raped Thrace thrice. His coming is announced by an off-key fanfare, and he enters with a lusty rendering of 'Bring me my Bride' whilst, unnoticed by him, his disgruntled army is pelted with rotten eggs and cabbages by an unruly crowd. The number serves as a parody of the usual 'heroic' entry of the star of the musical comedy, and also suggests something of the quality of Gloriosus himself, which will put a considerable obstacle in the way of Pseudolus's plan to unite Hero and Philia. Two characteristics stand out. There is, firstly, his impatience, emphasised by the song's martial rhythmic drive and by a lyric which suggests that this 'subduer of the Turk' must 'hurry back to work'. There is, secondly, his all-consuming vanity, which is supported by soldiers crooning about his mighty thighs and a 'St Trinians' girl's choir chorusing his praises. The camera's quickening montage and overlapping zoom shots are a hilariously obsequious homage to Gloriosus's orgasmic egomania.

Pseudolus has to substitute Hysterium, feigning death, as Gloriosus's intended. He convinces Hysterium of the viability of his plan by crooning 'You're Lovely' to him, a delightful parody of the song's original guise. The essential seediness of the plan is conveyed by three flies alighting on the pillow on which Hysterium is being serenaded. At first reluctant but won over by the argument, Hysterium turns slowly to look soulfully at us and then, as the camera angle switches to the front of the bed, sits bolt upright to take over the song. 'Who'd believe the loveliness of *me*,' he croons amidst Pseudolus's harmonising, and wonders whether he should complete his disguise as a beautiful female corpse by having some jewelry. Miles is harrowed by the death of his 'bride' ('Poor little moth. She fluttered too near my flame') and orders and leads a dirge, a suitable form for the epic scale of his suffering. The ceremony breaks up in chaos when fire is ordered to consume the body in flames and Hysterium and Pseudolus make a run for it, a harbinger of the chase which is to conclude the film's comic business and in which Ken Thorne composes a brilliant set of variations on 'Comedy Tonight' and 'Everybody Ought to Have a Maid'. The film concludes with a reprise of 'Comedy Tonight', which brings the characters together; unites Hero and Philia; establishes Miles and Philia as Erronius's missing children; and gives visual and verbal prominence to the word 'free' to emphasise the underlying purpose behind Pseudolus's scheming.

The musical numbers are clearly an indispensable part of the film's thematic and visual fabric. Even more, they are an indispensable part of the film's comedy. Ken Thorne's sparkling orchestral arrangements deservedly won him an Oscar. In addition to the orchestration of the songs themselves, he composes alternately exotic, jazzy and aggressive numbers for the displays of Lycus's girls in front of Pseudolus, arrangements which catch not only the rhythms of the dances but the turbulent emotional state of the beholder. The mock-fanfares and orgy music deliciously parody the epic methods of a composer like Alex North for a film like *Spartacus* (an appropriate reference, since that film is also about Roman brutality and the fight of slaves for their freedom). Sondheim's songs too are funny enough — full of internal rhymes, puns, alliteration, and with crazy rhymes that at one stage deliriously connect 'tunics' with 'eunuchs' — to continue and extend the comedy rather than provide a respite from it. For once, Sondheim has a film director who has style enough to rise to the wit of his lyrics (as in the visual send-up of the self-consciously saccharine 'I'm Lovely') rather than flatten them in the manner of Wise and Robbins' lumbering rendering of the songs of *West Side Story*. As a *musical* comedy the film is a delight. As a riot in colour, the film is triumphant, the vulgarity of the aspiring nouveau-riche, for example, exposed through the excessive decoration in awful purple of their interiors. Simply as a comedy, however, it is somewhat less successful.

More than the play, the film is not only an anthology of jokes, both ancient and modern (and various calculators have put the number of gags in the work at around 550). It is also an anthology of comedy traditions, the suave British (Michael Hordern) against the brash and breezy American (Phil Silvers, Zero Mostel); slapstick both old (Keaton) and new (Michael Crawford); and with styles that range from theatrical farce to visual parody (Lester's beautifully blurred point-of-view shot of what Erronius is actually seeing through 'these tired old eyes'). The comedy even ranges from ancient bawdry — a plot borrowed from Plautus — to modern film animation, with Buster Keaton, who has spent most of the film running in circles round the Seven Hills of Rome, filmically immortalised as an art object, becoming an animated frieze against which the end credits are projected. The diversity of comic styles in the film is fascinating, even if the different parts do not all attain the same levels of excellence.

For reasons previously mentioned, Buster Keaton and Phil Silvers are not seen to their best effect. Zero Mostel's ambitious performance is a more complex case. Much of it is very funny, notably his manic impersonation of a soothsayer ('How did you know I needed a soothsayer?'/'I'd be a fine soothsayer if I didn't know that') and his exaggerated assumption of the appropriate slavish demeanour, obsequious and grateful even when being struck. But he is an actor who often seems more subtle in long shot than in close-up. The low cunning of the character, discernible in Mostel's physical grace and insinuating movements, tends to emerge rather simplistically in close-shots of his infinitely malleable face. In a way, this is as much a reflection on the direction as on the performance. Lester's realistic context and hectic style do not coincide with Mostel's more theatrically conceived performance and his more deliberate delivery. The two best performances are probably those which are more consciously scaled to the size of the filmic image: Jack Gilford's Hysterium, whose harassed humility is enshrined in his obsequies to his master ('I live to grovel'), and Michael Hordern's Senex, cringing lasciviousness peeping out from under his crabbed exterior.

Within the comedy, there are two themes to which Lester draws particular attention. The first is the theme of vanity, which has always appealed to his sense of fun. The principal love song has the ineffable refrain, 'I'm lovely' and even Hysterium is so carried away by Pseudolus's compliments at one stage as to believe in his own beauty. In Pseudolus's opening monologue, he talks of his role as one of 'infinite nuance' requiring an actor of enormous 'range and subtlety' before adding: 'Let me put it this way — *I* play the part.' In the case of these two, the humour of their vanity derives from our perception of its transience and self-awareness. With Hysterium, who for the most part is cringingly self-abnegating, his momentary delusion of beauty is funny because of its unexpectedness, and the temporary wholeheartedness with which he embraces the concept. With Pseudolus, the vanity is part of his joke with the audience, involving us, like Richard III, in a complicity with his ingenious plans. However, it is significant that his asides are revealed to us but not to the other characters, for it is vital for his survival that his masters do not comprehend how clever he is. His genuine intelligence is what keeps him one step ahead of a potentially horrendous situation. With these two characters, Lester's laughter at their conceitedness is mixed with a certain sympathy.

However, no such sympathy is given to Philia or Gloriosus, who have the gall to take themselves with the utmost seriousness. Indeed, their unbearable vanity is the most sizeable clue to the plot revelation that the two are actually related. Isn't the song 'Bring Me My Bride' essentially the brother of 'I'm Lovely'? The arrogance of the rulers makes them ripe targets for Lester's satirical sword. In fact, Michael Hordern's Senex might come over so endearingly precisely because he has little of the vanity of the patrician class (it has been clubbed out of him by his battle-axe wife) and is rather modest and self-mocking. Speaking feelingly from his own experience, he tells Hysterium: 'Never fall in love during a total eclipse'. When Philia mistakes him for the warrior who claims her for his bride and says, 'You may have my body, but you will never have my heart,' Senex's pride is disarmingly undented. 'Well, you can't have everything,' he replies.

If vanity is one of the film's entertaining sub-themes, the main theme is essentially serious: that of freedom. Lester might have been attracted by the opportunity for a characteristic satire on film genre (in this case, the historical epic and the musical, the conventions of which are undermined or revised). Up to a point, he is prepared to go along with the basic strategy of the piece which is to use the Roman ambience as a vehicle for laughs — addresses to the heavens, soothsayers, chariots, parades, plagues, baths — and the kind of comic incongruity whereby Gloriosus can instruct his host to 'arrange food, entertainment and a sit-down orgy for 14' in an ancient variation of booking a table at a restaurant. But Lester was mainly attracted by the chance to recreate a brutal historical period with an unusual accuracy of detail.

There are two impulses at work behind this desire which might initially seem contradictory: a conviction that his comedy derives from his social observation and that if he does not know how a society works, he cannot make jokes; and a characteristic desire to give a serious undertone to his comedy, to get at the cruel social truth which the humour keeps under wraps. These twin impulses work together in a complex way in this film. Part of the humour of Lycus's character, for example, is the exclusive definition of the character in terms of money. 'Come and browse,' he cries, on the portals of his brothel, 'no obligation to buy.' Hearing the jungle of coins, he confides: 'I know that sound — and I love it!' Underlying the humour, though, is a criticism of an attitude which sees humanity as a commodity to be bought and sold. If Lycus comes over as one of the least sympathetic characters, it is not only because of Lester's difficulties with Silvers but because of the values that Lycus represents — a conviction that life is cheap. Philia's dozy obsession with her loveliness is amusing, but it also a reflection of a sexist society which educates women in the ways of beauty (that is, to be a decorative adornment for the world of men) whilst, in an adjacent house, a young man is being taught the complexities of astronomy. Even Gloriosus sings of 'women to degrade' after he has collected his bride.

Lester's intention behind all this is to show Rome as basically a horrible place to live, a conviction arrived at from his own research (the liberation of the film's final chase has something to do with the action at last escaping from the stifling confines of the city into the more open atmosphere of the country). What he attempts to achieve from this is social conviction and psychological motivation. The comedy is given a certain edge if it emanates not from an artificial proscenium arch but from the arches of a smelly, corrupt city whose physical presence one can almost feel. Further, the more one believes in the harshness of life there, the more one is sympathetic to and involved with Pseudolus's schemes. The unconventional evocation of Rome not only presents an ostensibly noble city as seen from the point of view of the underprivileged. It explains, and indeed justifies, the determination of the non-patricians to better themselves by fair means or foul.

In the event, the desperation extended from the situation of Pseudolus to that of Lester himself. *A Funny Thing Happened on the Way to the Forum* became a desperately serious thing for Lester happening on his way to the studio, in which his own freedom as a film-maker was involved. One is now at liberty, fancifully perhaps, to see the film as an allegory of Lester's working situation on it. Previously having worked for sympathetic masters, Lester now finds himself in danger of becoming a slave to a tyrannical producer and has to become as sly as his hero to plot his way out (if Pseudolus is Lester, then his helper Hysterium is probably Nicolas Roeg). No wonder Lester remembers the hardships, although his achievement in captivity, as he saw it, and his small victories for freedom are very impressive.

Notes

1. *Saturday Review*, 15 October 1966.
2. Interview with Joseph McBride, *Sight and Sound*, Spring 1973.
3. Melvin Frank has had a long career in films particularly in association with Norman Panama, writing and producing scripts for comedians like Bob Hope and Danny Kaye. His biggest recent success as producer-writer-director was with the George Segal/Glenda Jackson comedy, *A Touch of Class* (1973).
4. Interview in *Movie*, No. 16, Winter 1968/9.

Chapter FOUR

TRILOGY OF DISILLUSIONMENT

How I Won the War

During the train sequence of *A Hard Day's Night*, the Beatles have an argument with a stuffy businessman, who objects to their transistor and to their wish to open the window. 'Don't you take that tone with me,' he snaps at them, 'I fought the War for your sort!' 'Bet you're sorry you won,' responds Ringo, drily.

One could describe *How I Won the War* as a feature-length elaboration of that sequence. The businessman's boast about the war — as if fighting in it were a purely personal decision — is a small-scale variation on the kind of deluded egomania of Lieutenant Goodbody (Michael Crawford) which is to run rampant in the later film. The Beatles' crisp deflation of the businessman's 'war record' is to anticipate the whole tone of *How I Won the War*, where conventional notions of the glory and honour of conflict are to be comically and brutally undermined. Just as the Beatles put a brake on the businessman's aggressive remembrance, so *How I Won the War* is a young man's film that will not tolerate that kind of dangerous pomposity from his elders. War might sometimes be necessary, but it is never noble: that, in essence, is the theme of the film.

Lester has made all kinds of movies — musicals, comedies, thrillers, historical romances, a western — but the imagery he draws on most often is that of war. This might seem a surprising motif in a director most instantly associated with knockabout comedy, but then Lester has always been one of the most misunderstood of modern directors. The recurrent war imagery explains his frequent collaboration with the writer Charles Wood whose work for film and theatre has often concentrated on the behaviour of the military man, and whose play *Veterans* (dedicated to Lester) extends this military imagery into the making of a film.[1] Lester has intimated that he sees film-making as a sort of military operation, in which the director is ultimate dictator.[2] Warfare is a recurrent event in these films — from Vietnam on the TV screens in *Petulia*[3] to the nuclear holocaust of *The Bed-Sitting Room*; from the religious wars in *The Four Musketeers* to the Castro revolution in *Cuba*. But the most extensive and specific examination of warfare in his work is in *How I Won the War*, perhaps Lester's and Wood's most remarkable collaboration.

Said Wilfred Owen in the Preface to his War Poetry: 'My subject is War and the pity of War:/The Poetry is in the pity.'[4] In *How I Won the War*, Lester's subject is the lunacy of war and the obscenity of war movies: the artistry is in the anger. When the film appeared, it was frequently bracketed with the 'youth protest' movement and with artistic manifestations of that movement, such as Adrian Mitchell's poems, which were violently opposed to American involvement in Vietnam. (Probably the most controversial and extraordinary artistic contribution to the debate was to be Peter Brook's Royal Shakespeare Company production, *US* in 1968.)

In fact, the unconventional style of *How I Won the War* — its brutal alternation of black farce and shocking violence — has a variety of artistic precedents that goes far beyond the immediate 'protest' context with which it was linked. For literary precedents, one thinks of Evelyn Waugh's *Sword of Honour* trilogy, completed in 1961, which, like this film, offers an alternately serious and satirical thesis on the fate of class and honour in the theatre of war. Michael Hordern's Lt Colonel Grapple in *How I Won the War*, who is convinced that the real enemy is still the 'wily Pathan', is a real Waugh-like character. The film also evokes Joseph Heller's modern classic, *Catch-22* (1961) in that both share a similar lunatic logic. In the film, the lucid ravings of Musketeer Juniper (Jack McGowran) are perceived as madness by his commanding officer but as wisdom by his fellow soldiers, for Juniper has discovered what Yossarian finds in Heller's novel: in war, insanity is the key to survival.

Filmically, *How I Won the War* recalls Godard's *Les Carabiniers* (1963) in its alienating devices (though Lester has not seen the film) and Stanley Kubrick's *Dr. Strangelove* (1963) in its darkly mocking tone and irreverent use of Vera Lynn's voice to satirise war nostalgia. The film it most recalls, though, is Joseph Losey's *King and Country* (1964). Although very different in style, both films are fundamentally about the hypocrisies of war. Both Losey's hero and Lester's fight for a vague concept of 'King and Country' which neither has really thought about nor asked himself whether it was a concept in which he even believed. Both have court-martial scenes which are similar in their horrified and ironical look at the way in which the military echoes the prevalent Establishment prejudices about society even as they proclaim impartiality ('I had a grandfather who was a miner,' says Grapple, huffily, adding, 'until he sold it . . .') In both films, the insanity of the accusers seems more pronounced than that of the accused.[5] Above all, both films are highly individual responses to identical influences: Bertholdt Brecht and Stanley Kubrick's film, *Paths of Glory* (1957).

In *How I Won the War*, Lester's personal inflection of 'Brechtian alienation' — his attempt to destroy the illusion of narrative and present the film as a kind of political debate — takes various forms. To begin with, it takes a plot whose premise is absurd enough to be, in Lester's words, 'self-alienating': that is, impossible for any audience to involve or identify itself with. Recalling his war experience ('every word of this film is written in pencil in my own hand'), Lieutenant Goodbody particularly thinks of his most dangerous mission, which has been to set up a cricket pitch behind enemy lines for 'morale' and for the benefit of a visiting military VIP who will be impressed by this 'small patch of sanity' in hostile territory. (The rationale is not very different from Colonel Nicholson's justification for building his bridge in *The Bridge over the River Kwai*.) Accompanying him on his mission has been the afore-mentioned crackpot Juniper, a cynical Troop Sergeant Transom (Lee Montague), a cowardly Melancholy Musketeer (Jack Hedley), the kleptomaniac Gripweed (John Lennon), and Clapper (Roy Kinnear) who is being cuckolded by a 'suave' Insurance Collector at home. Each of these characters is introduced at a cricket match, in which Goodbody is captain and chief bowler, which is the reason that the opposition — with Hitler as scorer — is 569 for no wicket. It is an early indication of Goodbody's limitations as a strategist.

The film invites an audience not to accept the cricket match as a literal event but to read across it for various associations and thematic implications that are to be highly relevant to the whole film. The cricketing positions of the characters, for example Transom as all-rounder, Juniper very square, Gripweed in the outfield, are to approximate their positions in the platoon. The white cricket flannels anticipate the gleaming white straitjacket in which Juniper is eventually to be confined, though still advising the Americans on map strategy. The class-ridden aspect of cricket, its unquenchable atmosphere of Gentlemen and Players, relates to an important sub-theme of the film which is to be the mutual antagonism between officers and serving men. The fine weather necessary for cricket corresponds to the acts of madness that are to be committed under the sun in the film. (Mad Englishmen in the sun is another of the film's sub-themes, Grapple seeming to think he is Lawrence of Arabia, a connection reinforced by the film's allusions to and parodies of the style of David Lean). The cricket roller is linked to the mad circles within which Goodbody seems to move: he is first discovered circling crazily in a dinghy prior to his capture.

Above all, the cricketing theme links with the most murderous aspect of Lester's and Wood's critique: the kind of attitude enshrined in Goodbody's, 'War is, without doubt, the noblest of *games*.' It is the horror of this attitude, its sense of a desensitised attitude to suffering and death (World War Two as 'the Final Test'), that informs the film's sense of outrage. Games in Lester's films have often been lethal analogies to important main themes. In this film, the analogy is crucial. For some critics, of course, to take that attitude to World War Two — a 'just war', after all — was simply 'not cricket'. But again that is the film's point: war is *not* cricket, but a bloody business, and the class-ridden commanders who treat it as cricket are criminally insane.

War as a spectator sport has a long history in the cinema. This takes one to another aspect of Lester's criticism: the attack not only on war itself, but on war movies. Even ostensibly distinguished war movies sometimes have a humanism and a sense of noble sacrifice which Lester finds as suspect as schoolboyish heroics. 'You can't say to me *Paths of Glory* is a pacifist film,' he told me. 'The implication is that if Kirk Douglas had led the troops in the beginning, we would have been able to go out and kill the Germans more efficiently.' Clapper's line in *How I Won the War* — 'what we want are more humane killers' — is a sarcastic reference to the Kubrick film. Everything in *How I Won the War* is an attempt to deconstruct and demoralise the conventional war film. It derides the 'mission for morale' formula that appears in *The Bridge on the River Kwai*. It satirises films like *Cockleshell Heroes*, *The Guns of Navarone* with their sentimental vision of the excitement of the secret assignment, and scorns a film like *The Colditz Story*, which asserts the beauty of comradeship under adversity. In Lester's film, the mission is nonsensical and its morale-boosting strategy pointless (Field Marshal Montgomery sees the cricket match and comments, 'What wotten bowling, dwive on'). Comradeship is non-existent. The men hardly talk to each other, and the reunion of the platoon consists of

Goodbody and the coward — the solitary survivor under Good-body's command. The film sizzles with a hatred for the nostalgia and 'entertainment' of war. To those who said it did not treat war with sufficient respect, Lester replies: 'I feel it's treating it with real respect, and that is doing everything in one's power to say, "For God's sake, don't use war as entertainment: aren't you ashamed?" '[6]

To this end, Lester's style is a mixture of humour and horror, realism and surrealism, designed to keep an audience off balance, unable to indulge either its sympathies or its patriotism. It keeps an audience under constant pressure, and one could say that its tension is dependent less on plot than tone. Lester's claim that the comedy in the film has a deadly purpose is a valid one. Goodbody's intended morale-boosting opening speech to his platoon is drily deflated by Transom's one-line review of its drift: 'We're all going to die.' It is an effective comic anti-climax, but even then, has the ominous ring of literal prophecy: the feeling that their Commander's comic incompetence is not really funny, and is to lead to the annihilation of the Third Troop of the Fourth Musketeers. (Coincidentally, in Lester's future film, *The Four Musketeers*, slapstick swords-manship is also to be taken to the point where it is no longer funny). At one stage, when Transom is trying to teach military discipline to his men, he threatens Clapper with a bayonet. The gesture amus-ingly exaggerates Transom's exasperation, but it also foreshadows Clapper's ultimate fate, skewered through the heart by a bayonet immediately after murmuring to his enemy, 'Have a heart, eh?'

Charles Wood's savage sense of the paradoxes and incongruities of war leads to some particularly malevolent mirth, where the laugh-ter dies in one's throat. 'There's been some marvellous advances in surgery, thanks to war,' says Transom. 'If it wasn't for the British Army, you wouldn't be here today,' says Grapple to Goodbody, and he is right: Goodbody is being court-martialled at the time. There is a pervasive comic sub-plot about feet, deriving from Good-body's conviction, instilled into him by Grapple, that the essence of war is looking after your men's feet. 'I've looked after their feet as if they were my own,' is Goodbody's main defence at his court-martial. But the joke is booby-trapped. Goodbody's failure to look after the coward's feet — he accidentally shoots him in the foot — is actually to save the man's life, because he is unable to fight in the fatal final mission. Shortly after Grapple has given this advice, his own driver has his feet blown off by a mine, his agony being undercut by his wife's advice: 'Run 'em under the cold tap, love.' The film itself is structured like a minefield, ready to explode when an audience feels sympathy for the protagonists or the situation. In addition to the unpredictable and disconcerting detonations of humour and horror, another distancing device in the film is the use of actual newsreel and tinted monochrome footage from the war across which the actors will move. 'We knew that there would be four battles which the platoon would fight,' said Lester, 'which had to represent Montgomery's four classic battles, or blunders, or whatever begins with a b . . .'[7] The military strategies shown in the film correspond to those actually employed at Dunkirk, Dieppe, Alamein and Arnhem. In the film, each battle is given a dominant colour (green for Dunkirk, pink for Dieppe etc.). A soldier is coloured according to the battle in which he falls and then continues to follow the platoon around. Lester's intention here is two-fold. It demonstrates the 'immortality' of a platoon, in the sense that, however many are killed, it is constantly replenished with new bodies. It also emphasises that, as far as the officers are concerned, the individuals are interchangeable. Goodbody continues to address his platoon by the names of men who have long since been killed and candidly admits that 'they all looked the same to me'. It is a habit inherited from Grapple, who can never get Goodbody's name right, and is an attitude that conveniently ties in with Goodbody's belief anyway that '*I* won the war'. The ghostly presence of these 'coloured' soldiers is at once a morbid joke and a constant reminder of their deaths. They look like soldiers made out of plasticine, or characters in a comic strip. Interestingly enough, the officers have bubble-gum cards of their favourite military battles, a detail which relates back to the film's whole thesis on the difference between the romantic images and the actual reality of war, and its attack on the idea of war as comic-book adventure.

Lester was disheartened when the purpose of his film was widely misunderstood. The makers of the film were described as 'traitorous mod monsters' in *Films in Review*,[8] and the redoubtable Bosley Crowther, unbelievably, attacked the film on the grounds that 'war isn't funny'.[9] In England, Rank refused to show *How I Won the War* on Memorial Day on the first Sunday of release, whilst the other major circuit showed *The Dirty Dozen*, the absolute prototype of the kind of war film Lester was attacking in his movie. The film's anti-war sentiment was probably a little ahead of its time, preceding Richard Attenborough's acclaimed Great War wallow, *O What a*

Lovely War ('*Genevieve* with guns,' is Lester's acidly astute description of that) and Robert Altman's hugely successful *M*∗*A*∗*S*∗*H*, whose moral outrageousness and technical audacity paralleled the Lester film even if its attitudes to war were more ambiguous.

As well as being ahead of its time, Lester might well have got ahead of his audience, being, as the phrase was at the time, 'too clever by half'. Some French critics were baffled by the range and complexity of the film's references. If the significance of cricket, allusions to British war movies, the irreverence of its attitude to Montgomery (whom it treats as a forerunner of another Monty, i.e. Python) are not perceived, the film becomes difficult and obscure. Establishment critics who *did* pick up these references found the film all the more offensive, of course. Lester was adding impudent iconoclasm to off-putting intelligence.

The style undoubtedly caused problems. 'One has learnt over the years that Brechtian alienation is a euphemism for audience's backs seen disappearing down a street,' Lester said to me.

How I Won the War was an honestly felt attempt, in that technical sense, to try to avoid the trap of the Technicolour war film — the great toys, music and pictures, so you end that you can't make an anti-war film because you're going out rooting for one side to blow up the others. So we tried to get around that by constantly stopping the film when you're beginning to like the Roy Kinnear character, say, thinking that reminding the audience that he was an actor was preventing them from rooting for a character in the ordinary way. But all it did was to antagonise the audience. They said, 'Get your hands off me, you're manipulating me, and I don't like it . . .' — and they have every right to say that and I think now it was tactically a mistake. Although I'd do a lot of the film the same now, I'd have to re-think that, because I think it alienated the audience we wanted to attract. It's fine for cineastes to find it interesting, and for the young people who are going to like it anyway. But the people we wanted to have the polemic with were annoyed and closed their eyes to the argument.

For all its difficulties of structure and theme, it remains a remarkable film. There are some splendid performances. Michael Crawford skilfully negotiates all of Goodbody's moods of naive heroism and wistful bitterness. 'What they thought of me, I'll never know,' Goodbody says of his men, which is a really chilling moment: an inadvertent disclosure of the blindness of his self-knowledge; a tactless reminder that all his men are dead. If the structure seems wild, one should remember that it takes its form from Goodbody's journal, which is the diary of a madman. Equally unhinged is Grapple, and Michael Hordern conveys his indestructible derangement with wonderful flair, particularly in his closing moments when he mercifully puts a bullet through his injured tank whilst murmuring emotionally, 'Oh, my poor horses . . .' The one sane soldier is Transom and Lee Montague's powerful performance ensures that his bitter soliloquy about what war does to a man's attitude to death (whilst Goodbody in the distance practises press-ups over a mine-field) is one of the film's most telling moments.

'The tone is strident, tense, exclamatory; reasonable enough if Britain were in a deeply military mood,' said *Sight and Sound* at the time of the film's release. 'But in this country at this moment, *How I Won the War* seems to me to be stubbing its toes by kicking ferociously at an open door.'[10] Times have changed, of course, and, as often with Lester, a film which looked dated to some at the time of its release now looks remarkably prophetic and modern. (The same thing was to happen with *Petulia* and *The Bed-Sitting Room*, whose reputations have grown since their initial release.) At the time one probably responded to the film's anti-war fervour and its assault on the insanity of command and of blind obedience to authority. But the interrogation of media images of war and the ideology of war movies, which at the time might have seemed tangential to the film, now looks central. Certainly, in the wake of the conflicts over the Falklands and Grenada, its analysis of the relationship between war and the media is remarkably relevant. There is no warmongering in Lester's film, no glorification of conflict, and the potential for media insensitivity to war is vigorously dealt with. 'Take that camera away,' says Transom as one of his men is having a breakdown, 'haven't you insulted us enough without films?'

It is a perverse film that sets itself the task of making an audience feel ashamed of what it sees. But the film's profundity is in its perversity; in its ability to shake and antagonise an audience with its pacifist argument, and in its awareness of the terrifying responsibility of the film camera. Far from 'trivialising' its war theme, which was a common complaint about the film,[11] it has an almost painful sense of the moral urgency of its message, and there is method in its madness. 'If you play war with me, I'll play war with you,' says Goodbody to his men at one point. The film's own war games have an ugly ferocity designed to discourage people from ever wanting to play war again.

Petulia

Petulia is Lester's swansong to the Swinging Sixties, the period with which he is still (misleadingly) most closely associated, and an era whose positive potential he more than anyone affirmed on film. It is also the film in which his technique, human sympathy and social vision are given their sternest test and rise triumphantly to the challenge. In it, he confronts characters and emotions head-on for the first time; re-examines afresh a society he knows; and, with that nose he has for civilisations on the point of collapse, presents a picture of America that is uncannily prophetic of the convulsions which were to rip open the country in 1968.

The setting is San Francisco, a city whose 1967 'summer of love' is clearly in its death-throes. Lester had visited the city in 1966 to research the film, and returned a year later to shoot it, and he said to me: 'It had become people in Mustang cars in three-piece suits changing into beads and badges just before they got to the city limits. Optimism and the flower movement were turning into hard drugs and anger.' Unlike the flippant novel on which it is based (a modern romance between an LA surgeon and an 'arch-kook', Petulia), the film is a deeply serious and compassionate critique of an American middle-class dissatisfied by mere materialism but disorientated by the new morality. It explores the developing relationship between Petulia (Julie Christie) and a doctor, Archie Bollen (George C. Scott), both of whom are reeling from ostensibly satisfying but deeply unsuccessful marriages. Archie is separated from his beautiful blonde wife, Polo (Shirley Knight) who now wishes to remarry. Petulia is frustrated in her marriage to a rich American, David (Richard Chamberlain) whose handsome appearance disguises a psychological and sexual insecurity that is leading to uncontrollable bursts of violence. Archie is drawn to Petulia's youthful vitality, which might rekindle the passion for life and the excitement of risk that seem to have drained away at the approach of grey middle-age. Petulia is attracted by Archie's seriousness and concern, his healing hands a symbol of caring in a disruptive and turbulent world. Their relationship is a finally unavailing fight to make contact, in a sense to save each other's lives, in a savage and searing society where romance is being overwhelmed by emotional aggression.

On the level of characterisation, *Petulia* is easily Lester's most complicated film up to that time. The characters are reserved, deceptive, disclosing themselves only with great reluctance and therefore have to be built up in the film stealthily and through visual implication. Décor is very revealing about them. Petulia's bedroom, seen when she is back with her husband and his family, is like a doll's house, which says a great deal about the kind of attitude to her that has contributed to her feeling of suffocation: the idea of her as something decorative to be pampered rather than a person to be heeded. The naval paraphernalia and erotic Beardsley drawings in David's room hint at a confused sexuality behind a macho display, whilst the yellow sumptuousness of Polo's bedroom takes oppressive gentility to the point of near-nausea. Archie's apartment has great white spaces and no family pictures. If Petulia's room is claustrophobic, Archie's living quarters could induce agoraphobia. The chill of loneliness behind the desire for freedom is almost palpable there. One connects it almost subconsciously with that remarkable moment in the park, when Archie and his new lady-friend pass a girl who is playing solitaire with giant playing cards: a portent, writ large, of Archie's own potential solitude.

The revelation of character is oblique because the characters themselves are oblique. Petulia is a compulsive liar, inventing a grandmother who knew Cary Grant, and pretending to have stolen a tuba (her memory-flash of that revealed as a lie when she smashes a window soundlessly). It is part of the mystery, eccentricity and provocative mystique she wishes to exude, but it is also part of her desire to keep romance, reality, self-knowledge and sexual involvement at arm's length. Archie often seems distracted, being caught off guard in his first meeting with Petulia and drifting into an affair when he is actually searching for his coat. His mind wanders during conversations with his friend Barney ('Dammit, you're not even listening to me!'), as if his failing concentration is symptomatic of a more fundamental inability now to fix the course and destination of his future life.

Despite the title, Archie and not Petulia is perhaps the film's main character. Like Joseph Losey's *Accident* (1967), it is a supremely intelligent study of the anxieties and quiet desperation of the middle-aged male, made all the more perceptive by the quality of the central performance. Lester has waxed lyrical over working with George C.

Scott ('his instincts were the best I have ever known in an actor . . .
you could turn over with silent cameras on George's first rehearsal
because as long as he was dressed right, there were certain moments
when he produced insights that was like watching the eleven-year-
old Mozart turn up with things . . .'): the performance justifies such
superlatives. In a restrained and economical way, a complete individual is presented to us: his humanity and humour; his anguish and
anger. Archie is at that critical period when he realises that his past is
longer than his future. Thus, the film is concerned not only with his
present relationship with Petulia, but also with those that have con-
ditioned what he is. Explaining her hatred of Archie's ex-wife Polo,
whom she has not even met, Petulia says: 'I look at you, and I know
Polo.'

The scenes between Archie and Polo are peculiarly penetrating
and painful. As played by Shirley Knight, 'predictable' Polo has an
impenetrable cool charm that has solidified into a kind of bourgeois
frigidity. In becoming a habit to each other, they have slowly and
gently drifted apart, yet not quite enough to avoid resenting the
intrusion of someone else. Jealousy is the most intense flicker of life
that either of them shows in the film. Polo wishes for Petulia's death
at one stage and, when Archie protests that she has never even met
her, Polo replies (in a chilling echo of Petulia): 'I only have to look
at you.' Archie throws her gift of cookies at her when Polo tells him
of her forthcoming marriage to Warren, and Polo is momentarily
stunned: 'Well, this is a new side to your nature . . .' But the
moment — which could have broken the starchy surface of their
desiccated marriage — is irrevocably lost when, in a superb gesture,
Polo starts tidying up the cookies even as she tremulously speaks,
preserving the polite facade and resuming her role as model middle-
class housewife. She will never change: Archie is wondering if he
can, as he flounders after an ill-defined freedom in a desire, as he
puts it, 'to *feel* something'.

This desire is being complicated by the fact that Archie is steadily
being pushed to the fringes of people's lives without having any
secure relationship or fresh ambition to which he can turn. His
intimacy with his own children, sustained with increasing desperation and ingenuity, is being eroded by the presence of Warren, who
is even anticipating Archie's treats for the boys (his trip with them to
Alcatraz, for example, which, he discovers, Warren has shown them
the week before). A beautiful scene at the zoo, where Archie takes
the children to see the penguins and runs into Petulia, is particularly

eloquent about his situation. He moves across to sit with her but, noticing that they are being watched inquisitively by the boys, she squeezes Archie's hand for a moment and then quietly moves away. Wordlessly and unemphatically, this moment conveys with absolute precision Archie's suspension between two worlds of a receding past (the children) and an uncertain future (Petulia), each of which is bedevilling the other, and which paralyse Archie's progress.

Two other points should be made about this small scene at the zoo. The motif of watching and being watched is an insistent one in the film, contributing to its atmosphere of tension and paranoia. The other point has to do with the zoo setting itself. The film's most expressive settings are the hospital, Alcatraz and the zoo, and this implicitly reflects the situation of the characters, where they seem alternately patients, prisoners or predators. This absolutely encapsulates the role of Petulia throughout the film. The film begins with shots of people who have been road accident victims: it deals centrally with people who are emotional casualties. When passing Alcatraz, Warren tells the boys fulsomely: 'You can get out of anything if you want to bad enough.' It is not that easy. Archie might have broken out of the prison of his marriage, but he is still always hammering at doors that will not open (at the pawnbroker's, at the house of the Mendosas), and he is still locked inside the limitations of his own character.

Providing another perspective against which Archie's plight can be viewed is the presence of his friends, Barney (Arthur Hill) and Wilma (Kathleen Widdoes), who are clearly going through a similar nightmare. Their marriage is crumbling more openly than Archie's and they spend most of their time jibing at each other, but they lack the will to make a clean break. 'You were such a handsome couple,' drones Barney tactlessly, showing slides of Archie, Polo and the children to Archie, whilst chattering about the lenses he used to achieve those shots. This callous lack of real concern counterpoints the images just as the happiness on the slides themselves ironically contradicts the present situation. Yet Lester probes still further and, in a telling tracking shot towards the photo of the wife, he ends with a close-up of Polo's eyes, a shot to be repeated in various contexts in the film, and in which one can sense a desolation and desparation only just below the surface.

Admittedly, Archie has casually taken up with a lady he has known for a long time but not, one feels, with any great passion: Pippa Scott's excellent performance in the role economically projects the saddest aura of warm-hearted sexlessness since Barbara Bel Geddes in *Vertigo* (another great San Francisco movie where the topsy-turvy topography seems an expressive correlative to the psychological contortions of the main characters). Yet Petulia is not really the answer for Archie. To some extent, the film is about the collision of generations, as the young hunger prematurely for experience and the mature yearn nostalgically for idealism. Archie's maturity exposes Petulia's irresponsibility and impulsiveness ('You swinging young marrieds,' he sighs, with resigned humour, as she lures him provocatively to a motel and then refuses to make love). Yet her neurotic energy does at least afford the opportunity for change and undermines Archie's worldly-wise complacency and inaction. 'I'm fighting for your life,' she cries at one stage, to which Archie responds blandly: 'Who is trying to kill me?' Lester answers that question with three quick, cruel and, in retrospect, devastating flashforward shots: of the family slides; of Christmas presents to his children wrapped in red; of flowers thrown from a quay into the water — all stages of Archie's progressive disillusionment that, unknown to him, lie ahead, waiting.

'I would have turned those hands into fists,' Petulia says later of Archie. She means that she would have created a more assertive, dynamic man than the sensitive but rather weak figure Archie is revealed to be. Yet her comment has uncomfortable intimations of violence which are probably unintended but nevertheless significant. Hands heal, but hands can also kill, and Petulia has to endure a vicious beating at the hands of her husband after her one night of love with Archie. If she is fighting for his life, she is ultimately saved by his 'kiss of life' (a gesture that reflects the emotional urgency of the film). The attack on her has been presaged by a flashback to the Downtown Bull Ring, where we have seen a picador's spears dipped in blood: an image that seems ominously to relate both to Petulia as tease and David as possible killer. The bloodstained white dress is a shocking image, picking up a colour motif of red and white that has run through the film: the colour of ambulances, in a film peopled by casualties; the association of white rooms with icy relationships (like that motel room, with its nude bather and plastic water) where contact is desired but dangerous; Archie's red sweater, which he wears after the love scene and during the scene with the boys, when he seems most fully alive.

The intensity of the emotions flares and then dies down, and the characters settle back into the routine of their lives. Though she recognises the worthlessness of a life governed by appearances (her 'beautiful' husband David is, as he acknowledges, a potential monster), Petulia will compromise. Though her appreciation of beauty now goes more than skin deep (when she and David are discussing ideas of beauty, she mentions in her list 'men of science': cut to a shot of Archie's door), she will stay by the imperfect husband she has. Archie makes defiant gestures — clambering angrily up the Danner hill rather than take the lift, after his meeting with the Danners' appalling family — but they are all equally impotent and futile. The main characters continue to lead totally different, disconnected lives, but there are certain parallels. Polo and Petulia never meet but they 'know' each other, are often similarly dressed, and seem to have had a similarly castrating effect on their men. Archie and David meet and even phone each other but they never speak; and yet both seem full of a similar kind of frustration, indefinable disappointment, silent rage. Their lives cross, but no connection is made, which might be the reason that the shot late in the film, where Petulia and Archie catch a glimpse of each other on trams that are pulling them in opposite directions, seems so appropriate and powerful a metaphor both for the relationships and for the narrative structure.

When Archie and Petulia meet for the last time, Petulia is in hospital and having her baby. 'So things go better for Mr and Mrs Danner,' Archie comments drily. The scene — with its doubts, uncertainties and hesitancies — consciously and movingly echoes their first meeting. Archie proposes that they go away together: Petulia agrees: Archie picks up the phone to arrange transport and then, resignedly, replaces the receiver. Again a momentary movement of commitment is broken and the two are left, suspended, frustrated. 'When I lay dying and wondering what my life has been all about, you won't even across my mind,' Petulia says to Archie, but as he leaves, she says: 'Wait — I lied. I'll never forget you — Arnold.' Archie silently mouths 'Arnold' in mock horror (magnificently acted by Scott here) before moving over to kiss her goodbye. The poignancy of the moment when he kisses her hand depends enormously on context and cumulative force, for it refers back to one of their earliest scenes together in a lift when she has taken his hands and kissed them ('Real, honest-to-God tears, Petulia?' he had asked then), and her whole association of Archie's hands with tenderness and life. In the final moment of the film, feeling a doctor's hand along her face, she whispers, 'Archie?' It is the last word of the film, the name of the man she loves and has lost, in the form of a question. It provides a coda of haunting, shivering uncertainty about the future.

Apart from the unusually downbeat ending, the relationship between Archie and Petulia might have formed the basis for a fairly conventional romantic melodrama. But, there are two things which give a complex modern resonance: the style and the context. The plot is not the thing: it is the way the story is told. *Petulia* is a major advance in the mainstream cinema's attitude to film narrative and film form. Complex matter discovers a new maturity of expression through the Hollywood cinema's belated recognition of some of the advances of the modern novel by practitioners such as Joyce and Virginia Woolf. Lester's style moves freely between time and space, past and future, reality and imagination. A good primer for an understanding of the method would be Virginia Woolf's seminal essay, 'Modern Fiction' in *The Common Reader*, with its call for a new kind of fiction constructed on psychology as much as on plot and developing not from a linear narrative about character in society but from a process which truthfully reflects the mind in action. Both *Petulia* and the essay are aiming for a different way of representing reality and a form of art which can give the impression of the randomness of life without sacrificing aesthetic construction and control. Examples previously quoted indicate how the flash-forwards and flashbacks can give a particular moment an enriched accretion of meaning and implication. It makes *Petulia* seem more tightly structured than less, for disparate images interlock and similar lines echo and reverberate in unexpected directions.

For example, there is a moment during the first scene between Petulia and Archie when Petulia says, 'Money can't buy me', and at that precise point, she sees a gleaming white car that is being offered as first prize in a hospital raffle. With an immediacy almost involuntary, a split-second flashback indicates that she connects it mentally with a memory of a car that has run over a small boy who has been following her (ever since, she has been trying to buy off her guilt by helping the boy and his family). The subliminal process whereby Petulia links an object of status with an act of destruction is an elaboration in miniature of a key theme of the film: an exposure of a society sensing the dissatisfactions of materialism, a society whose surface glamour only thinly conceals its inability to cope with people's basic needs. In a generous tribute to the film in the November 1968 issue of *Films and Filming*, Mike Nichols perceptively said:

'What I liked so much about *Petulia* was that it seemed to me it was about suffering in a time and place where there was no expression allowed for it . . . I kept thinking of Chekhov — that there are immense feelings under the words that are never expressed *in* the words and the environment doesn't permit an expression of the feelings.'

The gap between appearance and reality in relationships is paralleled by that in society and becomes more and more apparent. There are numerous fleeting images of a community cluttered with artificial and useless objects which are imposing barriers between people and their feelings for each other. This is sometimes revealed in ostensibly comic detail: the automated motel for your affair, with a radar-controlled key; a dummy TV set, which a lady in hospital is invited to stare at all day; Archie's climate-controlled greenhouse, a present from Petulia, which has to be protected from the sun. Yet all of these details have their sinister side. The automated motel is an image of a loveless liberation, sex without feeling, that will ultimately demoralise the permissive generation as much as it disgusts the repressed. The dummy TV set is an uncomfortable symbol of a hollow society, a society with its own frame of reference but no substance. The artificial greenhouse has implications of the superficiality of the 'flower movement' which will wither the moment it has to come out into the open ('the sun'll kill it') and confront reality.

The deceptions of appearance build up a frustration that ultimately can only lead to violence, which is a crucial theme in the film and felt on many levels. Sexual violence: Petulia is a kind of ice goddess, gorgeous to behold but who freezes at a touch, and whose idealisation of the men in her life leaves them impotent and raging. Polo is not dissimilar: also an immaculately beautiful, cool blonde who patronises Archie to the point where he explodes. These small detonations (Archie with the cookies, the fight at a roller derby, a ferocious row at a supermarket over a tin of sardines) are ultimately to lead to the one big explosion of violence (David's assault on Petulia which almost kills her). But there are complex causes at the root.

There are two particular frameworks — sexual and social — which provide the context for the feelings of the film. First, the so-called sexual revolution, whose manifestations vary from 'free love' to topless bars. It has promised so much — a freedom from inhibition, guilt and repression — but it has failed to make people feel any more liberated, especially those whose who have the material means to exploit it. Petulia flirts with the idea of an affair, but seems to enjoy the atmosphere of menace and danger more than the reality of commitment. As the film progresses, she seems to become more and more the conventional romantic, forced into hollow gestures of promiscuity and outrageousness to vindicate her membership of what Archie calls 'the Pepsi generation' (a variation on Jean-Luc Godard's famous axiom in his 1965 film, *Masculin Feminin*: 'we are the children of Marx and Coca-Cola'). Both she and Archie seem victims of the new morality in that it gives them a liberation which they have no idea how to handle. The converse of such freedom is the vengeful brutality of Petulia's husband, partly a legacy of the old-fashioned paternalism represented particularly by his father (Joseph Cotten), for whom murder could still be a justifiable response to marital infidelity by a wife. The reactionary backlash has begun.

The social context is Vietnam, an insistent presence on the television set which will eventually explode the 'summer of love' and the youth revolution into destructive and divisive protest. Vietnam serves a complex function in the film. In being so insistent a presence, it surrounds the film with an atmosphere of violence that gathers enormous tension. It becomes part of the underlying ideology of the film: nobody refers to it and the sound on the television is invariably switched off when the pictures appear to show the level of the people's concern, but it is there eating into the country's subconscious and self-confidence. This ebbing self-confidence in the national psyche parallels the way in which the character of Petulia's husband, David, is presented. He is the all-American boy with everything — the power that goes with looks, with money — whose discovery that he cannot live up to this superman image is leading to fear and arbitrary violence.

Petulia has had a somewhat chequered critical career. It was America's entry in the 1968 Cannes Festival, which was to have been its commercial launching pad, but as the festival itself became caught up in the May riots, the film was withdrawn and its launch postponed. Its reviews ranged from the enthusiastic and respectful to the angry and downright vicious (Pauline Kael describing it as 'obscene, disagreeable, dislikeable'; *Newsweek* talking of a 'rotten, dishonest comedy' and contemptuously referring to Lester as 'an opportunistic deracinated entertainer'). From a period of relative obscurity, in which a survey of sixties' Hollywood by John Baxter fails even to give it a mention,[12] *Petulia* became a film whose stature and influence has grown as it underwent revaluation. A recent poll of critics placed it third (behind Coppola's *Godfather* and Altman's *Nashville*) in a survey made of the best American films made between 1968 and 1978. When it first came out, it was rather submerged by jazzier, more commercial movies such as Mike Nichols' *The Graduate* (1967), Dennis Hopper's *Easy Rider* (1968) and Paul Mazursky's *Bob and Carol and Ted and Alice* (1970), which offered whimsical, apocalyptic or ironic visions of late-sixties' America. With the passage of time, *Petulia* has emerged as the deepest and most wide-ranging of them all, precisely because of the way it moves from confused characters responding to a specific time and situation (kooks and conservatives, eccentrics and eunuchs at loose in permissive San Francisco) to the sense of a society and a country whose conviction in itself is similarly beginning to wilt under the pressure of rapid and confusing change.

Two other film comparisons suggest themselves. Rather like Alexander Mackendrick's *Sweet Smell of Success* (1957), *Petulia* is a film by an expatriate American, revisiting home territory and, from an outsider's perspective, offering a lacerating vision of the country's ills that an insider might have had neither the courage nor the perception to pursue. Mackendrick's film specifically picks up the atmospheric legacy of fifties' McCarthyism, with its society of snoopers and informers. Lester's film unnervingly X-rays the cancerous guilt about Vietnam, the imperialist war that marks the death-knell of the sixties' egalitarian dream. The film it anticipates is Nicolas Roeg's *Bad Timing* (1980), an extraordinary study of psychological chaos in a post-Freudian era and the complexities of so-called sexual revolution. Roeg is, of course, the outstanding cameraman of *Petulia*, and the title of his film might even have been inspired by an exchange in the final scene of Lester's film ('Why did you let me get away, Archie?' — 'Bad timing. Dumb Archie'). Both films have complicated narrative structures and a grisly motif of surgical dissection that is a metaphor for self and social laceration. Both films deal with a romance between a seemingly liberated heroine and an inhibited older hero in a context of socio/sexual dislocation, where the border between liberty and licence, self-expression and self-indulgence, is well nigh indistinguishable. Both works have, as a significant central image, the hospital, which serves as a microcosm of both films' world. An aphorism by Sir Thomas Browne in his great seventeenth-century text, *Religio Medici* might actually be summarising the main theme of the two films: 'The world is not an inn, but a hospital: a place not to live in, but to die in.'

Petulia is a difficult film, but an inexhaustibly rewarding one and one in which repeated viewings reveal a warmth, honesty and depth which Lester has yet to excel. In an ambitious attempt to comprehend the innate violence of urban society and the absence of fulfilment in personal relationships through the shallow obsession with material pursuits, Lester has fashioned an extraordinary mosaic of contemporary feeling, painful, deeply moving, superlatively acted. The pessimism is undeniable, but a work of art — and that is what *Petulia* is — is a sure sign of hope.

The Bed-Sitting room

There is one remarkable moment in what is otherwise Lester's most modest achievement, *The Mouse on the Moon*. Having landed their craft on the moon's surface, the astronaut and the professor take their tentative first step in Space. They are immediately assailed by their own garbage which, discarded during the flight, has been balefully following them through the atmosphere. 'Wherever civilisation goes,' the professor comments, 'garbage is sure to follow.'

Man's potential for reducing practically the whole of civilisation to garbage is the main idea behind *The Bed-Sitting Room*. The sole survivors of a nuclear strike on England wander around picking up the pieces of their lives. This phlegmatic journey across a sea of desolation becomes an absurdist reverie on the theme of human alienation brought about by social annihilation. Lester's main dramatic strategy is to counterpoint the comic foreground with the tragic background, the withered landscape either echoing the eccentric disorientation of some characters or mocking the attempts of others to recreate vestiges of their former existence.

The situation itself offers an enormous challenge to Lester's visual and dramatic imagination. The film opens with traditional shots of molten lava, the earth as a red crust, a burnt doll. It then moves into a more unconventional vision of the effects of a holocaust: a devastated motorway with the skeleton of a toy dog nodding back and forth in a back seat; an underground escalator which smoothly deposits its passengers into a total wasteland. A beach strewn not with seaweed but with reels and reels of tangled film is an obliquely chilling metaphor for failed communication. Rather than resort to a brutal literalism, Lester stimulates a viewer's imagination of disaster by the use of an inventive visual metonymy. Thus, the effects of the Bomb are presented not through the sight of rows and rows of emaciated corpses, but through death-ridden images of the absurd appurtenances of human existence: a twelve-foot mound of boots and shoes; set after set of false teeth being fished out of a polluted stream. It might seem incongruous to compare *The Bed-Sitting Room* with another work of an American emigré similarly responding to a London recently devastated by war — T.S. Eliot's *The Waste Land*. Yet some of Eliot's lines are remarkably applicable to the imagery of this film:

> A heap of broken images, where the sun beats,
> And the dead tree gives no shelter.

Society has effectively been fractured. Famous London landmarks are identified by fragmented icons of their former existence. Conventional heredities and hierarchies have also broken down. The Queen is now Mrs Ethel Shroake, who, of the twenty or so survivors, was the next in line for the throne. The Prime Minister is selected on the basis of his inside-leg measurement. Because of the diminution of the population, institutions have become individuals. A man on a bicycle is the Electricity Board. Mate (Spike Milligan) seems to represent the complete postal system. The National Health Service is embodied by Marty Feldman. Only an employee of the BBC in *It's Trad, Dad*, Frank Thornton, is now the entire organisation, wandering around with news bulletins which he relays through hollow television sets, itself an eloquent image for a world which has had its guts blown out. In fact, now that news itself has been rendered extinct by the atomic explosion, the newscaster is open to requests for favoured headlines from the past, such as the Fall of Singapore. It is from him that we learn what has happened — a nuclear misunderstanding whose devastations have unfortunately outpaced the almost instantaneous signing of the peace treaty. No one seems to have known who the enemy was, or who won, but as a policeman remarks about the British situation: 'When you've forty million dead, it's hard to see the wood for the trees.' Interesting hints are given about the survivors, though, notably in the news about a Sportsman of the Year event which, we learn, is to be contested by Charlton Heston and the Pope.

If institutions have become individuals, the effect has not been to individualise the institution so much as to institutionalise the individual. He is still going around with the vestiges of his Establishment role, his civic values unchanged by the total disappearance of a society in which they can usefully operate. Not even atomic mutation can radically alter people's values or their conception of their roles in society. During the course of the film, a housewife is to change into a cupboard; the Prime Minister into a parrot; and a policeman into a sheepdog. These are all highly evocative images, a surrealistic comment on their function in conventional society. So a housewife becomes a cupboard because she is ordinarily treated as a piece of furniture; the Prime Minister becomes a parrot because such people are *in essence* mere talking heads; a policeman becomes a sheepdog because his customary social role anyway consists of a mode of snappy obedience and keeping things in line. The concept of atomic mutation provides Lester with some marvellous images: a brick dropping out of Lord Fortnum's coat ('I've dropped a brick,' he comments heavily) and wallpaper beginning to sprout on his sleeve as he begins to change into a bed-sitting room; a wooden drawer popping out of the mother's breast pocket as her transformation to cupboard begins, a startling and direct quotation from Salvador Dali. 'Surrealism' is a word which has often been used, rather loosely, of Lester's style, but the term is appropriate for *The Bed-Sitting Room* conceptually as well as visually, for the film not only has the visual originality of Surrealism but also its attack on the madness of bourgeois norms.

The former social roles of the characters give particular piquancy to their present situation. This is felt most powerfully by Lord Fortnum (Ralph Richardson), a Parliamentary survivor, it seems, by virtue of his Early Warning Hat. 'It gives you that extra four minutes in bed,' he explains, which, as the war has lasted only two minutes and twenty-eight seconds, has enabled him to sleep through World War Three. But Lord Fortnum is now, like everyone, in desperate search of food (the Third World War has reduced everyone to Third-World poverty and malnutrition). Also the effects of atomic mutation are slowly changing him into rented accommodation. This is seen by him as a horrific image of social decline. It is not the transformation itself that appalls: it is being transformed into an ignominious bed-sitting room and not, say, Woburn Abbey. In an extraordinary image as he staggers across a lurid night sky encumbered with encroaching gas-meters, Fortnum cries to be taken to a proper respectable area. 'Belgravia, Belgravia,' he moans, before shouting,

'My freehold for a guide!' Possibly because of Ralph Richardson's hilarious yet dignified immersion in the role, the image is oddly reminiscent of the mad King Lear on the heath: a king without a kingdom who is also railing against his transformed social status in a mockingly unfriendly climate. Lear is to wind up in a hovel. Fortnum is to wind up at and as 29 Cul-de-Sac Place, Paddington.

Shakespeare's *King Lear* could well be felt as an interesting touchstone to the atmosphere and themes of *The Bed-Sitting Room*. Both are investigations of worlds of 'nothingness' and irrationality, in which life is felt as meaningless and absurd. *King Lear* is a play whose tragedy has an intensity and bitterness that almost tips it into farce; *The Bed-Sitting Room* is a film whose comedy has a forlornness and pain that almost tip it into despair. Both suggest that the only way of perceiving society's madness is by becoming mad yourself, in the process offering a radical revaluation of what social sanity is.

This links to the film's pessimistic thrust — its feeling that, if contemporary society is torn apart, what will replace it is not revolution but merely a fragmented version of what we have already. Even in this new situation, people are still acting out the values of the old (think of Edgar's comment in *King Lear*: 'The oldest hath borne most; we that are young/Shall never see so much nor live so long'). Penelope (Rita Tushingham) still has to pop into the smokers' compartment for her cigarette, despite the fact that she, her boyfriend and her parents are the only survivors on the whole underground system. When her boyfriend is introduced to her family, Mother (Mona Washbourne) instinctively starts making knitting motions with her fingers, the meaningless repetition of an instinctive ritual overcoming the absence of materials. Harry Secombe gets Mother to act out a fondly remembered domestic situation by pelting him with crockery. Occasionally this kind of detail is funny — Bules Martin (Michael Hordern), for example, carving a banana as if it were the Sunday roast. Sometimes the humour is a little more disquieting. The Bomb has not exploded Lord Fortnum's prejudices. 'No coloureds. No children. And especially no coloured children,' he stipulates as a bed-sitting room. On his window has been spelt out the slogan: 'No Wogs', even though, as far as can be seen, there are no 'wogs' who have been 'fortunate' enough to survive.

The tragedy forces these characters to act out a travesty of bourgeois existence. 'It's family life that's important,' intones Father (Arthur Lowe) as he watches pregnant Penelope playing with Alan (the daughter's child is to end up as a mutant and Father is to end up on a plate). But Lester's strategy is also to compel the thought that bourgeois existence itself is a travesty. By taking the trappings away and placing these activities against a harsh, alienating context, the hollowness of the activities is exposed. By showing the absurdity of these rituals after, he highlights their absurdity before.

There is a superb sequence of events where Bules Martin proceeds on a bizarre display of courting rituals over Penelope. He puts his mac over a puddle, like Sir Walter Raleigh; attempts to go for a punt across some unspeakable sludge; plays on a beach which sinks under their feet; and comments, 'I love St Paul's, you know' as he sees a dome alone visible, the rest submerged in water. The marriage service itself is a (literally) diluted version of the real thing. Water in the organ pipes mutes the effectiveness of the church music. Mate provides an 'Instant God Kit' with fitted cash register, and a trendy vicar conducts a service not from *the* 'good book' but from *a* good book — *Lady Chatterley's Lover*. It makes a mockery of the traditional marriage service but it also causes one to question this traditional institutionalising of love in our culture, compelling people to swear by standards and by an authority in which many of them do not believe.

Horror is never far away from the surface of the film. Birth provides the most sinister moment of the film, and the mutant child — deformed by the fetid atmosphere — is a chilling anticipation of certain trends in seventies' horror movies, where 'monstrous' births are seen as the legacy of the corrupted adult world. It is a world of pollution, of continual hunger, and of cannibalism, in which the new Prime Minister is finally to be consumed as a cooked meal ('That'll mean a by-election,' says Mate). The peculiar mixture of cannibalism and comedy is summed up in the strange confusion of Mate's version of the story of The Three Bears with a classic comedy routine: 'That's no porridge, that's my wife.'

The London Lester celebrated in *The Knack* has been completely devastated in *The Bed-Sitting Room*. Baker Street is a mere sign on the underground, Regents Park a muddy swamp, St Paul's a sinking dome. When told to keep her chin up because she is British, Penelope replies: 'British? What a lot of use that is. We don't even know who's won the war.' But even more disturbing is the feeling that, fundamentally, nothing has changed. When the atomic dust starts up again, they all run to the safety of the bed-sitting room — that is, Lord Fortnum, a figure of authority. At the end there is a strong feeling that it could start over again, with the BBC man declaring that 'Great Britain is a first-class nuclear power again' and a sense that a renewed outbreak of devastation could be caused with Britain's nuclear *deterrent* (ironically referred to as her 'detergent' at one stage, a clever metaphor for the conventional soapy euphemisms that particularly characterise the discussion of nuclear holocaust.) This kind of paradox is the kind of absurdity in which Lester delights — and despairs.

The film was a critical and commercial disaster when it first appeared in 1969. Many felt its Goon-like humour was as anachronistic as its nuclear disarmament theme. Both elements have, of course, come back into prominence since, the success of the Monty Python films making the humour of *The Bed-Sitting Room* look fresher than before (one could imagine the Python team responding in a very similar way to the theme of the bomb), and the renewed Cold War hostilities of the 1980s once bringing the possibility of nuclear confrontation to public consciousness. The film's observation of bellicose British Imperialism also looks more relevant now than it did then, as does its proferring of the Bomb as the ultimate four-letter word (so risqué that no-one in the film, until the end, can bring himself to say it). At the time, the tone of the film particularly reflected Lester's disillusionment with Britain's development at the end of a decade that had promised an extraordinary era of optimism and prosperity and had ended in compromise and cynicism. There are two comically forlorn images of the golden era of the mid sixties which gain particular potency when set against the prevailing devastation: a torn poster of *The Sound of Music* on the London underground; and the Union Jack on the mother's cup, which recalls the whole euphoria of 'Swingin' London', 'Buy British', 'I'm Backing Britain' — before the bubble burst. ('At the height of that period,' Lester said to me, 'you could have exported your boots with a Union Jack on them, and somebody would have bought them.')

Nevertheless, the film is flawed in some ways. The writing has many brilliant passages, but there are some rather teeth-grinding puns (e.g: 'I'll have it made up in Boots' — 'It'll be better in bottles. More hygienic.'). 'Enough of your cheek and impotence,' says Father to Bules Martin after the latter's virility test. When the police balloon soars over St Paul's and one of them enquires whether the architect was Wren, the other says, 'Looks a bit cloudy, but there's no rain . . .'

With sharper playing, this kind of wit would not have weighed so heavily. But, unusually for a Lester film, the performances are rather uneven. There is a variety of performance styles which never quite cohere, with Ralph Richardson, Michael Hordern and Spike Milligan providing brilliant comic flourishes from a solid human base that is not matched by the different styles of Marty Feldman, Harry Secombe, Jimmy Edwards, Peter Cook and Dudley Moore, who all seem searching for a spot in which to do their familiar humorous routine. The casting as a whole does not quite 'jell'. The survivors are a bit too incongruous and self-conscious an amalgam of actors who can play comedy and comedians who cannot act. Arthur Lowe only comes into his own when he is turning into a parrot. Although turned into a cupboard, Mona Washbourne's Mother seems less wooden than her daughter and the boyfriend. Rita Tushingham is made to represent a rather schematic humanism, privileged with a soliloquy over her boyfriend, with the repeated refrain, 'I will say this for him . . .' The role is sentimentally conceived and played, and both actress and director seem rather embarrassed by it.

One of the problems is that the film has a landscape characterised by absences, whereas Lester's films tend to thrive on an abundance of detail. It is a film in which Lester (as he was also to attempt in *Butch and Sundance: The Early Days*) seems to expect the context more than the content to provide the drama. This puts a strain on his visual inventiveness, which would need to surprise and nourish an audience in every frame. Although the result is interesting, in the final analysis it is perhaps not quite interesting enough. There is a certain thinness which is partly a narrative thinness (that is, nothing much happens) but mainly attributable to the surprising linearity of the film's development, with none of the complex time-adjustments one had in *Petulia*, for example. We are required to bring our own cross-references to the film (comparing the devastated motorway we see, for example, with our present knowledge and our imagination of what a nuclear holocaust would do). Lester usually supplies this sub-textual density in the body of the films themselves rather than asks for a shared consciousness to be applied from the outside. He either seems to need a lot of narrative or contextual energy in his films or some kind of correlative to which he can refer. What he has here is, inevitably, a lot of blank space, a passive rather than dynamic situation and society, and a correlative that is implied rather than visualised. It makes for a somewhat skeletal texture.

'Keep moving' is the motto of the film, but its even temper and tempo tend to impede its progress through its very quietism (unlike *Petulia*, say, whose positive rage banishes any hint of flippancy or self-pity).

In retrospect, Lester's approach to the piece as a 'nostalgia piece' might have been mistaken, since it blunts the cutting-edge of his anger and subdues the energy and thrust of the original play (by Spike Milligan and John Antrobus). Whereas Milligan's world is one of disintegration through violent distortion, a movement towards dehumanisation through an exaggeration of humanity, Lester's approach here goes the opposite way, taking a deformed world and superimposing normality upon it. The effect is intriguing, but the final result a little bland, the form of the film certainly the most conventionally structured of Lester's pieces up to that date and perhaps not sufficiently deformed for its subject. In a way it seems an extended version of *The Running, Jumping & Standing Still Film*, a vision of eccentric Britain in a bare landscape. It realises to the full some of the uneasy implications of the earlier film in its portrayal of isolation, insanity and violence, but has not quite enough of the sustained inventiveness needed to fill the larger context of a feature film and a destroyed England.

There is much to admire in the film, nevertheless. One always admires the quality of Lester's intelligence, even when one is not completely convinced by what he is saying. 'Keep thinking' is the motto behind Lester's method, reflecting an analytical rather than an emotional response to experience. Ideas rather than characters modify Lester's sensibility. It can make some of his films appear a little cold. But it is this intellectual quality that is also the most attractive aspect of Lester's films, his refusal to wallow in emotional indulgence, the determination to engage the mind of an audience rather than its handkerchiefs.

Although Lester told me that it was the work of Kurt Weill· that was giving him the reference for the music, mood and montage of *The Bed-Sitting Room*, the musical analogies that occur to me whilst watching the film are Ibert's *Divertissement* and Nielsen's Fourth Symphony, the 'Inextinguishable'. Ken Thorne's brilliant score often recalls Ibert in its perky humour. Ibert's programme is remarkably similar to the film's, including a satire on the marriage ceremony, nocturnal ruminations, and rude noises at conventionality. Thorne's plangent main theme, which cuts through the nuclear clouds like a knife, has the nobility of Nielsen. Nielsen's music, like Lester's film, is also a response to war and, particularly in the opening stretches, an evocation of a stenching, smoking chaos. But he also offers, like Lester, the sense of psychic health not morbidity, an outward-looking rather than introspective temperament, and a hard-won confidence that is felt in the full flowering of the glorious main theme at the work's climax. 'In case all the world was devastated,' said Nielsen, explaining the programme of his symphony, 'then nature would still begin to breed new life again, begin to push forward with all the fine and strong forces inherent in matter . . .' It is a statement which comes to mind when one watches the sudden flood of natural imagery at the end of *The Bed-Sitting Room*, with its weird evocation of the evolution of life and its capacity to survive almost any catastrophe. Even if he occasionally gets stuck in the nuclear mire, Lester refuses to submit to a Romantic 'easeful death' but attempts a counter-attack of irony and resilience. *The Bed-Sitting Room* is still one of the cinema's most thoughtful dramatisations of the unthinkable.

Notes

1. Charles Wood's play *Veterans* (Faber, 1971) is generally believed to be about Wood's experience of working on Tony Richardson's film, *The Charge of the Light Brigade* (1968). In his preface to the play, Wood writes: 'All the films I have worked on have contributed to *Veterans* and more interestingly than gossip I hope the play is concerned with deceit, exploitation and treachery within an empire/industry run by gangsters, funny in their pretensions, vicious in their actions, showing a pathetic regard for skills and talent, and how these gangsters can be used by talented people who have acquired other talents like deceit, treachery and the ability to be totally selfish yet remain on the best of terms with everyone, but for what?'
2. Interview with Lester in *Film*, Spring 1967.
3. Even the poster for *Petulia*, which is set in San Francisco in the sixties, picked up the film's implicit war imagery: 'The oldest battlefield in the world. You know it by another name. Marriage.' Melodramatic perhaps, but not inappropriate, and certainly reinforced by the dialogue (Petulia: 'I'm fighting for your life.' Archie: 'Who is trying to kill me?') The background of the political and military violence of Vietnam and its increasing impingement on the American conscience via the TV screen finally explodes into America's domestic and social foreground in *Petulia*, when the heroine is beaten almost to death by her husband. 'Only a crazy man hits a woman,' he says, 'or a coward.' The alignment between violence, madness and cowardice links *Petulia* directly with *How I Won the War*.
4. *The Collected Poems of Wilfred Owen* (Chatto & Windus, 1963).
5. I have remarked before on certain similarities in subject between the films of Lester and Joseph Losey in my comparisons between *The Knack* and *The Servant*, and *Help!* and *Modesty Blaise*. (One might also mention *The Bed-Sitting Room* and Losey's 1961 film, *The Damned* which, in different ways, are urgent warnings about the possibilities of nuclear annihilation.) There are also similarities in technique, the flashforwards of *Petulia* anticipating similar dislocations of time-structure in Losey's

The Go-Between, and Losey's witty use of mutterings over the soundtrack during the cricket match in *The Go-Between* recalling a familiar Lester device. Both are articulate, self-critical film-makers with an intellectual cinema style that likes to dislocate narrative and submit it to a judgment. Curiously, both men worked on the same television series in the fifties, *Mark Sabre*.

6. *Movie*, No. 16, Winter 1968/9.
7. Interview with Joseph McBride, *Sight & Sound*, Spring 1973.
8. Gwenneth Britt, *Films in Review*, November 1967.
9. *New York Times*, 9 November 1967.
10. Penelope Houston, '*How I Won the War*', *Sight & Sound*, Summer 1967.
11. For example, see Richard Schickel's review in *Life*, 17 November 1967.
12. John Baxter, *Hollywood in the Sixties* (Tantivy, 1972).

Chapter FIVE

ALL FOR ONE AND EVERY MAN FOR HIMSELF

The Three Musketeers; The Four Musketeers

Lester's film adaptation of Alexandre Dumas's *The Three Muske-teers* is a remarkable achievement. It is at once social satire and political allegory. It mixes comedy and period adventure, recreating not only a historical past but paying homage to the swashbuckling cinema past of Fairbanks and Flynn. Underpinning the action and spectacle are Lester's humour and intelligence and a characteristic disenchantment that particularly overtakes the second part of the film. *The Three Musketeers* (*The Queen's Diamonds*) is the part in which Lester's flair for visual grandeur, offhand humour and manic action is given full rein. *The Four Musketeers* (*The Revenge of Milady*) occupies a larger, more turbulent canvas, as the religious wars erupt, the social, political and personal divisions deepen, and a series of villainous vendettas undermine the invulnerability of the Musketeers and result in violence and death. The whole work is a remarkably sustained performance of inventiveness and excitement, and can certainly be counted as one of the cinema's most successful adaptations of a literary classic.

This final point might need emphasising, for when Lester was announced as the director of the film, some apprehension was expressed that his zany comedy and statements about social realism might be at odds with swashbuckling heroics and Dumas's nine-teenth-century romanticism. Even though the first part of the film, in particular, was generally well received, there was some complaint that the comedy was false to the spirit of Dumas. In fact, the adapta-tion is very much in the spirit of Dumas and does reflect Lester's professed admiration for the novel, and the revelation to him of a re-reading.

It is straightforward enough to see the elements of appeal. Because the novel necessarily moves through an exciting historical period and a wide social stratum, it provides ample opportunity for

Lester to display his facility as social historian. Lester is interested in the grandeur of the seventeenth-century Court at Versailles and the brutality of the religious wars, but he is also intrigued by the day-to-day life of this society: for example, how the people dispose of rubbish (by tipping it out of the window) or how people had teeth extracted. He has said that it is only by knowing this kind of detail that he can generate humour, by playing it off against this social reality. A conversation can be enlivened if it is crosscut with a primitive game of tennis, which was beginning to become popular in France at that time. Indeed, the games people play can be very revealing about society and the different levels of society. The contest between two peasants on a greasy pole (the winner takes the food) is a revealingly different affair from the games played and observed at Court. These alternate between baroque indolence (a game of chess, with hounds as pieces) and sadistic cruelty (the delight of the French royalty as a hawk snatches a dove out of the air — 'Did you hear it cry?'; the circumscribed deer hunt in which Buckingham participates).

There were two other qualities in Dumas which would particularly appeal to Lester — namely, his wit and his irony. It is often forgotten that *The Three Musketeers* is a very funny novel, and Lester and his excellent screenwriter, George MacDonald Fraser, were sometimes unfairly criticised for introducing an inappropriately farcical dimension to the film, when such an element is quite loyal to the spirit of the original. Spike Milligan's extraordinary performance as Bonancieux in *The Three Musketeers*, for example, was greeted by some critics as an eccentric aberration: it is, in fact, an ingenious elaboration of Dumas's creation of the original character, who in the novel is presented as a comic amalgam of cowardice, panic and obsequiousness. Similarly, Raquel Welch's performance as Bonancieux's wife Constance is a slapstick elaboration of Dumas's hint in his novel that Constance is peculiarly clumsy and graceless: 'Her feet did not indicate a woman of quality'[1] (in the film, they get stuck in a chamberpot during an amorous embrace with d'Artagnan). Roy Kinnear's Planchet is also funny and authentic and, as with most great adaptations, the relationship between him and his master d'Artagnan is conveyed in a gesture. When Constance first appears and Planchet is rather obviously taken with her, d'Artagnan slaps him sharply across the face. 'Thank you,' says Planchet placidly, accepting this brutal rebuke as part of the natural order of things and a perfectly proper element of the relationship between master and servant. It is a quick visual equivalent to something that takes Dumas a paragraph to convey:

> D'Artagnan reflected and resolved to thrash Planchet provision-
> ally, which was executed as conscientiously as he had acted in all
> other affairs. Then, after having drubbed him soundly he for-
> bade him to quit his service without permission . . . Planchet was
> seized with . . . admiration and spoke no more of leaving him.[2]

One suspects that the quality of Dumas's irony was even more appealing to Lester than his wit. For all their romantic associations, the Musketeers are essentially mercenaries, which often results in a conflict between morality and money. They can be devious, and many of their more spectacular deeds (the mock fight in the inn, or the breakfast on the battlements) are primarily motivated by a play-ful sense of greed and selfishness. With his scepticism about heroes, Lester would clearly respond to the dualities and ambiguities of their situation. This quality of irony provides the means by which Lester can reproduce the swagger of the original without having to endorse an anachronistic heroism, for their daring deeds are often for causes which are discredited or in which they do not themselves believe. They are not morally pure, nor are they supermen: they are accom-plished survivors in a mad, slippery world. The underlying serious-ness of this is emphasised by the casting of straight actors and playing with and against their image, rather than by casting comedy actors in the leading roles and letting them loose within the legend. It is emphasised still further by the intensely powerful performances of the villains, menacing in a subdued way in *The Three Musketeers* but rampantly destructive in *The Four Musketeers* — Charlton Heston's devious Richelieu, Christopher Lee's satanic and volatile Rochefort, and in particular, Faye Dunaway's deadly Milady, alternating winsomeness and ferocity, delicacy and danger.

If Lester's adaptation is faithful to the spirit of Dumas, it is not absolutely faithful to the letter. The liberties taken are original, emphasising the particular interpretative shading of the film. Some changes might seem minor, though the implications are quite inter-esting. For example, unlike the novel, d'Artagnan in the film is made illiterate. It is a detail one notices particularly because of Lester's recurrent interest in literacy and education in his films, the way it reveals social position and often social deprivation and vul-nerability. It has the effect in this film of making one continually aware of d'Artagnan's modest origins, set out imaginatively in the film's opening sequence. It places him in a social position between the peasants and the royal personages with whom he increasingly comes to deal, becoming in effect their go-between. It is a detail also which alerts one to a shift of character. He confesses his illiteracy quite openly to Buckingham in *The Three Musketeers*, but in *The Four Musketeers*, he tries to brazen it out, as if aware that such a deficiency is inappropriate for a man of his rising station. D'Artagnan the pure is becoming d'Artagnan the pragmatist, the politician.

Another major difference between film and novel is the film's characterisation of Rochefort, the 'Cardinal's living blade' as he is characterised by Athos. The enmity between him and Richelieu is not present in the novel. In the film it makes him a rather more complex, divided figure, being committed to two people (Richelieu and Milady), one of whom he serves, one of whom he loves, neither of whom he trusts. *The Four Musketeers* invents a final fight between d'Artagnan and Rochefort which is not in the novel and which is violent, overtly blasphemous and, unlike their nocturnal fight in *The Three Musketeers*, wholly without comic diversion. The fight has been provoked by the murder of Constance who in the novel is poisoned but in the film is surprisingly, savagely garotted with rosary beads by Milady dressed as a nun.

It is in the second part, then, that the film diverges most clearly from the novel. *The Four Musketeers* intensifies the violent imagery of Dumas, and of the first part of the film. As the adaptation is known as two separate films, it is probably necessary eventually to discuss them individually. Nevertheless, although freely conceding that splitting the film into two was a shrewd commercial decision, Lester feels that it works best when seen as a single film, shown without an interval and with the awkward reprise at the beginning of *The Four Musketeers* deleted. Before dealing with the films separately, one should certainly draw attention to the structural unity of the whole adaptation, which a severing of the work into two films inevitably disguised. (It had little effect on the critical reception of *The Three Musketeers*: it had an enormous effect on the reception of *The Four Musketeers*. How the whole package would have been received is anybody's guess: probably less enthusiastically than *Three* and more enthusiastically than *Four*.)

The Four Musketeers brings down the fantasy structure of *The Three Musketeers*: it is mock heroic with a sharp edge, a savage twist of Fortune's Wheel (a recurrent image of both films) which is some-times brutally to upend one's expectations. If *The Three Musketeers* is to end with fireworks, *The Four Musketeers* is to end with fire. The pastiche and panache of Legrand's score in the former film gives way to the heavier dramatic style of Lalo Schifrin in the latter. It repeats the structure of the earlier part, but with dark variations. For example, *The Three Musketeers* contains a fight between the Musketeers and the Cardinal's men outside a convent; a fight between Rochefort and d'Artagnan; a trip by Milady to England and a meeting with the Duke of Buckingham; a secret meeting in the rain; a journey by Planchet to England to warn Buckingham of treachery; a concluding fight between Constance and Milady. All of these events are repeated in *The Four Musketeers*, but, in every case, the staging and the outcome of events are significantly darker. The fight between the Musketeers and the Cardinal's men (like that at the end of the film between d'Artagnan and Rochefort) is now murderous and to the kill. Whereas there were many fights and no deaths in *The Three Musketeers*, in *The Four Musketeers*, the peo-ple who are stabbed now fail to get up. The fight on the ice in the latter ostensibly seems to take the atmosphere close to pantomime. But the ice becomes bloodstained, not only recalling the blood-stained white sheet on the washing line in *The Three Musketeers*, but also indicating the chillier atmosphere of the second part. When Aramis in his fight here stabs someone and realises he has actually killed him, he hovers over the body, startled.

Similarly, the secret meeting in the rain in *The Four Musketeers* is not part of a romantic assignation (as it was in the earlier part, arranging a meeting between Buckingham and the Queen of France) but a plot of political assassination, hatched between Richelieu and Milady. Milady's trip to England in *The Four Musketeers*, unlike that in the earlier part, is to lead to Buckingham's murder. Planchet's journey this time is to be too late, an omen of this sug-gested by the second journey's having none of the comic interlude of sea-sickness of the first. Whereas the fight between Constance and Milady in *The Three Musketeers* has some comic by-play, notably in Constance's crude but effective tactic of pelting her honourable lady opponent ignobly with fruit, the struggle between them in *The Four Musketeers* is to be brief and savage, and to lead to the death of them both.

There are numerous other details that one can read across both films, details which would probably escape the viewer if the viewing of the two parts were separated substantially in time. For example, when Milady and her maid Kitty first see d'Artagnan from their carriage early in *The Three Musketeers* (he is occupied in an altercation with Rochefort at the time), they both comment on him. 'He's very handsome,' says Kitty, to which Milady adds: 'Even with his broken rapier'. This anticipates the romantic relationship d'Artagnan is to share with both ladies in *The Four Musketeers*. The comment about his broken rapier might even anticipate that impudently suggestive shot of the wilting flower in the morning after d'Artagnan's night of love with Milady.

To view the two parts as a single film is to make one more aware of the development of d'Artagnan's character and situation. He needs help at the end of *The Three Musketeers*, but he does not need help at the end of *The Four Musketeers*. By the end of the latter, he seems to have grown somewhat away from his friends. Porthos's concluding narration talks of 'the old days, you see . . . when we were indeed all for one and one for all,' implying that these days are now over and that d'Artagnan can now fight his own battles and go his own way.

The character whose motivation suffers most in the separate releases of the films is that of Athos (Oliver Reed). In *The Three Musketeers*, Athos is given a melancholy gravity and intensity which is not accounted for. For example, when he fights there is not the sense of play that is observable in Porthos or Aramis, or the sense of foolhardy enjoyment that is in the style of d'Artagnan. Yet the explanation for this is not furnished until *The Four Musketeers*: that his behaviour is the product of bitter dishonour and emotional disillusionment.

When Athos, Porthos and Aramis are introduced, the most striking feature is the fact that Athos is the only one of the three to be introduced seriously. Porthos (Frank Finlay) is modelling for a portrait and trying to conceal the full extent of his ample girth and the fact that the gold sash he is ostentatiously displaying does not extend fully around his apparel. When d'Artagnan collides with him, Porthos's antics as a *poseur* are revealed and he is angry enough to demand a duel, but the immediate purpose of this scene is humour, Aramis commenting on his friend's discomfort that 'discretion is the better part of vanity'. Similarly, Aramis's dandified nature is wittily extolled in his nonchalant sword display which consists of slicing new candles in half that have just been placed in their holders by increasingly exasperated servants. (An important class point is being made here, but again the immediate purpose and effect is one of humour — the detail acquires different connotations as the film develops.) But Athos is presented sitting on the stairs, suffering from the pox (reflecting his sexual despair?), in pain and drinking. He does grow increasingly drunk throughout *The Three Musketeers* and, at one stage, even falls backwards into a well. It is not until *The Four Musketeers* that we learn that the well into which he has fallen is that of romantic despair.

If there is a primary distinction to be made between the films, it is in the quality of their romanticism. *The Three Musketeers* is characterised by romantic excess and extravagance, particularly conveyed in the expansive phrases and gestures of the Duke of Buckingham and d'Artagnan as they pay court to the respective objects of their ardour, the Queen and Constance. The theme is further extended by the bumbling approach to romance of a broadly comic character like Bonancieux (his keys rattling on his chest as he contemplates the delights of Thursday nights with Constance) and the nervous gestures of love made by the King, who is a rather complex, pathetic figure. *The Four Musketeers* is suffused with romantic anguish, the dreadful love in the past between Athos and Milady hanging like a dark cloud over events and eventually and violently severing the love relationships of the earlier part — Constance from d'Artagnan, Buckingham from Queen Anne, Rochefort from Milady, Milady from Buckingham, Rochefort, d'Artagnan and Athos. The power of Oliver Reed's performance in *The Four Musketeers* overwhelms the film with such a sense of romantic loss that d'Artagnan's seemingly swift recovery from the emotional shock of Constance's death is almost flippant, an exposure of a certain superficiality in the hero's character — an effect Lester surely intended.

It is appropriate here to begin with some comments about the individual films. In *The Three Musketeers* the main romantic interest is provided by the secret love affair between Anne, Queen of France (Geraldine Chaplin) and the English Duke of Buckingham (Simon Ward). Cardinal Richelieu (Charlton Heston) is scheming to discredit Anne, thus giving him a greater hold over the King and the destiny of France. When Anne gives Buckingham a love memento in the form of some diamond studs which were a present to her from the King (Jean-Pierre Cassell), the Cardinal sees his chance. He sends Milady to England to acquire two of the studs by seduction and plans to reveal Anne's dishonour at an elaborate ball. But at the instigation of the Queen's loyal dresser, Constance, d'Artagnan and

Planchet ride to England to warn Buckingham, who arranges to have two identical studs manufactured and entrusts d'Artagnan to return them to the Queen before the King discovers their absence.

One can disentangle a number of separate points from this summary. Richelieu's deviousness is prepared for in that delightful mini-epic arrival of his in Paris, attended by a small, surly crowd who are provided with flags and money for a 'spontaneous' display of affection. Richelieu is seen almost in profile looking stonily towards the camera and the impression is given of a man who habitually shows only one side of his face to the world. D'Artagnan's zeal leads him into a situation where he is acting against the Cardinal and his King in favour of the Queen, which in effect means acting for England against his beloved France. These kinds of uneasy alliances run through the film. They undercut the ostensible patriotism and the purity of the Musketeers' actions, and emphasise them as opportunists and men spoiling for a fight at the least provocation, irrespective of justice or country. After vanquishing the King's guards at the laundry and hence saving Buckingham, they are curious to know what they were fighting for. 'Who was that?' asks Porthos, to which Athos replies, 'I don't know but he sounded a touch foreign to me.' Ostensibly the King's men, they are sometimes instrumental in working against their monarch's interests.

Both the King and Buckingham are the Queen's men, both in thrall to her, a link which is stressed visually when both men, at different points in the film, check their reflections prior to a crucial meeting with Anne. But they are rather differently treated. Buckingham might have his own private shrine to the Queen, but he is still not averse to sexual dalliance with Milady. ('A pretty price to pay for infidelity,' he says when he discovers that the diamond studs are missing.) This anticipates the d'Artagnan of *The Four Musketeers* who also professes loyalty to Constance whilst enjoying other women's favours. The full significance of such infidelity is kept in check in *The Three Musketeers*, since the cuckolds are the comic Bonancieux and the foppish King. In *The Four Musketeers*, the consequences of such infidelity are to be much more savagely felt, both in the imagery (Milady's bathwater stained with Rochefort's blood, which is his designed shock effect and warning to her not to become romantically involved with d'Artagnan) and in the events (the action and atmosphere being dominated by Athos's destructive romantic obsession over just one woman).

Nevertheless, in *The Three Musketeers*, it is possible to feel more for the King than for Buckingham in the struggle for Anne. Jean-Pierre Cassell's performance is interestingly conceived. The King's foppishness does not entirely conceal his sadness and his isolation. Cassell's performance is characterised by little gestures of dismissal, largely to himself, the nervous reflections of a man whom no one attends to or takes seriously. Even when he offers a morsel to his dog at the concluding ceremony of *The Three Musketeers*, the dog refuses to take it. Some prominence is given to the look of wistful pain that comes into his eyes when looking at Anne as Richelieu is ironically assuring the King of the warmth of Anne's devotion ('I'm not scorched by the heat'). Similarly, one notes his anxious leaning forward when the Queen at the concluding ceremony seems to be giving d'Artagnan a gift for services rendered.

Aided by an unselfishly unflattering performance by Geraldine Chaplin, Lester makes Anne an unworthy object of romantic obsession. She is introduced at Court on a carousel being whirled around by servants at a somewhat slower speed than she requires. 'Come on, make them go faster, *whip* them!' she snaps, before adding, 'I feel . . . I feel . . . sick.' Anne's sadistic petulance is not only an expression of character, but of something vital about the relationship which exists between the upper and lower orders. Indeed the carousel is a magnificent visual image of that society. The servants turn the bottom wheel and the top spins, the seats occupied by the languishing nobility. Although the lower orders are ignored, buffeted and abused by that society, they are essential to the smooth running of it. Without them it could not function, whether they merely provide the entertainment or are the laundry girls who wash the gentry's shirts. 'So that's how it's done,' says Buckingham smugly, during his secret assignation with Anne in the laundry — a witty visual pun on washing his dirty linen in public. 'In future I'll wear my shirts with more respect.' Needless to say, when he is later bustling through the court while effecting a change of clothing, the servants are completely depersonalised, merely a series of hands servicing his requirements, and he does not even look at them. It is not only an indication of Buckingham's arrogance, which further complicates the rightness of d'Artagnan's and the Musketeers' endeavours on his behalf. It is preparing for the moment in *The Four Musketeers* when a servant is to strike back, and Buckingham's abused valet, Felton, becomes the instrument of the Duke's destruction.

In *The Three Musketeers*, the social abuses, cruelty and poverty are perceptible, but registered with an appropriately unemphatic eye, recognising that this is a period of isolated protest rather than revolution. D'Artagnan's servant, Planchet, occasionally grumbles at his lot, but when he first lines up for inspection to be selected by his new master, he is clearly pleased to be employed and even leans over curiously as d'Artagnan is paying for him to see how much his master thinks he is worth. Roy Kinnear's marvellous performance is a giddy mixture of hilarity and harassment, happiness and hysteria, but it is not until *The Four Musketeers* that he has the temerity to murmur, 'All right for some', as he is sent off on another impossible mission which could cut short his clowning with a nasty, brutish death. The dwarfs at the Ball too are very keen to serve, clucking over whether the King will deign to eat one of their sweetmeats ('He's having one of mine!'), and Lester as usual has a lot of fun with the exasperated mutterings of a servant body straining to transport an upper society which is becoming heavy with its own debauchery. (Milady's carriage-bearers grumble about this in *The Four Musketeers*: 'She's put on weight . . . why doesn't she get a horse?') The main feeling is of a society that sees these divisions as natural and right, which adds all the more force to the clear presentation of its inequities and its denial of individual recognition. Rochefort can make Bonancieux disbelieve the evidence of his own eyes. In the search for Constance and d'Artagnan, Bonancieux seems to see a finger sticking out of a cupboard, but because Rochefort does not see it (it's on his blind side) then clearly it cannot be there. When d'Artagnan and Planchet are trying to board a ship to England with a pass stolen from Rochefort, the official seems dubious. 'This pass is only for one,' he says, to which d'Artagnan returns with ineffable logic, 'I *am* only one. That' — pointing to Planchet — 'is a servant'.

D'Artagnan is interesting here, because he traverses the various class divisions so insistently and speedily. His first confrontations with both Rochefort and Aramis are instigated by his adversaries' snobbishness, but also checked by their reluctance to involve themselves in a brawl with a social inferior. 'I was speaking *at* you, sir,' says Rochefort, 'if you were a gentleman, I would speak to you'. Similarly Aramis: 'You see a deal too much. It is a fault among country folk.' D'Artagnan acts as a sort of go-between across the societies of master and servant. Indeed, the film *The Go-Between* (1970) is actually evoked when d'Artagnan passes a message of love and warning to Buckingham who has just been hunting and who stains the letter with blood. As in the Losey film, this is a portent of the blood-letting to come, and a reminder of the same situation of a naive romantic acting as messenger for two people unworthy of his attentions. Through the haphazard progress of d'Artagnan, various echelons of society are exposed that otherwise would not have been, yet d'Artagnan, a man in a hurry, pays little attention to them. He is a mercenary not a moralist and, rather like the hero in *Cuba*, he precariously professes commitment and nobility to a cause he only dimly understands.

This is particularly striking in the Musketeers' involvement in the religious wars in *The Four Musketeers*. If romanticism and social justice are treated with a mixture of satire and severity by Lester, this is equally true here of his attitude to religion. In *The Three Musketeers*, religion is satirised principally by its intrusion in incongruous contexts. This is first elaborated in the fight outside the convent, eagerly watched by nuns. Aramis, who is supposedly going to enter the church, insists that he and a Cardinal's guard should pray before they fight, using their swords as a cross (a motif which is powerfully to recur in *Robin and Marian*). 'Gentle Jesus, meek and *mild*,' he says, on the last word knocking his opponent's sword from under him and gaining an immediate advantage for the fight. Here the connection between religion and trickery is treated amusingly, but, of course, throughout *The Three Musketeers*, this sort of deception is disturbingly personified by Cardinal Richelieu, a figure who exemplifies an equation between religion and a possibly murderous duplicity. In *The Four Musketeers*, these tremors of demonism are to come insistently to the surface. This film takes place against the background of the destructive religious wars. A picnic scene for royalty includes a moment when a cleric climbs a ladder to intone the last rites for rebels and criminals who are hanging from a tree: 'Look down upon these sinners *hanging* here.' It is a variation of the hawks and doves scene in the first part — the casual cruelty of the upper orders — but it is a variation with a sadistic twist. If religion is part of the ironic humour of *The Three Musketeers*, in *The Four Musketeers* it is part of the film's apparatus of violence — rosary beads as a murder weapon; Rochefort being skewered by d'Artagnan's blade, the sword piercing him and a bible on a lectern. Lester's atheism has rarely been inspired to such lethal imagery.

Part of the interest for Lester in this society is its insecurity, the peculiar tension between privilege and paranoia. The upper orders do not fear revolution as yet, but they certainly fear each other, and it is this fear which makes the suspense in the film crackle, taking it beyond light adventure. The dominant motif of this comfortable society is that of spying, as if this luxuriance and privilege are bought at the cost of constant vigilance. The Cardinal has his spy to report on the Queen (Rodney Bewes in a funny cameo, embroidering with relish the fulsome insults to the Cardinal that were overheard). The King has his spy; true to the terms of Hollywood iconography of female evil, she is dark-haired. Milady spies on Buckingham. Rochefort is a resentful spy for Richelieu and is almost executed for it in *The Four Musketeers* (Richelieu: 'Spy. It is a foul word.' Rochefort: 'It is a familiar word to me, your eminence — in your service.'). Another of the Cardinal's spies is Bonancieux, with his spectacular spy-glass, or periscope, to spot the Queen and Constance in the garden together. Connected with this motif is the apparatus that goes with spying: concealed doors, keys and weapons (Richelieu's passage to the dungeons behind a portrait of the King; Buckingham's concealed doorway to his shrine to Anne; d'Artagnan's present of a sword from Buckingham, which, he discovers, has a concealed dagger in the handle). The impression given is of a society whose power base is dependent on its line of communications being cunning, secret and concealed.

This is particularly apparent in the elaborate Royal Ball, which is the concluding set-piece of *The Three Musketeers*. It is a visual feast in delicate whites and greys, offset only by the flaring red of Cardinal Richelieu. Yet the purpose behind this splendour is to expose the infidelity of the Queen. The ease with which the decorative can be turned into the malevolent is demonstrated by Milady's rapid transformation of hair-grip into sword during her fight with Constance. It is, in fact, a society of masks. Richelieu cloaks his deviousness under a demeanour of impeccable decorum and the Royal Ball is a perfect symbol of this. The dance between King and Queen almost breaks down because the man is trying to count the diamond studs and catch out his partner. The awkwardness of the occasion comes partially from its being so public. Chaos and unease lurk beneath the formality, the masks disguising guilt and corruption, and even the horns on the costumes are a pointed signifier of the King's fear of being cuckolded.

The motif of a masked society is central to the film. Milady's first sight of Buckingham in *The Three Musketeers* is through a transparent eye-shade and, felt in its full context, the effect is strikingly sinister, an image of both Milady's duplicity (the lace is supposed to be a blindfold) and, even at that stage, marking out Buckingham as a potential dead man in his inability to see approaching danger. The powerfully mounted sequence in *The Four Musketeers* in which Buckingham is killed is a logical extension of that, the relentless forward movement of an assassin whose danger no one comprehends. The motif of the mask recurs at the very end of the film when Milady is executed. Throughout she has reacted violently when her own mask, hiding the brand on her arm which signifies harlot, has been torn aside. When d'Artagnan inadvertently does so, she attacks him with an acid-filled knife. At the end she attempts to talk her way out of her destiny but her seductive stares this time cannot penetrate the Headsman's mask of death.

Faye Dunaway's characterisation of Milady is in some ways at the core of the film's meaning, certainly in *The Four Musketeers* where the character's presence and influence quite overshadow that of d'Artagnan. We learn in this part that she has been married to Athos (the Comte de L'Affaire), the marriage being destroyed at the discovery of the fleur-de-lis on the woman's arm, the symbol of dishonour. Beneath the glamour and the guile of the character is a real sense of pain, her actions a reptilian repudiation of her guilt, directed particularly at people who come too close. In the scene at the Inn with Richelieu in *The Four Musketeers*, when the Cardinal talks of the Queen's being 'paraded in dishonour', there is a telling close-up of Milady: a woman who really knows what that means, and whose progression has been permanently poisoned by that experience. There is a real chill in the scene that follows between Athos and Milady, his former wife. It is a familiar situation in a Lester film, of a hero and heroine meeting again after a past romance and, for various reasons, finding in the occasion intimations of tension and tragedy (the end of *Petulia*, or *Robin and Marian* and *Cuba*). It gains especial intensity here because it takes place at night during a violent thunderstorm, in sharp contrast to Athos's flashback reminiscence of the romance. (This has been done in a stylised series of tableaux like a courtly fairy tale: the Comte de L'Affaire is light, boyish, spruce, very different from his subsequent persona as the dark, unshaven, embittered Athos.) When he comments on her 'beauty', there is a clap of thunder, as if in a horror film. Milady unites beauty with fearsomeness in a striking and disturbing way, and the confluence of these qualities is surprisingly characteristic of the film.

The Three Musketeers represented a great come-back for Lester after five years in the wilderness. As he has admitted, it was very much a make-or-break film for him. The timing was right, the critics and the public generally applauding the film's adventurism as a change from the heavy neurosis and violence that characterised the cinema of the time. The tone was right. It seemed to offer a skittish view of heroism; a sharply witty picture of political paranoia that was an appropriate analogue to Watergate, as well as a ruefully funny look at the uneasy alliances developing between the shifty French and the smelly English that seemed hilariously apposite during the period of England's tentative tip-toe into the Common Market.

Considering that most critics saw (and still see) him as a farceur, it is perhaps as well that the two parts were released separately. Lester did at least receive rich plaudits for *The Three Musketeers* as it conformed more obviously to the oversimplified impressions of him as a comic satirist, a sender-up of unconsidered trifles. Nevertheless, one does need the more audacious fragmentations of *The Four Musketeers* to get a full measure of the adaptation's achievement. After *The Three Musketeers*, one might be forgiven for feeling a certain premonition that Lester might be in danger of losing his cutting edge under the trappings of costume spectacle. After *The Four Musketeers*, such fears are completely allayed. The whole adaptation is full of Lester's customary vision of social chaos and injustice, religious hypocrisy, savage divisions between rich and poor, as well as a continual clash between moral and mercenary values. The line between love and hate (Athos and Milady), admiration and apprehension (Richelieu and Rochefort) is very thin. It is in many ways a pessimistic vision of a violent and treacherous world, in which nobody is to be trusted, everybody to be feared. When a spy is poisoned by wine intended for the Musketeers ('I always had my doubts about the Anjou 22,' muses Aramis), Porthos comments pointedly: 'The sooner we get back safely under fire, the better.'

The recognition of treachery is important in these words, but so too is the amused irony of the tone. It is characteristic of Lester to carry these weighty undertones beneath a glittering sheen of witty entertainment, transmitted in fair measure by the drollery of Frank Finlay's performance and the fresh-faced acrobatics of Michael York. It is one of the reasons why Lester's films can be seen again and again. The richness of detail both on and below the surface is so'clever and provocative that one's curiosity never palls. *The Musketeers* adaptation is less of a historical romp than a historical inquisition: typically, putting fictional characters next to actual ones to enquire into the truths and illusions of an age, its romance and its realism. There are dark undercurrents, but the narrative verve never flags. 'In a picture where there is so much plot,' Lester said in a *Films and Filming* interview, 'there isn't time to sit quietly and let the thought seep through that the people might look marvellous but that their hair hasn't been washed for three years'.[3] The lice under the coiffure might not be the most immediate image of the traditional *Three Musketeers* but it is quintessential Richard Lester, and not at all an inappropriate image for a resplendent seventeenth-century society that is slowly rotting from within.

Notes

1. Alexandre Dumas, *The Three Musketeers* (translated by William Barrow, Collins, 1962) p. 118.

2. Ibid., p. 100.

3. *Films and Filming*, October 1974.

Plate 1: Lester and Buster Keaton on the set of *A Funny Thing Happened on the Way to the Forum*

Plate 2: *The Knack*, the four main characters in the park

Plate 3: *Help!*, Lester, the Beatles, and Eleanor Bron

Plate 4: *How I Won the War*, Roy Kinnear and John Lennon

Plate 5: *A Hard Day's Night*, Lester and Paul McCartney

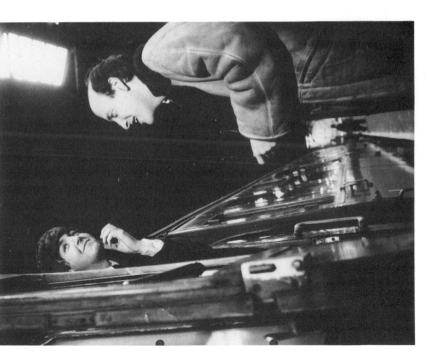

Plate 6: *Butch and Sundance*, the tight-rope walker

Plate 7: *The Bed-Sitting Room*, the marriage ceremony with the Instant God Kit

Plate 8: *The Bed-Sitting Room*, Ralph Richardson and Lester

Plate 9: *The Ritz*, Rita Moreno and Jack Weston with portrait of Jean Harlow

Plate 10: *Petulia*, Julie Christie

Plate 11: *The Three Musketeers,* King, Cardinal and Queen at the masked ball

Plate 12: *Robin and Marian,* the fight

Plate 13: *Juggernaut,* bomb disposal men scaling the *Britannic*

Plate 14: *Cuba,* Sean Connery

Plate 15: *Superman II*, Superman and Lois Lane

Plate 16: *Superman III*, Clark Kent fights Superman

Chapter SIX

HOLDING THE COUNTRY TO RANSOM

Juggernaut

Bombs are put aboard an ocean liner, the *Britannic*, which goes to sea before this is discovered. A ransom is demanded ashore by a mysterious, unseen terrorist whose code-name is Juggernaut. Whilst the government and the shipping company negotiate with this unknown figure, a squad of bomb disposal experts are landed on the ship in an endeavour to defuse the explosives. Meanwhile the police comb London in their search for Juggernaut.

Richard Lester was invited to take over the direction of *Juggernaut* at short notice after two previous directors (Bryan Forbes and Don Taylor) had been fired. Lester had already read the script and liked the original idea (based on an actual event when a bomb had been placed on board the *QE2*), but insisted on bringing in Alan Plater, with whom he had already worked on an eventually aborted project, *Send Him Victorious*, for some rewriting. In fact, according to Lester, in the two and a half weeks they had prior to shooting, they 'rewrote every line'. (Lester had further insisted that he should have freedom of casting and he supplemented the existing cast of Richard Harris, Omar Sharif and David Hemmings with some familiar faces from his repertory company, such as Shirley Knight, Roy Kinnear and Michael Hordern.) Two things emerge almost instinctively from this intense and pressurised period of preparation and writing. First, that the character of the bomb-disposal expert Fallon (Richard Harris, in his best-ever screen performance) might have been the closest that Lester has ever come to a self-portrait in his films: an expert technician, a self-deprecating and humorous professional who, in a very short space of time, must save a ship/film in peril. Secondly, that the nature of the material and the urgency of the writing situation might have locked almost subconsciously into the mood of the country at a time of great political turmoil (the early months of 1974) to produce a statement on the condition of the country. For there is no doubt in my mind that *Juggernaut* is essentially the most mature comment on contemporary British politics that the national cinema produced during the seventies. It is not a disaster movie as such: more a film about a *society* heading for disaster.

None the less, when *Juggernaut* first appeared late in 1974, it was immediately categorised as being part of the contemporary cycle of 'group-jeopardy' films that had been a feature of the popular cinema of the early 1970s. It does indeed share some of the characteristics of films like Ronald Neame's *The Poseidon Adventure* (1972), Irwin Allen and John Guillermin's *The Towering Inferno* (1974), Mark Robson's *Earthquake* (1974), Jack Smight's *Airport 1975* (1974) and Joseph Sargent's *The Taking of Pelham 123* (1974) which comprise the most popular examples of the genre. There is the usual large group of stranded people to represent a supposed cross-section of humanity; an emphasis on gadgetry which is connected to the technical accomplishment of the heroes; a distinguished all-star cast; and even an abundance of water, which seemed to be one of the odder manifestations of this cycle. All that *Juggernaut* failed to contain, to link it with *The Poseidon Adventure* and *The Towering Inferno*, was a popular song to be crooned before the holocaust (possibly on the theme that only a bomb could tear us apart). There is a pop group aboard the *Britannic*, complete with electronic instruments, but its only contribution is to wonder at one stage whether the ship is earthed.

Of this cycle of films, *Juggernaut* probably has most in common with *The Taking of Pelham 123* and *The Towering Inferno*. It shares with *The Taking of Pelham 123* the stress on terrorism and also a welcome, abrasive humour, which in the latter film takes the form of manifesting through an inventive flow of four-letter words the impotence of hapless civilians in the face of the kind of cool ruthlessness of people who can hijack a subway train. In *Pelham*, however, the motives of the terrorists are merely part of the suspense mechanism rather than a contribution to a political sub-theme. It more or less assumes that terrorism is a form of insanity ('Don't take this personally,' says the hero Walter Matthau over the intercom to the terrorist leader, 'but when all this is over, might I suggest you go and see a psychiatrist?'). In *Juggernaut*, the terrorist is a much more complex figure, whose position is taken seriously and who makes an important contribution to the film's debate on human and political issues. *Juggernaut* shares with *The Towering Inferno* an allegorical sub-theme, though it expresses itself in a very different way. Although superficially about the burning of a huge tower block, *Inferno* can be read as a modernised version of Man versus Nature, in which the former's technological arrogance is undermined by Nature's imperious forces, culminating in a situation where man is a helpless onlooker as the final elemental struggle takes place between fire and water. At the end, eyes which have formerly looked sky-wards in admiration of the building now look heavenwards in grati-tude for divine mercy and in humility at divine admonition of human aggrandisement. (The expression of this message is very ambivalent, of course: whilst criticising man's technological arro-gance, the film celebrates it also through the grandeur of its special effects; whilst asking God's forgiveness for man's conceit, the film ensures that its superstars, Paul Newman and Steve McQueen, are ultimately equal to everything that is thrown at them and will prob-ably collaborate on future tower buildings.) The religiosity of *Inferno* is completely eschewed by *Juggernaut*, which is invested instead with Lester's usual devout atheism. Religion as a solution, consolation or explanation is offered only as a joke: the First Officer (Mark Burns) ironically suggesting that he might consider entering the Church if they survive this; the Social Director (Roy Kinnear), when passed by two nuns on deck, regarding them slyly as early arrivals for his Fancy Dress Ball. In the place of a washy religious message, *Juggernaut* substitutes a sharp moral allegory in which the thriller format gives particular emphasis to the urgency of the issues involved.

The other thing *Juggernaut* shares with *The Towering Inferno* is the Hawksian stress on male cameraderie and professionalism. In fact, one of the important recurring motifs of *Juggernaut* is the respect that is due to proper leadership, and the pride that comes from professionalism in work. The close relationship between Fallon and Braddock (David Hemmings) of the bomb disposal team basically derives not simply from Fallon's skill but from his will-ingness to lead by example and put his expertise to the test (the whole strategy behind the dismantling of the bomb is that of Fallon's taking the initial risk and making the first move and the others following when that has proved safe). This is very different from the niggling and hostile relationship between the ship's Captain (Omar Sharif) and his First Officer, largely because the Captain uses his position to *avoid* danger: he assigns the First Officer to the hazardous task of collecting the bomb disposal team from the sea; he selects a junior officer to assist the team when one of their men has been drowned. Attitudes to work and jobs inform the film on many levels. Fallon's definition of death is that it is 'Nature's way of telling you you're in the wrong job'. One could say that Juggernaut's whole motive for terrorism stems from his resentment at an undervaluation of his talents ('I'm still good at my job,' he insists to his accusers); and the ship's Social Director, Mr Curtain, is ultimately devastated by the events on board because he has failed in his job — that is, to cheer people up. In the context of the miners' dispute and the three-day working week in the Britain of early 1974, these themes of *Juggernaut* might have seemed all the more relevant to Alan Plater as he was writing it. Fallon's throwaway remark when he emerges from the art gallery after defusing that explosive device —'Doesn't anybody work in this country anymore?'— is actually at the heart of the film's meaning.

The most immediate analytical line on *Juggernaut*, and the one understandably taken by most critics at the time, is to approach it as a superior disaster movie. In this respect, it can be related to preceding Lester essays on the subject of genre — stimulating, quizzical forays into the musical (for example, *A Funny Thing Happened on the Way to the Forum*), the historical romance (*The Three Musketeers*), the war film (*How I Won the War*). What Lester does in *Juggernaut* is to take a traditional disaster theme and perform some fascinating variations around it. He intensifies immediacy by an attention to detail of people at work: in the engine room or the kitchen, or on deck. Traditional doses of nobility and heroism, like Shelley Winters' grotesque underwater display in *The Poseidon Adventure* are entirely eliminated. Here the passengers start becoming irritable and uneasy and, as the full situation dawns on them, credibly work their way up to a blind terror that even cures one of them of sea-sickness. He undercuts sentimentality by taking a notably astringent attitude towards the children, who are bright, cheerful nuisances throughout, get on the adults' frayed nerves and cause one man's death. Above all, the pomposity of the genre is punctured by wit. In *Juggernaut*, even the bomb has a sense of humour, sometimes capriciously assuming the personality of a birthday cracker, leaving fun messages when a false trail has been pursued, and going off like an alarm clock at one stage when a mightier explosion has been feared. The humour increases the tension rather than alleviates it, since it makes the film that much more edgy and unpredictable; and the imaginative fusion of fun and fear is extended in Roy Kinnear's remarkable performance as Mr Curtain, whose task is to provide entertainment for the passengers to distract them from their perils and whose strained good cheer is reduced by events to near-hysteria. 'A night to remember,' he mumbles nervously, unwittingly evoking an uneasy analogy between the situation of the liner and the ill-fated *Titanic*.

The film's unusual confluence of quirky humour and rigorous unsentimentality probably reaches its high-point at the Fancy Dress Ball, in which the passengers gather together listlessly, fully aware that beneath them is a team working on a bomb that could blow them all to pieces. The costumes themselves add a bizarre touch to the event (a man showing up as Dracula; someone else even dressed as an Arab terrorist and clutching a toy bomb). What is on view is not a picture of social cohesion, but of people glumly marooned within their own anxieties, their own isolation intensified by parallel shots of a motionless *Britannic* at sea (literally and metaphorically), and of the manager of the shipping company alone in a huge tower block, unsuccessfully grappling with the terrorist threat. Whilst her husband, a 'liberal policeman', attempts to discover Juggernaut on shore, Mrs McCleod (Caroline Mortimer) has to cope alone with her misery on the ship, receiving little consolation or compassion from her blithely unconcerned children. Mrs Bannister (Shirley Knight), who had started an association with the Captain, has been abruptly ejected from his life at the onset of the crisis; and shares a dance instead with Mr Curtain which becomes a poignant, disconsolate little two-step of loneliness and fear. In the scene's potentially most tricky moment, when his wife asks the American politician (Clifton James) whether he has ever been unfaithful, Lester beautifully side-steps the dangers of overt sentimentality by playing on the noise around the couple; the man's embarrassment at the question; an ambiguity about whether his denial is true or not (in his job as politician, he has said earlier, he has learnt to lie convincingly); and, finally, by having the man's party hat fall over his face immediately after this proclamation of fidelity. This last touch is a lovely, utterly typical piece of Lester observation of the perverse way in which life can place an abrupt banana skin beneath human solemnity.

The opening scene is a particularly interesting example of Lester's confident way with the genre. It is full of clues to the subsequent development of the film, as the *Britannic* pulls out of Southampton. One curious shot watches the departure of the ship from behind the blue light on a police car, a shot which links Superintendent

McCleod (Anthony Hopkins), whose car it is, with his wife and children who are on the *Britannic*, and anticipates the involvement of the police in the subsequent debate about the fate of the ship. McCleod tries to shout and wave to his family, but his efforts are submerged by the noise of the band and the crowd. His frantic hand movements convey the sense of a man not waving but drowning, a gesture which implies foreboding and inadvertently forecasts the fate which could overtake his family. Mrs Bannister is to refer to the Stevie Smith poem, 'Not Waving, But Drowning', when the passengers have learnt about the bomb and, in various ways, are failing to put a brave face on it. Obviously, all this only becomes apparent as the film develops, and this opening — an oblique, unsettling, seemingly disconnected sequence of shots of farewell waves and anxious departures — is a sort of game with the conventions of character and situation to see if the audience can make the correct connections and relations before Lester chooses to reveal them.

The motif of game is a crucial one in the film. Throughout, the bomb disposal expert, Fallon, treats the whole occasion in the manner of an intellectual challenge, like chess. (During his scene with the Captain, there is an ornamental chess set directly in front of Fallon on the table.) The suspenseful scenes where stage by stage Fallon attempts to defuse the bomb mechanism are simultaneously presented as an exercise by Fallon in reading Juggernaut's mind, guessing his intentions, anticipating his opponent's next move. Fallon's procedure has the clinical precision of brain surgery: in the process the psychology of Juggernaut is slowly dissected. The game Fallon masters is, essentially, 'What's My Line?' in which stage by stage he proceeds to the identity of the 'mystery guest'. By fathoming how the bomb works, he simultaneously fathoms who put it together.[1] 'I'm beginning to recognise his style,' he says. 'There's something about his brush-strokes . . . about his tone of voice' (ultimately everything will depend on Fallon's reading of that tone of voice). Nevertheless, as in all games, there is an important element of chance and luck, the sense of Superintendent McCleod's bitter comment earlier that 'it's all a bloody lottery anyway'. In the central climax of the film, with all the psychological expertise at his command, Fallon has to decide whether his opponent is bluffing and has to gamble on which of two wires to cut — one of which would defuse the danger, the other of which would blow up the ship.

The motif of game is woven very consciously into the film's visual surface. At one stage what seems to be a radar screen turns out to be a video ping-pong machine. Elsewhere there are numerous shots of games on deck, of a table-tennis room, of a game of what Mr Curtain calls 'cut-throat Bingo'. Even one of the suspected terrorists is interviewed at a greyhound track where he works. This recurrent image of play can, on one level, be take as an ironic contrast to the deadly earnest affairs which occupy the film's main action. The children in particular are involved with this, creating their own world parallel to that of the adults. 'It's Action Man,' says a boy, as he sees one of the bomb disposal team descending from the plane to the ship, the adult drama translated instantly and ironically into childhood fantasy. They also play 'I-Spy', which could actually put them ahead of the adults in their perception of the real situation on board (seeing the ship's flag, the child interprets quite correctly that the *Britannic* is carrying explosives, but converts this knowledge back into the currency of 'play': 'Give myself fifteen points'). The children play a game of 'pick-up sticks' which offers an innocently amusing, if grisly, parallel to the main action — the steady hands needed for dismantling bombs.

However, it becomes apparent that this obsession with game is not an ironic variation on the film's main concerns, but a crucial expression of them. A characteristic of these games is the presence of numbers and coloured lights, which visually link such diverse aspects of the film as the game of 'Shipwreck', the lights of the greyhound stadium, the plan of the *Britannic* doors, and the timing mechanism of the bomb itself. The link is not simply visual but thematic, stressing the fascination of mechanical devices, technological impersonality, and the processing of people as data. This clearly implicates Juggernaut, who has created his master-bomb which endangers helpless and, to him, faceless people. But it also implicates the people in London who are trying to deal with this dilemma. 'It's a much bigger game than you imagine,' the ship's Captain is told when he angrily enquires why the ransom money is not being paid. Should one put twelve hundred lives at risk, or should one pay Juggernaut his £500,000? The manager of the shipping company, Nicholas Porter (Ian Holm) and the politician, Hughes (John Stride) disagree: and it is here that 'playing with numbers' moves away from the realm of game and into the dimension of morality.

In addition to being at the mercy of the device of Juggernaut and the skill of Fallon, the passengers are also dependent for their fate on decisions taken in London by various power groups of different viewpoints, each with their own image to sustain, their own particular axes to grind and their own method of dealing with this particular problem. The shipping company, represented by Porter, fears for the lives of the people on board and wants to pay Juggernaut the money. The government, represented by Hughes, is afraid of what might happen if the country is seen to give in to 'extortion by terror' and veiled warnings are uttered about the withdrawal of government subsidies and loans if the company decides to act contrary to this principle. The police feel that the best chance of catching Juggernaut is to promise him the money and attempt to snatch him at or after the pay-off. The line between strategy and morality is a thin one, and for the moment Juggernaut has them dangling on a wire.

Although each point of view has its merits, the film is very direct in its distribution of sympathies. The main conflict is between the humanist, Porter, and the pragmatist politician, Hughes. Porter is agitated, sensitive, obviously feeling the situation personally (with the terrorist, he is the only character in the film who is given a home life), whilst Hughes is suave, withdrawn, until giving the government's position, at which point the camera moves in as if for a party political broadcast and he discusses the fate of the passengers whilst coping with the *Times* crossword puzzle on his knee. The crossword puzzle is a clue to the way in which Hughes sees the situation in terms of an abstract problem to be solved rather than in terms of human lives at risk. Much is made in the film of the difference between conceiving of the passengers as an anonymous mass of twelve hundred or feeling them as separate frightened individuals. The theme is intensified by the film's judicious visual contrast between large and small. An aerial shot of the *Britannic* can make the ship look tiny, whereas a single screw on the bomb mechanism can be magnified in close-up so that it looks enormous — both images suggesting that a sense of scale is very much dependent on point of view. Twelve hundred people can seem minimal in the eyes of a detached observer like Hughes, whereas a woman and two children can seem enormous to someone closely involved like Superintendent McCleod, whose scrupulous expression of neutrality on the moral question ('No opinion,' he says, consciously omitting the personal pronoun) is belied by the visible deterioration of his appearance as the suspense of the night wears on. Indeed, the film's strategy in putting McCleod's family on board the *Britannic* seems a device not so much to intensify emotional involvement as to undermine the notion of police objectivity — admirable in theory, impossible in practice.

As the dilemma focuses on the attitudes of different institutions to terrorism, it is inevitable that the moral dimensions of the situation expand into the political arena. It is here that the concealed allegorical import of the film is felt. Without displacing the suspence structure with a political essay and without tying itself to specific correspondences between characters and events in the film and in real life, *Juggernaut* is a brilliantly imaginative evocation of the Condition of England, an ingeniously structured enquiry into the physical and spiritual condition of a particular social organism in a questionable state of health at a crucial time in the country's history.[2] The time is 1973–4, which saw the final weeks of the Heath Conservative Government and the miners' strike, a time of power cuts and the three-day week. The *Britannic* is implicitly England, sailing into choppy waters when the stabilisers are not working, a so-called luxury liner which is, in fact, being re-built around people's ears and which seems to be going to seed (tomato juice spilt on walls; soggy streamers on deck; drink on the Captain's cabin wall). When the bomb is discovered, the Captain seals off some areas of the ship from the passengers ('Because of the re-fit, we're used to that anyway'), with the result that the ship becomes only partially operational — like England itself, in those early months.

'Looks like Ted Heath,' says an observer, when the Captain is spotted on the bridge. The ship is run by a man who seems ill-equipped to deal with the evolving crisis and whose authority and effectiveness progressively diminish, the Captain becoming essentially a spectator when matters are at their most critical and decisive, even though feebly insisting, 'It's still my ship'.[3] He is not consulted about the company's initial decision to withhold the money; he is not on the life-boat to help his men bring in the bomb disposal team; he has not the electronics expertise to help Fallon and his associates, having to delegate this task to a junior officer and then envy the man's position in the thick of things. His passivity is clearly unhelpful for a ship which at times seems run like a cross between a betting-shop and a sports arena, with its own anachronistic Court Jester offering to demonstrate the Lambeth Walk to people who are on a vessel in which they can scarcely stand upright. With the intervention of Juggernaut — the undervalued working man, good at his job, who decides to take revenge on the system — the *Britannic* is compelled to go round and round in circles before coming to a complete halt; and the situation of the ship/country is crystallised by that ghostly shot of the unoccupied canteen in which everything seems to be shaking, unstable, unsafe, trembling as if with terror.

The underlying political allegory (the English way of life under siege) is emphasised verbally by irreverent references to the BBC, Princess Anne and the Queen Mum, and visually by a range of imagery which, despite the restricted settings, manages to embrace evocative icons of England and Englishness: Whitehall, Big Ben, the National Gallery, the Royal Ballet. The allegory is also relayed through an emphatic colour symbolism. Fallon is the man who, with care, can restore the stability and mobility of the Britannic — implicitly, the country. He is introduced against a *red* background and wearing a *white* sweater with a *blue* shirt-sleeve showing. When later he is about to start defusing the bomb with his second-in-command Braddock, he rings through with instructions to the Captain, wearing a blue shirt and holding a red telephone with a white cord. Alternatively, the explosive wires are coloured simply red and blue, which emphasise the disruptive political polarities involved in this struggle and reinforce the image of the Britannic itself as an England sitting on a powder-keg of potentially divisive and destructive social forces.

The struggle over the future of the ship, then, with various factions fighting for power and influence, forms the basis for a stimulating filmic essay on the theme of 'Who runs the country?' (the issue on which Heath fought the election). Significantly, there is a wide gap, physically and socially, between the people who are taking the decisions and the people whom those decisions affect. This is emphasised by the film's recurrent use of a stylistic device, whereby we hear a voice over the soundtrack describing what is to happen (for example, Juggernaut's first phone-call, or the Naval Officer's description of the actions of Fallon's men on the ship) whilst what we see is this narration's being translated into action. It is a device effective for narrative economy, and it also appropriately suggests the voice as an important trigger-mechanism for the action: as indicated previously, everything, finally, is to hinge on Juggernaut's voice to Fallon, and Fallon's interpretation of the sound he hears. Mainly, however, it seems to draw attention to the distance between the character who has activated the visual events and the people whose lives are particularly affected by his behaviour.

In this power game, women and children especially are afforded only a marginal role, being roped off from the main action. This is plainly a deliberate part of the film's political allegory, in which women are seen as helpless vessels. The potential romance between the Captain and Mrs Bannister, the equivalent of which one finds in other disaster movies, is introduced, it seems, only to heighten our awareness of the absence of romantic love, the relationship obstinately refusing to develop when the action proper starts. She is made to feel irrelevant and a spectator, merely someone to be 'impressed' by what is happening rather than someone who has a useful role to play. After saying that it is hard to care about the lives of twelve hundred people but that there is usually one whom one cares about, she asks the Captain pointedly, 'Is it me?'; and the question remains, equally pointedly, unanswered. When she asks Mrs McCleod if she will join her in getting drunk, the latter gestures to her pregnant state and, by way of explaining her moderation, says, 'Responsibilities'. One cannot help comparing this with the politician's comment early on to Porter and McCleod that the moral dilemma is one essentially of 'responsibility'. In the woman's realm, the term means not having too much to drink, which might affect one life; in the male realm of political and economic power, it means the power to decide the value of twelve hundred lives. One is made constantly aware of the helplessness of the passengers — in effect, the general public — who are incompletely informed by the crew about what is going on and reduced to drawing or taking photographs of the people and events that could drastically affect their own futures. When one passenger does attempt to intervene and transform a passive situation into an active one (his concern about the member of the bomb disposal team who falls into the ocean), he is forceably rebuffed by a naval Officer.

'You don't give the orders,' says Fallon to the Captain. 'That good and gifted man who planted the bombs gives the orders.' Never has that ludicrous phrase, 'holding the country to ransom' been given a more ingenious and exciting dramatic context. Of recent films, only Claude Chabrol's *Nada* (1972) rivals *Juggernaut* in the way in which psychology and suspense are judiciously balanced with mature political commentary. The theme of *Nada* — that the only difference between the terrorism of the State and the terrorism of the anarchist is that the former offers only Death but the latter offers Revolution — is modified in this film, but the material still allows Lester to expound his anti-authoritarian sympathies and draw an uncomfortable parallel between terrorist and state. The Captain offers the following ironic toast: 'To the insanity of governments and the insanity of those who oppose them'. The tactics of the politician are not very different from that of the terrorist: he too is prepared to see twelve hundred people die to achieve what he wants; he too is prepared to apply financial pressures on the shipping company to bring the latter into line. 'And you think we should give way to people like that?' he says in disgust as Juggernaut exits after being interviewed by the police, to which Porter replies sharply, 'You *make* people like that.'

This retort gives an extra twist to that moment earlier in the film when Porter has decided, against the politician's advice, to pay the ransom. 'I'll have to inform the Minister,' says Hughes, 'and I can't answer for the consequences', to which Porter replies, 'These *are* the consequences. We're living through them.' At the time it seems a comment on the immediate situation, but, in retrospect, it has a broader implication: people like Juggernaut are the 'consequences' of the kind of insensitive Government represented by Hughes. It is interesting that, when the identity of Juggernaut is discovered by the police and Sid Buckland (Freddie Jones) is arrested, Buckland's nose suddenly begins to bleed — perhaps an extension of the colour symbolism of the film (red equals anarchy) but also a moment which makes the man seem suddenly vulnerable, human, sympathetic. (It is the only blood we see in the film.) Forceably retired four years previously (an explicit reference to the time when the Heath Government took office?), he now lives on a pitiable pension in a noticeably cramped house watching glossy advertisements which mock his own life-style, a 'good and gifted' man who has been callously discarded by the State he has served. In retaliation at his dismissal as an inessential figure (the analogy with the mood of the miners in 1973–4 is striking), he proceeds on a course of action which dramatically emphasises his continuing value and power, as, through his potency, the *Britannic* is completely immobilised.

The film builds to the wonderful final scene between Fallon and Buckland. Fallon has little time for the enthusiastic amateur anarchist, but he has much in common with Buckland, the old master whose 'brush-strokes' he recognises and a man who in the past has saved his life and taught him all he knows. Fallon does, however, implicitly align himself with 'those poor simple sods who have to pick up the pieces' made by the actions of 'insane governments' and their 'insane' opponents. As he hears the dancing on the upper deck of the ship whilst busying away at the bomb, he comments wryly, 'Civilisation must be preserved', not a ringing declaration of faith in western civilisation but a muted, mocking and moderate one cheer for democracy, recognising its failings and that it is, alas, all that we have.

It is the final contest. Fallon has got through to the red and the blue wire, but recognising that there is no way of knowing for certain which would activate and which would defuse the bomb, he asks to talk to Buckland as one professional to another, indeed as the contender talking to the champion. Buckland is led into the main Operations block and, in a brilliant stroke, even though there are only about two minutes to go before the bombs explode, he looks with irrepressible professional pride at the diagram of the bomb on the blackboard — his own handiwork — before turning to talk to Fallon. 'Is it the red or the blue?' asks Fallon. 'Cut the blue wire,' says Buckland. After an agonising moment in which Fallon debates within his own mind, he chooses to cut the red wire — and the ship is saved.

It is a magnificent moment, essentially the final move in the battle of wits between Fallon and Juggernaut. In what is probably a piece of psychological probing and one-upmanship, Fallon has freely admitted to Juggernaut that 'you're still the governor', almost inviting the latter to demonstrate his superiority to the patronising upstart by giving him false information. (One even fleetingly recalls Mr Curtain snapping back at Mrs Bannister when she compliments him on the job he is doing: 'Don't patronise *me*, darling'.) Further, the tension is increased by the fact that, with our sympathy being elicited for Juggernaut, we are far from certain whether he is lying or not. The beauty of the moment is that his misleading instruction to Fallon ('Cut the blue wire') is perfectly logical: not simple malice, but the proud refusal of the expert to the end to give away his professional secrets and concede defeat to the contender until the latter has actually *proved* his superiority. Fallon, who has been reading Juggernaut's mind throughout the film and who had indeed been checked by Braddock at one stage when making a lazy assumption about Juggernaut's strategy ('Isn't that what Juggernaut would want you to think, sir?'), correctly anticipates this last move and Juggernaut is finally outguessed and outmanoeuvred. Characteristically in Lester (one thinks also of Tolen and Colin in *The Knack*), the pupil has taken over the mantle of the teacher who has instructed him. 'In his master's steps he trod,' as Braddock has said earlier, a man who is killed when he inadvertently gets out of line with Fallon in an imperfect attempt to emulate his mentor. At the end Fallon is ready to take over. He can with some justification clap his hands and chant quietly, 'Fallon is the champion' — seen as a small figure in a long corridor isolated by his own skill.[4]

The film's ending is notably quiet and restrained. The relief of the passengers is muted because they have remained locked in their own isolation and therefore cannot share their feelings of relief. Fallon comes out on deck, but he is not congratulated for no one knows him or what he has done, and the camera pulls away, losing Fallon in the crowd and leaving us with the ship, moving slowly, uncertainly forward. Ken Thorne's subdued end-title music reflects with characteristic subtlety not triumph but melancholy, the feeling of a crisis having been survived but the sense of anti-climax suggesting that this might be a temporary respite. Considering the strong bond between Fallon and Buckland, the lack of recognition of Fallon at the end is rather disquieting. Might he become another Buckland? A warning note is sounded not to undervalue or abuse the working skills of men like Fallon or Buckland lest they turn them against the State they are serving. Men like the Captain, the politician, the policeman, the manager have a clear stake in the ship, the country, but ultimately it is men like Fallon who keep the ship/country going.

Notes

1. Compare Juggernaut's conceit in the bomb — a delicate mechanism of wit and cleverness which Fallon eventually recognises — with the attitude of the cold-blooded Irish terrorist (Cyril Cusack) whom Superintendent McCleod visits in prison in the hope that he might give him a few leads. This is one bomb expert who will not show off his talents. 'I really don't care who gets blown up,' says the prisoner and, tapping his head in a very significant gesture, he adds: 'It's all up here you see. And that's where it stays.' By contrast, by putting his brain into his bomb and, in a sense, allowing it to be analysed, Juggernaut unwittingly reveals his identity.

2. The 'Condition of England' was a phrase first used by Carlyle in *Past and Present* in 1843 and was the title of a highly influential book by the Liberal politician, C.F.G. Masterman in 1909. It is a term used in literary contexts for novels which seem centrally to be pessimistic prognostications about the state of the country; which often use London as symptomatic of the country's declining health; and analyse a 'cancerous growth in the body politic' which is only discovered when it is well advanced and possibly beyond cure. Novels which are traditionally discussed in these terms are nineteenth-century novels such as George Eliot's *Felix Holt* and Disraeli's *Sybil*, and, in the present century, E.M. Forster's *Howards End* and H.G. Wells', *Tono-Bungay* (David Lodge's discussion of the Wells novel in these terms in his 1966 book *The Language of Fiction* is particularly fine). Clearly a similar kind of genre could be defined for the cinema, and Raymond Durgnat's *A Mirror for England* (1971), Charles Barr's *Ealing Studios* (1976) and Jeffrey Richards' and Anthony Aldgate's *The Best of British* (1983) are three books which offer hints on how this study could be pursued. Joseph Losey's 1963 film, *The Servant* (coming in the wake

of the Profumo affair) seems to cry out for such an approach. Philip French has done a very entertaining reading of Hitchcock's *The Lady Vanishes* (1938) along these lines, seeing the film basically as an allegory about British society being threatened by a turbulent Europe and in which the British will pull themselves together at the last minute and fight the foe (the appeaser is shot down).

3. The casting of Omar Sharif as the Captain might seem to count against this allegorical interpretation. One should remember though, that Sharif was cast before Lester and Plater came onto the film: and what a deliciously comic touch that the man in charge of England's destiny is played by an Arab, as is the location of the explosives in oil drums (the price of oil about to blow the country's economy sky-high).

4. This may well have been the last thing in Alan Plater's mind, but I am intrigued by the similarity between the way in which Fallon's character is conceived and Billy Wilder's characterisation of Sherlock Holmes in *The Private Life of Sherlock Holmes* (1970) — and, after all, Fallon's dismantling of the bomb and simultaneous unmasking of the villain is essentially brilliant detective work. Like Wilder's Holmes, Fallon is cursed as well as blessed by his skill, admired but isolated (a man with no family). 'I do have one small talent, developed to near perfection,' says Fallon, and then adds: 'I wish it were a talent for playing the violin.'

Chapter SEVEN

FAME AND MISFORTUNE

Royal Flash

'We were coming out of the old age into the new,' comments the narrator-hero of George MacDonald Fraser's novel, *Royal Flash*.[1] Richard Lester's film of the novel also hovers between two worlds: between Rabelaisian ribaldry and Ruritanian romance; between elegant Victorian pastiche and sinister modern analogue. The material evokes both a Land of Hope and Glory (through Flashman's Imperialist arrogance) and a Land of Anthony Hope and Ignominy (through the cavalier use of the heroics of *The Prisoner of Zenda* to satirise the Victorian hero and to allegorise the growth of modern Germany).

Fraser's ingenious conceit in the Flashman novels was to take the bully, Harry Flashman, of that classic Victorian text, *Tom Brown's Schooldays* as being more representative of the Victorian age than Tom Brown himself. Fraser then proceeded to create friction by rubbing Flashman against the nineteenth century, allowing him to extol traditional virtues of the age in public — religiosity, sexual morality, obedience to elders, abstemiousness, bravery — which he despises and discards in private. His hypocrisy becomes an elaboration of D.H. Lawrence's description of the century as 'the age of the mealy-mouthed lie'[2] and, in satirical vein, uncovers the cruel degeneracy of certain of the upper classes of the time that Steven Marcus elaborated more seriously in his book *The Other Victorians* (1966). Lester's film of *Royal Flash* seizes on this, and grafts onto it something more: his own instinctive iconoclasm, which makes Flashman's coward/hero and Bismarck's great man/bore seem characteristic Lester figures. Similarly, his fascination for societies on the point of disintegration makes the plot of the film, with its conflicts between royalists and anarchists, between mealy-mouthed Victorianism and Prussian pomposity, ideal for his dramatic purposes.

What he brings to it as well is a specific cinematic and social awareness, a 1970s perspective which gives a darker, more serious inflection to the events. Part of George MacDonald Fraser's dedication in his novel is to 'Ronald Colman, Douglas Fairbanks Jr, Errol Flynn, Basil Rathbone, Louis Hayward, Tyrone Power, and all the rest of them'. Lester, by contrast, aligns the swashbuckler to both slapstick and sadism, and his perspective on the tale is essentially informed by James Bond, by the state of British cinema and by a view of contemporary England. Flashman has all of Bond's sexual prowess and is confronted by very Bond-like villains. Lionel Jeffries' Kraftstein is a kind of Ruritanian Oddjob, whilst Tom Bell's De Gautet has a way with seemingly innocent objects that is every bit as deadly as the lethal bowler hat of Goldfinger. However, unlike Bond, Flashman's bravery is all bravado, his athleticism a means of avoiding trouble. His alternate cockiness and whining contain the changing face of British heroism and an image of national decline, an arrogance that is wholly unsupported by achievement. The image is mocking and even painful, given the confidence and prospective social revolution of the sixties in England that Lester's films, more than those of any other director, had enshrined.

In a way *Royal Flash* is to seventies' British film what *Tom Jones* was to the early sixties. Both are glossy period romps, risqué, adventurous, with heroes of ravenous sexual appetites, played by actors whose performances had already set the tone of a decade (Albert Finney's in *Saturday Night and Sunday Morning*, Malcolm McDowell's in *A Clockwork Orange*). But the difference between them is symptomatic of what has happened to the British cinema between 1963 and 1975. *Tom Jones* is essentially a home-grown product, whereas *Royal Flash* is an elaborate co-production, with international names, and reflecting the more volatile film financing situation of the seventies. *Tom Jones* is about the adventures and integration of a young and seemingly low-born man into the aristocracy, and bubbles with the confidence of a film industry intoxicated with success and a society coming to terms with the concept of class mobility. *Royal Flash* is about an over-privileged bully with a contempt for the lower orders, and it creaks with a peculiar unease. Its hero represents a society whose self-confidence is cracking even as its prejudices are hardening. In its international perspective, it reflects a crisis in national confidence. In its rather desperate and uncomfortable sense of what constitutes popular appeal, it reflects a crisis within escapist entertainment.

Both the society and the industry seem to preclude the possibility of Lester's making a film as close to the pulse-beat of mid 1970s England as *The Knack* was to the national spirit of a decade earlier. Lester now makes 'period romps' because the cinematic climate is no longer conducive to the urgent contemporaneousness of *The Knack*. Yet the fact that he feels that he has to make these 'romps' — that these are the appropriate films for the time — makes its own comment on the conservatism of the industry and on the change of a social mood. British society has closed in on itself again after the euphoria of the mid 1960s, has become static and is sensitive to criticism. Yet the very sourness of *Royal Flash* reflects the decline of a dream and the return of outmoded forms and ideas. The film's air of frivolity seems perversely dark, strained and tense, halting and self-aware, as if it were both an elaboration and a critique of escapism.

One should beware of a Lester film which begins with a close-up of its hero. It invariably signals a character who is making an inflated attempt to button-hole our attention and a film in which stereotypical notions of heroism are to be thoroughly undermined. *Royal Flash* opens with a shot of Flashman framed in just such a way against an oppressive red background which only gradually reveals itself to be a Union Jack, and with the camera recoiling from this image of spurious patriotism. The casting of Malcolm McDowell as Flashman links the shot to the similar close-up of *A Clockwork Orange* (1972), Stanley Kubrick's fearful vision of a future authoritarian England, just as Lester's is an ironic but nevertheless quizzical vision of an oppressive and self-righteous former age. With the shot of the flag and the hero mouthing what could almost be a parody of nationalistic platitudes, the opening also invokes Franklin Schaffner's *Patton* (1970).[3] The significant difference here is that Patton is a genuine warrior whereas Flashman is not and Patton believes what he says whereas Flashman merely pays lip-service to it. 'Even heroes must work,' intones the headmaster of his young gladiator, at which point Lester cuts immediately to a scene of Flashman at his club, the lurid red baize of the gambling table being his spiritual home much more than the red of the flag.

This first sight of Flashman is profoundly significant. The close-up adulation of the camera to introduce him contrasts vividly with the first appearance of a genuinely brave man, the bomb expert Fallon (Richard Harris) in *Juggernaut* who is framed slightly off-centre and visually dominated by the bright red background. The contrasting visual presentation pinpoints the imperfect perception of both societies of what true heroism is, as well as the way in which the values of a society are implied in the people it choses to value. There is a mighty discrepancy between the account offered by the headmaster at Rugby of Flashman's legendary valour at Afghanistan and the catalogue of ignominious accident and surrender we actually see. (He comes on rattling a sabre which ostensibly symbolises the sabre-rattling of British Imperialism but it is actually rattling because he is shaking with fear.) Just as in *Juggernaut*, where society's inadequate valuation of courageous professionals like Fallon is revelatory of its own mean-spirited soul, in *Royal Flash* society's blind admiration of a charlatan like Flashman becomes symptomatic of the hypocrisy at the heart of Victorian society.

Flashman is not an evil man, nor really, in Lester's eyes, an authentic anti-hero. He is a rather pathetic fool, who has been made what he is by various Victorian precepts, by his social status and by his education. The pre-credit scene at Rugby is so good because it concisely suggests the origins of Flashman's more obnoxious Victorian certainties: maleness, Englishness and class snobbery. The emphasis on maleness (an audience of young boys and a line of approving masters, redeemed only by a matron who seems conspicuously unimpressed by Flashman) links the public school with the following scene at Flashman's club (where hostesses, plainly there simply for the pleasures of men, look weary and bored, disporting themselves on bicycles which are significantly going nowhere). It is as if public school leads directly to gentleman's club. The values of such establishments inform Flashman's whole attitude to women in the film as subservient, inferior objects to be used for his own sensual gratification, an attitude which is to lead him into strife when he tangles with Lola Montes (Florinda Balkan). The emphasis on Englishness in the Rugby scene (Elgar is pressed into service by music arranger Ken Thorne to underline the 'theme' of Flashman's speech) is expressive of a patriotism that has become less a matter of quiet pride than a complacent belief in national superiority and a sneering xenophobia. This in turn is to lead Flashman into an injudicious confrontation with someone whom he terms a 'dirty foreigner'. This man turns out to be Otto von Bismarck (Oliver Reed), and his humiliation by Flashman leads to his planning an ingenious and uncomfortable revenge. The final legacy which Victoria and Rugby have bequeathed to Flashman is insufferable aristocratic arrogance. Lester needs only one close shot of Flashman's old school audience — a shot of a smirking boy with a face radiating flushed brutishness — to conjure the attitudes with which Flashman was inculcated and which he in turn imparts.

Lester sometimes makes a simple joke out of social incongruity, as when a cleaner is happily mopping the dungeon whilst, around her, Flashman and Rudi (Alan Bates) are engaged in furious combat. Her smile seems to say, 'Boys will be boys', but typically there is something harsher underneath: men in this society have all the adventure, whereas women are merely expected to clean up the mess. On another occasion Flashman exchanges a lewd conversation with Lola whilst, standing between them, a young footman must maintain a poker-face and an air of repose. On one level, the footman provides a comic counterpoint, but the shot is held long enough to be uncomfortable. The impression is that, because he is a menial, they literally do not see him (it recalls the moment in *The Three Musketeers*: 'This pass is only for one' 'I am only one, this is a servant'). Flashman passes his glass to the boy as if putting it on a table, a gesture which summarises a whole attitude of one class to another — the aristocrat's sense of the lower orders as furniture, not people. Flashman's arrogance reaches its logical summation when, as part of Bismarck's plan to unite Germany, he has to impersonate a royal prince. His perfection of the role is signified by his attacking Bismarck from behind ('You're beginning to behave like royalty already,' says Bismarck); unconcernedly standing on the foot of a lackey; and murmuring, 'That's it — grovel, you commoners' when entering the Queen's palace. For Flashman (and for the film's disenchanted vision) royalty is the ultimate expression of the arrogance and insensitivity that go with privilege and power: a dream come true. But it is appropriately coupled with the ultimate royalist nightmare: social unrest and intimations of terrorism and anarchy. Flashman attains grandeur only to be immediately engulfed by the threats of kidnap and murder. *Royal Flash*, then, is a work which allows Lester first to elaborate and then to pull the rug out from under crucial Victorian concepts — misogyny, xenophobia and snobbery — using Flashman as whimpering fall-guy.

Royal Flash recalls a number of Lester films (the Beatles' films, the Musketeers films, and, to come, *Butch and Sundance* and *Cuba*) in the way it plays between the interstices in history and fiction, juxtaposing actual historical figures with creatures of pure fantasy. If *Royal Flash* offers an entertaining revision of nineteenth-century history, it also offers an ironic perspective on one of the nineteenth century's greatest fictions, *The Prisoner of Zenda.* 'The romance,' said Anthony Hope, explaining the intention and appeal of the romantic school, 'can give to love an ideal object, to ambition a boundless field, to courage a high occasion; and these great emotions, revelling in their freedom, exhibit themselves in their glory. It shows men what they would be if they could, if time and fate and circumstance did not blind, what in a sense they all are, and what their acts would show them to be if an opportunity offered. So they dream, and are the happier, and at least none the worse for their dreams'.[4] Fraser cannot accept Hope's idealistic escapism, and retrospectively revises the plot into a much more sardonic vision of English heroism and Prussian ambition. The swashbuckling tradition is maintained though, in the character of the witty villain, Rudi von Starnberg, who is Fraser's equivalent of Rupert of Hentzau and who is devious and dangerous but also charming and a man with a rough code of honour. Lester shares Fraser's vision and probably felt obliged to push it even further. What Hope would regard as part of the age's inspiriting dreams, Lester proposes as one of the age's dangerous illusions about itself.

'We live, I regret to say, in an age of appearances,' said Lady Bracknell in *The Importance of being Earnest.*[5] Lester's world in *Royal Flash* is an age of appearances. An ostensible hero is a fool and a coward; a beautiful heroine discharges her beauty for deadly ends; and a brothel can instantly be changed into an establishment of surface respectability. The public facade can sometimes only be maintained at the cost of private pain. (A hapless railway man is knocked senseless when inadvertently stepping into the path of a celebratory champagne bottle and there is more concern about the disruption of proceedings and the inconvenience to royalty than for the health of the man himself. 'Get him out of here. Get another bottle.') No wonder Lester gives great force to the moment when Flashman confronts his double in the dungeon, who is played noticeably straight, pitifully: a confrontation between the original and the forgery (which Flashman is through and through), the face being presented to the world and the *real* face. The contrast here is significant for the whole world of the film.

In dealing with a superficial hero and a superficial society, the film runs the risk of seeming superficial itself. Would it be too harsh to suggest that the film itself has a lot of the slick heartlessness it purports to criticise in its hero?

One of the problems with *Royal Flash* is that it is a sequel without an original. After *The Bed-Sitting Room* Lester was scheduled to make a film of the first of the Flashman stories, which included Flashman's school experience at Rugby and an account of what really happened to him at Afghanistan, but United Artists pulled out of the film in 1970 only a month or so before it was due to start shooting. After the success of *The Three Musketeers*, which was from a screenplay by the author of the Flashman books, George MacDonald Fraser, and which seemed to stimulate a taste for period adventure, the idea of filming the stories was revived but the second of the books chosen, *Royal Flash*, because it offered an entertaining variation of a classic adventure. The outline of the narrative remains stirring enough, but the character of Flashman now emerges in something of a vacuum. The problem was compounded by the fact that the release version of the film was cut from 118 minutes to 102 minutes, eliminating Roy Kinnear from the film despite his mention on the credits and, more importantly, a flashback section in which the hero's infamous school behaviour was recorded. (Some details of that are recounted in Gordon Gow's review of the film at the time in *Films and Filming*.)[6] One can only conjecture about the effect of the missing sections. However, given the importance of Victorian values in the film, the absence of material which would flesh out the background and the development of Flashman's character serves rather to unbalance the structure of the film.

After the success of *The Three Musketeers* and the successful collaboration with Fraser, Lester was a natural choice for *Royal Flash* but, having already prepared one film on the Flashman theme, he might have assumed too much of an audience's acquaintance with the tone and intention of the works. Also, there are significant differences between *The Three Musketeers* and *Royal Flash* as source material. Both books have a modern sense of irony and humour to which Lester can respond, but the irony is differently inflected: in Dumas, through authorial comment; in Fraser, through first-person narrative. It might be that the adaptation of *Royal Flash* does not take sufficiently into account this difference of point of view. Unlike d'Artagnan, Flashman is caught up in a romantic adventure of which he wants no part, but, in the transposition from book to film, Flashman's role is shifted from retrospective commentator to passive victim. He becomes overwhelmed by the adventure, and the character — and hence what he stands for — begins to diminish. The experience is consistently filtered through Flashman's eyes in the novel: in the film he seems to be consistently upstaged.

This is partly attributable to the casting of Malcolm McDowell in the leading role. He brings a youthful iconoclasm to the part and a lively athleticism to the action scenes, but the modernistic associations attached to his persona (through *If* and *A Clockwork Orange*) seem distinctly unhelpful in this instance and he is not really imposing enough to convey the romantic attraction of the character. What is required is something more calculated, like Ryan O'Neal in Kubrick's *Barry Lyndon* (1975): it is one of Lester's rare casting miscalculations. With the reduction of the hero's background, however, and a lightweight performance in the main role, the film's emphasis begins to drift away from the portrait of the Victorian bully and the centre-stage is stolen by Alan Bates's Rudi and Oliver Reed's Bismarck. Starting out as a satire on Victorianism, the film moves to an equally sardonic depiction of the growth of modern Germany, and a film which began with Elgar at his most solemn ends in a blaze of Wagnerian splendour. Flashman is displaced by Bismarck and Rudi (perhaps another modern reference — England's victory in war upstaged by Germany's economic recovery?), but this seems less thematically meaningful than the consequence of Bates's and Reed's performances seeming so much more subtle and strong than McDowell's. It leaves the film structurally broken-backed and hazily focused in its centre of attention.

Another unsatisfactory aspect of the film is its attitude to women. *Royal Flash* perhaps raises in its most acute form the occasional criticism of sexism in Lester's films. Although it would be unfair to label Lester's films as misogynistic — truer to call them bracingly misanthropic — one could not entirely defend him on the grounds that his films reflect the sexist attitudes of male-dominated societies. His disinclination to examine feminine psychology in any depth could lead to the charge that he is not simply reflecting but also endorsing a dominant ideology. Women tend to play a marginal role in his films and invariably inspire rather lewd attention (from the characters rather than the director). Lester's attitude is balanced between criticising their deadly docility or acknowledging dark-haired dynamic heroines who attempt to take control of their destiny — like Lola Montes in *Royal Flash* and, to come, like the Rita Moreno character in *The Ritz*, Alexandra in *Cuba* and Lois Lane in *Superman II*. But their fierce independence leads often to neurosis, and friendship between women in Lester's films is non-existent. Polo and Petulia in *Petulia* hate each other, although they have never met. On the rare occasions when Lester does stage a scene between two women, the enmity is electric enough invariably to provoke a fight: between Lola and the affronted soprano in *Royal Flash*; Constance and Milady in *The Three Musketeers*; Alexandra and Therese in *Cuba*; and between Lois and Ursa in *Superman II*.

Lester has always been reticent in his handling of romance and sexual relations in his films. This austerity and puritanism lead him to parody romantic effects, like the slow dissolves which accompany the undressing scene while they dance between Flashman and Lola, or to contrive imagery that seems sometimes too harsh for its context. There is a love scene between Flashman and Lola where the narcissism of each is not only underlined by showing it through a mirror and observing Lola's posters about herself on her wall, but by accompanying the scene with Wagner's Liebestod from *Tristan and Isolde*, a far remove from the self-centred lovers of this scene. Irony is grafted onto narcissism and the characters are criticised both on and below the surface of the film, which is a little excessive.

Given this reticence it follows that Lester would have difficulty in dramatising the adventures of a sexual rake. The attempt seems to lead to exaggeration in both directions. There is a certain relish when Flashman's appetites lead to the threat of castration (only to be rescued by Rudi who, in the ensuing struggle, slices a sausage in a suggestive manner). But there is also a certain embarrassing overstatement in suggesting female frigidity, so that Duchess Irma (Britt Ekland) wears white fur, takes a foot-warmer on her wedding journey and is as rigid as a board when Flashman first approaches her on their marriage-bed. The bawd takes over and the Snow Queen is thawed. Lester tries to humanise this as best he can, with Flashman coming close to a speech of love: 'I really love her. I think.' But, significantly, it is said to himself, and the absence of warmth in the performances not only nullifies the effect, but makes the scenes between the two lovers seem vaguely sleezy.

In the novel, there is a sneaking admiration for Lola Montes, particularly among the women: 'the women hid their satisfaction that one of their sex was setting Europe by the ears'.[7] Not much of this really comes through in the film. Lester has fun with the celebrated incident where Lola is alleged to have bared her breasts before King Ludwig of Bavaria. There is also a nice moment when she summons Flashman to meet her in Munich and the new setting is introduced by a shot of a cake on which her face has been inscribed in decorative icing. The image is at once eloquent (an immediate signifier of the mythic status she has acquired), impudent (many men have had a piece of her), prescient (the association of Lola and ice anticipates her wintry final meeting with Flashman) and meaningfully subjective (Flashman's view of her — and women in general — as icing on the cake, decorative, tasty, marginal to proper sustenance). Lola is egotistical, vital for survival in a patriarchal society, but Florinda Balkan's performance only gently penetrates the character's supposedly irresistible allure. She certainly has none of the extraordinary force of Faye Dunaway's performance of Milady in *The Four Musketeers*, for example, which genuinely magnetises in its savage switches of mood. Miss Balkan's imperfect English blurs some of the nuances of her character, and the sound-track has to provide an ironic dimension lacking from her insufficiently shaded performance, as in the moment in the film when she realises that Flashman has a fortune. The surge of Tchaikovsky's *Romeo and Juliet* over the soundtrack conveys both a sense of the romanticism she has to pretend in order to lure Flashman back into the carriage and the genuine emotion she feels on seeing the jewels, diamonds being always her best friend.

'Courage — and shuffle the cards' is Lola's credo for coming to terms with life and the caprices of fate. Rudi and Flashman conclude with a game of 'Hungarian roulette' (Flashman is nevertheless alarmed to find that the revolver is loaded — 'I could have been killed!'). If there is an air of flippancy about the film it is, to be fair, partly because it is dealing with spoilt and self-centred people who see life as a sport. Flashman is most deeply wedded to the gaming table — that is, he wants excitement and profit without pain to himself — and he howls like a wounded animal when his own flesh is torn (another of Lester's characters, like Superman, to be startled and stunned by the sight of his own blood). Bismark's pomposity — he even kills a rat with a crossbow — is signalled by his attachment to the ritual of the *schlager*, with its noble scars. The absurd duel between Lola and the soprano over their honour, and Rudi's toying with a new pistol that can kill at a distance and can easily be concealed, each tell their own stories of the characters, as does that clumsy game of musical chairs in a fashionable house in Munich where the participants seem ungainly, portly and old — like Europe herself. The hostilities between individuals (codified in these gaming rituals) do begin to acquire nationalistic overtones — 'Each country to its own game,' says the host at Flashman's club. The violence of the film — from Bismarck's boxing match with Gully, through Lola's duel, to the death of De Gautet, the murder of Eric Hansen and the storming of the castle — becomes noticeably more extreme. It is pointless but dangerous and destructive, with uncomfortable intimations of a future in which conflicts of nationalism and pride might well overwhelm the whole of Europe. When Rudi accidentally tears Bismark's map, the latter is unconcerned: 'Already it is out of date. I go to re-draw it'. If, by the end of the film, Victorian England seems on the wane, modern Germany is on the march.

It is a sumptuous-looking film. Geoffrey Unsworth's photography has an almost Teutonic richness, responding to castles shrouded in mist, Victorian drawing rooms whose pictures reflect the brutish pleasures of the aristocracy, and opulent décor that is stunningly dominated on one especially evocative set by a huge golden peacock. Appropriate for *mise-en-scène* directors like Kubrick and Fosse, Unsworth's photographic style seems a little plush for Lester. Whereas the crystalline clarity of David Watkin's camerawork seems an ideal visual match for Lester's sharp satirical eye, Unsworth's seems to weigh down the sprung rhythm of his style. Lester's visual flair is best reflected in the enthusiasm with which he recreates an historical era — the musical instruments of the time, Victorian showers — and the ingenuity of his sight gags, as when a shot of Bismarck riding a horse against an artificial backcloth turns out to be a shot of him as he taps his foot whilst a landscape painting is carried past behind him.

Royal Flash represents perhaps the best and worst of Richard Lester. The best means visual inventiveness, satirical skill, and a bold reworking of screen stereotypes. It also means providing plenty of room for acting flair and idiosyncrasies of character, like Kraftstein's gesture of kissing his claw better when it has been attacked, or Rudi's spectacular rescue of Flashman by leaping through a window even when the door is open ('Well, I do like to make an entrance'). The best of Lester also means a true sense of the spectacular, which reaches a breathtaking climax here in Flashman's encounter with a murderous De Gautet on the bridge and which culminates in a staggering fall that seems to spell certain death. (Flashman dies several deaths in this film, which, as Shakespeare said, is the fate of all cowards.) Typically, the film is full of offhand comic detail — Flashman's rude inspection of a wine bottle even when he is offered it in prison, or a duellist objecting to his opponent's breath smelling of garlic — that is the particular hallmark of this director's style.

Royal Flash is a clever film, but without being an especially compelling, convincing or likeable one. There were a number of critics who were beginning to write Lester off as a shallow poseur, all display but no substance. But, as Flashman says when he has inadvertently knocked Rudi senseless and is momentarily tempted to repeat the treatment: 'Never hit a man when he's down. He may get up.' *Royal Flash* might seem an expensive trifle, but Lester was to follow it with a jewel: one of the most original and unexpected films of his career as well as one of the greatest, *Robin and Marian*.

Robin and Marian

There is a delightful scene in *Robin and Marian*, when Robin Hood (Sean Connery) wakes up in the morning in Sherwood and has to rouse his sleeping companions, Little John (Nicol Williamson), Friar Tuck (Ronnie Barker) and Will Scarlet (Denholm Elliot). He cleans his teeth with a twig; kicks Little John awake and spits at Tuck; thinks again about relieving himself when he remembers Marian (Audrey Hepburn) is amongst them; and dances manically on the spot to try to pump some life into his stiff limbs. It is an amusing piece of observation, the kind of attention to unusual behavioural detail that forges a bond between character and audience, but, typically, the humour emerges naturally from the context and is absolutely germane to the theme. A seemingly light and throwaway scene is actually adumbrating ideas that are to be crucial to the film: the theme of ageing; the revelation of the ordinary men behind the myths; and the split between their legendary personas and what these people have now become.

Richard Lester sometimes feels that critics are too much inclined to judge a director's work as a linear progression, with the result that they respond to a new film as if it is a straight continuation of the preceding one. *How I Won the War* suffered critically from coming after four comedies, because there was a mistaken tendency to judge it by its (deliberately limited) humour quotient and not to consider carefully the relation of its Brechtian style to its serious themes. Lester feels that *Robin and Marian* also suffered from succeeding the *Musketeers* films and *Royal Flash,* some critics responding to it as if it were a swashbuckling historical exercise in the same vein.

'The number of critics who said about it that "it's quite funny, but not up to his usual standard!" ' Lester exclaimed to me. 'There was not a purposeful joke in the film, it's not that kind of film. To me it's a simple, sombre film of ideas.'

In fact, *Robin and Marian* not only throws fresh light on the legend of Robin Hood: it subverts the 'myth' of Richard Lester's personality as a director. For too long glibly associated with films of flashy visual surfaces, two-dimensional characterisation and flippant farce (totally inaccurate and misleading but a parody image of the director that has been perpetuated by several standard reference books on the cinema),[8] Lester, with *Robin and Marian*, has made a film that studiously reverses every one of those critical clichés about him. It is visually sombre and austere, and the characterisation is complex and unusual, focusing on once famous, now forlorn figures who are half in love with easeful death. The film is an elegiac, even tragic work in which Robin's Merrie Men are seen almost as the Wild Bunch of the Middle-Ages: men who came too late and stayed too long, and who are now scarcely sprightly enough to climb a tree, let alone launch an ambush from one. The violence[9] has no swashbuckling flair but an uncomfortable edge of savagery and barbarism, because it represents the clumsy fight for life of tired and desperate men who are no longer quite in control of their own reflexes (one might compare the unexpected extremes of violence in Howard Hawks' final films, *El Dorado* and *Rio Lobo*, which are similarly about aged protagonists reacting wildly to a fearful sense of declining potency). It is also Lester's most romantic film, in which the setting in the past allows him to confront more openly than usual the feelings of his characters, and in which the emotions of the protagonists seem more deeply ingrained than the whirlwind passions of youth. But the romanticism emerges not so much through verbal rhetoric as through imaginative visuals. The film's elaborate array of evocative imagery — withered fruit, the moss-covered horn, golden cornfields, a forest which is both an enchanted repository of sunlit memories from the past and an inadequate refuge from the cruel insurgences of the present — has an intensity that oddly recalls a director whom one would not normally associate with Lester, Andrzej Wajda, particularly the Wajda of *Lotna*. As in Wajda, a world in transition and a mood of last-ditch romanticism are viewed with a piercing, sympathetic but unsentimental sensibility.

Establishing the quirky and original tone of the film through a disconnected but intriguing 'trailer' of images, the film's credit scene also offers a concise exposition of some of the main ideas. The still shot of the decaying apples on the ledge is not simply a comment on the inevitability of ageing: it implies that, if things stand still (a danger for both England and some of the characters), they do not simply age but rot from within. The shot of the one-eyed, 'mad old man' (as Robin will call him) anticipates the appearance of this character in an early scene, single-handedly defending a castle from King Richard and his men. But, more importantly, it anticipates the theme of 'mad old men' which is to run right through the film. This theme implicates King Richard, who is now corrupt, moody and deranged: his Crusade has degenerated into sadistic and indiscriminate butchery. (The subsequent slaughter of the children in the castle is economically and suggestively conveyed by screams set across a perversely beautiful image of a burnt-out castle at sunset.) The theme of madness and age also looks forward to the conflict between Robin Hood and the Sheriff of Nottingham, which is similarly crazy, irrelevant, socially damaging (what will happen to Nottingham after the Sheriff has gone?) and personally perverse (the two men over the years seem to have developed a respect and even liking for each other). Tuck, Marian, even Little John describe the Sheriff's battle tactic (just sitting out on the field waiting for Robin to abandon his cover and come out into the open) as 'mad'. Robin accepts the bait nevertheless. Their legendary enmity, whether true or even relevant anymore, must be played out to the finish.

Several other details of this early confrontation with the 'mad old man' are to be elaborated later. 'I speak for Richard Lionheart, King of England . . .' says Robin, to which the man replies: 'I'm here speaking for myself'. It is a declaration of individualism that Robin is actually to repeat when he defies the King's orders to attack the castle and is imprisoned with Little John. The castle is being invaded because someone has dug up a rock and a rumour has gone round that it was a 'gold statue'. That early indication of the progress and process of myth-making is to be recalled later when Robin returns to England, burnt-out and disillusioned, and finds himself regarded as a hero whom the people wish to convert into precious metal. Robin's discovery that they are actually fighting not for gold but for a rock has the kind of considered anti-climax that is typical of the film's method, as it unearths the flinty truth behind the golden mythology. The mad old man in the castle stops a round of arrows by holding up a pan to his face. It is a gesture that anticipates

Robin's desperate flinging of pans at the Sheriff's approaching men when he and Little John are trapped in Nottingham castle: the old man at whom he had laughed has, by now, become a portent of himself. Sensing King Richard's imminent attack on the castle, the old man flings an arrow that seems 'magically' to strike Richard in the neck ('magical' in the sense that it seems impossible that he could have hit him from that distance). The 'magic arrow' that kills Richard and, in a sense, precipitates everything in the film, is to be recalled at the end at the point of death for Robin and Marian. Asking John to bury them where the arrow lands, Robin draws his bow and, in a breathtaking visual conception which transcends mere inventiveness and touches screen poetry, the arrow flies through the window and lands not on the earth but seems to wing its way unstoppably into legend.

For defying the King, Robin and Little John have been imprisoned in the dungeon, and their disillusionment with the monarch, their relationship with each other, and individual traits of character are sketched in quick, sure strokes. John is philosophical about the possibility of their being executed ('If we go, we go'): Robin is more agitated and defiant ('I tell you something — I won't go quietly') and is looking to escape. In fact, a guard enters to escort them to the King before they can take advantage of their laborious creation of an opening. The slowness of their progress is indicative of their waning vitality, and the passage of time from night to morning as they claw their way out is an indication that time-changes are to be very significant in the film. 'Let's come back tomorrow,' is a common refrain of Robin's, until the point right at the end when the realisation is thrust upon him that there are no tomorrows, and that they will never have a day like this again. The meeting with the King (Richard Harris) is a grisly dance of death, in which the mortally wounded monarch taunts his most loyal subject in a manner that reveals the remnants of a noble dream closing in shabby recrimination. 'You're not for hanging, you're for cutting up,' the King says (a ghostly premonition of Robin's blood-soaked fight to the death with the Sheriff), but, with the effort of pulling a sword from its scabbard, the King collapses. 'What will you do without me now, jolly Robin, now I'm dead?' he asks. Watching the funeral procession, Robin says to Little John: 'Let's go home, John.'

The opening section of the film has been all rock, dust and metal: an arid background for harsh, unyielding man. The film cuts from stone and steel to green fields and flowers as Robin and John return to England. This is not so much Lester's romanticism as Robin Hood's, this distinction clinched in a marvellous moment where Robin's excitement is so pronounced that he heedlessly rides across the peasants' carefully cultivated crops: so much for the champion of the poor. The forest is more a dream to him than a reality and, for a time, Robin and Little John are as lost in the wood as the two war-lords at the beginning of Kurosawa's *Throne of Blood* (1957). The reunion with Will Scarlet and Friar Tuck turns from tense conflict to cackling reminiscence as they recognise each other, and later over the campfire, Robin asks casually about Marian. 'Lovely girl. Haven't thought of her in years,' he says, an ironic preface to another romantic relationship from the past which will be revived with tragic results (something of a Lester trademark). When Will comments about the songs which have grown up about Robin and his Merrie Men's exploits, Robin interjects, 'We didn't do them,' to which Will laughingly responds: 'I know *that*'.

It is not simply that the characters are twenty years older and can no longer do the things attributed to them. (Robin even finds it difficult to carry Marian in his arms anymore: 'You've put on weight,' he grumbles.) It is that the characters have changed in the interim; they are, in some cases, unrecognisable from their former selves; and the legends therefore seem to be about different people. This is especially pronounced in the case of Robin and the Sheriff of Nottingham — in the legend, the embodiment of good and evil, respectively — whose shifts of attitudes over the twenty years provide the film with some of its richest irony. For all his reputation as a righter of wrongs and a defender of the underdog, Robin has been out of the country during the years he has been most needed. James Goldman's script presents him as an intriguing mixture of royalist and rebel, anarchist and patriot, around whom an aura has formed which might not be entirely true to the reality. There is no evidence that he feels keenly anymore about social injustice: his progress in the film is more towards self-vindication, personally valuable, politically and socially negligible. In contrast, the Sheriff of Nottingham (Robert Shaw)[10] has stayed behind, becoming something of a political maverick. 'You see, I can read and write,' he tells Robin, 'it makes you suspect'. In presenting the Sheriff as a rather bookish, intellectual character, the film considerably complicates the usual contrast between him and Robin, the Sheriff representing a cultured and civilised intelligence against Robin's ragged and rascally rebelliousness. But they are equally outsiders, and Robin's occasional outmoded forays against the State might well be less dangerous now than the Sheriff's sustained political cunning. It is significant that King John (Ian Holm) sees them both as more or less an equal threat: if he cannot have Robin's head, he says, he will have the Sheriff's.

In the scene in which the Sheriff is introduced, he is disturbed from his books by the feeble swordsmanship of his men. Murmuring resignedly, 'They never learn,' he goes out to give them some instruction. The bruising demonstration which follows has something of the humour of the gladiator training scene of *A Funny Thing Happened on the Way to the Forum* but also the flavour of the master-pupil subtheme of *Juggernaut*, whereby the leader attains respect not by position alone but by deeds and personal example. (There has been an echo of that theme in the early antagonism between Robin and King Richard, in which the former has found it impossible to follow his increasingly fallible leader in blind obedience. 'Robin judges me. He always does — the peasant bastard,' grumbles Richard.) What also emerges in this scene is the antagonism between the Sheriff and the Establishment, here represented by Sir Ranulf (Kenneth Haigh) who is in the confidence of King John and who resents the Sheriff's aloof, arrogant manner. The Sheriff's opinion of Sir Ranulf seems not very different from Robin's: the man has an insufferable pomposity that derives entirely from social privilege and not from genuine worth. 'My idea of the Sheriff,' said Lester, 'was that if you are English in a basically Norman society, and are clever and sensible and realise that there is no promotion or opportunity, your disappointment would manifest itself in looking after your own people and their social welfare, and in teaching yourself to read and write in the interim. The Sheriff is basically a liberal: he's become a genuine grass-roots politician.' One of the implications of that is the irony of the final fight. Robin kills the one person in that society who is genuinely trying to help the kind of people about whom, by legend, Robin is most concerned.

Another implication of the Sheriff's situation is that, because of his static social position, he has spent much of his time simply waiting. The image of waiting is something that the film reinforces on a number of occasions: waiting for Robin to come into Nottingham, or to come out and fight on the battlefield. For the last twenty years it is as if he has simply been waiting for Robin's return. Strikingly, the Sheriff recognises Robin more quickly than Marian does and seems genuinely glad to see him. 'Robin,' he remarks genially, 'still not dead?' The relationship develops into the mutual respect of worthy adversaries, like Fallon and Juggernaut in *Juggernaut*, a respect that Lester crystallises in a single gesture: kneeling in prayer before their fight, using as crosses the very swords with which they will try to kill each other, each helps the other to his feet. The fight is a tense, sweaty, ugly affair, the long shots emphasising the passage of time and adding to the suspense. Because of the complex sympathies of the characterisation, one is not certain of the outcome (if Lester had been allowed to keep his preferred title for the film, *The Death of Robin Hood*, the tension might have been even more acute). As the fight develops and the Sheriff begins to gain the upper hand, he starts begging Robin to stop, and one has the sense that the Sheriff cannot kill Robin, any more than King Richard could: it would be killing a vital part of himself, almost an act of suicide. In that moment of hesitation — of waiting — Robin rushes in and stabs the Sheriff to death. Personally the fight restores Robin's reputation in his own eyes, but behind him, it unleashes the wrath of Ranulf and his men who are to storm the forest and bring to an end Robin's old social dream that has long since dwindled into memory.

The revival of the rivalry with the Sheriff might have restored Robin's reputation, but the revival of his romance with Marian is to lead to his death. On his return to England, Robin has been horrified to discover that Marian has become Abbess of Kirkly Abbey. In her first scene, she is preparing a potion for a sick woman, saying, 'This will help the pain'. It is a scene to be replayed in her final scene with Robin when she poisons them both and convinces him that this is the right thing to do: that this is euthanasia not murder and that this, finally, will help the pain. 'We are celebrating our demise,' King Richard has said in one of the early scenes: the end of Robin and Marian is also a kind of celebration, as the lovers find consummation in death.

In entering the convent after a failed suicide attempt (even, at that stage, as throughout the film, love being closely associated with death), Marian has gone to ease the pain of her separation from Robin. 'My confessions were the envy of the convent,' she says simply. It is not a conversion but a retreat, a denial of her capacity for life. But, as D.H. Lawrence put it in *Lady Chatterley's Lover* (a novel that makes explicit reference to the Merrie England of Robin Hood and in which the wood is a sanctuary from conventional society): 'The world allows no hermits . . . And if you do keep clear, you might almost as well die.'[11] Marian acknowledges this when she renews her commitment to Robin. 'I felt so little for so long,' she says to him. 'Hurt me. Make me cry.' As they make love in the cornfields, they seem to melt magically into the earth, anticipating the end when they will also lie together where Robin's arrow lands. The natural imagery beautifully merges with the film's theme: like nature itself, the legend is imperishable and will rejuvenate the land like the spring.

The performances of Sean Connery and Audrey Hepburn as Robin and Marian are amongst the finest either of them has accomplished on screen. Connery brings to the part of Robin a quality that also distinguished his performances in John Milius's *The Wind and the Lion* (1974) and Huston's *The Man Who Would be King* (1975): an engaging streak of self-mockery that resides in characters conscious of their own image. His performance elicits all the humour without diminishing any of the grandeur. Coming out of retirement to play a character, Maid Marian, who also comes out of retirement, Audrey Hepburn seems more beautiful than ever in a way entirely appropriate to the part, her former pixilated charm having matured into a new warmth and strength. The give-and-take of Connery and Hepburn's scenes together is screen acting of consummate ease and timing, with Connery at times playing Punch to Hepburn's Judy ('I never mean to hurt you and yet it's all I ever do'), finally playing Tristan to her Isolde, as he quietly listens to her death-ridden aria of love. During the film there have been many highlights in their performances: Robin's bitter soliloquy about the sickening brutality of the Crusades, the slaughtering of his dream; Marian's inspection of her image in a stream to see if she can spy any trace left of Mother Janet. When Robin reminisces nervously about the King on the night before the battle ('The day is ours, Robin, Richard used to say — and then it was tomorrow. But where did the day go?'), he suddenly turns to Marian and says, 'You're so beautiful'. The line is invested by Connery with a soft simplicity that gives it the quality of a valedictory caress. 'I won't go quietly . . . I'll have a lot to say when the time comes,' Robin has said about death. When the time does come, Marian does the talking for him, in a speech that Hepburn makes sing with a tender emotionalism, and to which Connery mutely reacts with an extraordinary fluctuation of expression that ranges from confused anger to final grateful acceptance. It should also be said that the poignancy of the leading performances is supported by an equally sensitive performance by Nicol Williamson as Little John, doggedly devoted to Robin, ambiguously wary of Marian, and with a troubled sense of having for years stood between them.

Robin and Marian is a deeply moving film, but it is not a sentimental one.[12] Aided by cameraman David Watkin and editor John Victor Smith (indispensable members of Lester's team), Lester keeps the texture of the film hard. There are no dissolves, often terse transitions between scenes, and a prominence of sound cuts that fractionally anticipate the visuals in a manner that keeps the film bustling forward. The handling of historical and period detail (from the reconstruction of Nottingham market to the detail of the ink-stained fingers of the tax-collector) is brisk and natural rather than lingering or indulgent, and the writing in the modern idiom has a kind of racy realism rather than a period pomp. When Lester injects his modern perspective into his historical films, the intention is never to satirise the past but often to suggest a continuity with the present: that these too were periods of inequality, injustice and confusion and people have responded to adversity with similar kinds of stoical humour and sardonic endurance. The major characters of *Robin and Marian* are ordinary people who have become figures of myth in spite of themselves, but who still, like all of us, have to come to terms with their own mortality. The film does not debunk a legend but humanises it, in the process giving an old tale new heart and fresh dimensions of heroism.

Butch and Sundance: the Early Days

Early in this film, as the eponymous young outlaws have robbed a safe and are making their getaway by hearse rather than by horse, they pass an incongruous looking cowboy who stares after them in pained confusion. The cowboy, who is not seen again, is played by Richard Lester.

Lester's presence at that point encourages a temptation to read more into the moment than seems immediately apparent. (It is not his only screen appearance, of course: he is seen in *The Running, Jumping & Standing Still Film*, fleetingly in *A Hard Day's Night*, and scowls at us in *The Knack* as a voice over says, 'Well, I come from Hampton Wick myself, so I'm used to innuendo.') The unusual getaway vehicle might reflect the film's comic irreverence and the characters' unholy high spirits, but the hearse is also a dark foreshadowing of the fate which will overtake them all too speedily because of their lawless pursuits. Lester's appearance there is partly a joke of recognition — the director taking his bow — but his observer is also an outsider whose tense expression seems to foresee the implications of the characters' actions more clearly than the characters themselves. It is also a defiant declaration of personality, bringing to the foreground of the film a question in the back of one's mind: what is Richard Lester doing directing a western?

The answer is: not making a western, a genre he has always disliked, but making what he called 'a piece of American Victoriana'. What attracted him was the opportunity afforded by Allan Burns's intelligent and witty script for the three roles he likes best: comic, iconoclast and social historian. The comic reveals itself in odd details such as two outlaws exchanging casual pleasantries as they pass on the road, a miniature exchange made all the more strange by the huge expanse of country around them; or the linguistic peculiarities so beloved of Lester, as when one of Butch's gang insists that there is a detachment of 'calvary' on the hold-up train; or character portrait by décor, as in the evocation of the prison governor's mental confusion through a room and desk cluttered with bizarre adornments such as an egg-timer, a skull, a pair of horns, a stuffed eagle and framed portraits of hanged criminals. The iconoclast in Lester reveals itself in the impish inversion of western expectations, such as the moment when Butch jumps into a clear pool to wash off the grime of prison and the result is not purification of soul but near instant frost-bite, the director typically undercutting his hero's gesture of romantic release. The presence of the social historian discloses itself in the unusual visual detail of the old West, like the observation of the number of children and Chinese labourers who are working for the railroad, the cost of common goods, even the ritual of queuing at the butchers. What must have seemed particularly congenial to Lester about the material is the way these three elements merge imperceptibly into each other.

For example, the social historian in Lester would inevitably lead also to the comic and the iconoclast in this film, simply because of the gap between the legend of the American West which so many directors have elaborated and the reality which Lester actually uncovers. Most westerns present a society which, for the purposes of the film, seems temporarily frozen. We might observe a saloon bar piano, but Lester's film reminds us that such a piano might occasionally need tuning. Characters might be seen eating their food, but

Lester's film reminds us also of the way in which the family pet can be handily used to turn the cream separator. A train might stop for water, but Lester's film pauses to depict with some fascination the complex and elaborate process by which the train is actually filled up with water. It is a film very much concerned with how a society physically operates. An early scene in which Butch buys a gun and bullets is primarily important to Lester not as a portent for action, for Butch never shoots his gun in the entire length of the film, preferring to burst paper bags: it is part of his *image*, more than his equipment. What interests Lester are the economics involved. Bullets were expensive and the kind of fancy and indiscriminate shooting in the usual western would actually have cost the equivalent of a washing machine. In fact, economics has a lot to do with Butch's getting together with Sundance in the first place. He joins a posse that trails Sundance after the latter has shot up a saloon simply because Sundance has taken his gun in the melée and it is the only way Butch can think of to retrieve it. Never mind justice: he simply cannot afford a new gun.

Lester, then, is mainly concerned with recreating the tempo and texture of nineteenth-century American society rather than the more conventional aggressive delights of the typical western. The film's appeal comes through this kind of oblique detail and the striking use of location for some scenes, like the gunfight which takes place in a Mormon town, the streets of which are under two feet of water and some of the walls of which are inscribed with portentous religious warnings ('And now my brethren/How is it possible/Ye can lay hold of everything good?'). Because he was charmed by the comedy of the script, Lester clearly felt that its dramatisation against a vital, interesting and unusual background would carry the film's casual structure. As is (sometimes) the case with the films of Robert Altman, an audience's attention would be held not so much by narrative expectation as by the sheer sense of life going on. However, Lester might have overestimated what he could get away with: because of genre expectations, a western cannot live by observation and charm alone. Also, unlike the eponymous characters of Altman's *McCabe and Mrs Miller* (1971), Lester's Butch and Sundance are essentially loners. For all the interest in the background detail, there is only so much that can be done with two characters against an often unpopulated landscape.

The film's interest in the social context was, in any case, tempered by studio interference. Lester had wanted to have a variety of foreign languages audible over the soundtrack to convey the sense of America at that time as a burgeoning polyglot society. (This would certainly have given a different inflection to that moment when a Swedish skier emerges out of nowhere to assist Butch and Sundance who are stuck in the snow: it could have seemed charming but natural, whereas, in the film now, it seems funny but arbitrary.) But the studio eliminated the sound of Russian and dubbed in instead the reassuringly conventional sound of the howling coyote, which, as Lester said, 'was exactly what I'd been avoiding'. By subduing the vitality of the background, the studio unwittingly exposed the impoverishment of the central narrative.

There is no doubt also that Lester was restricted by the spectre of the film's illustrious predecessor, George Roy Hill's *Butch Cassidy and the Sundance Kid* (1969). Lester had fought against this connection, feeling that the new film could stand on its own, and believes that the title — which insists on this relationship — was a mistake. The connection meant that Lester had to find new camera angles for routines that might seem overfamiliar from the earlier film. In fact, Sundance's shooting his way out of the saloon — with the abstract montage of guns and holsters and the gradual destruction of the impressive set — is a strikingly original piece of filming, as is the finely controlled farce of the final train robbery. The bank robbery is most memorable for the reaction of a guard who, when kicked on the shin by Sundance, limps towards the desk, saying, 'That's it, that's it — I quit' and hands in his badge with a gesture that implies years of simmering exasperation behind this sudden decisive outburst. In all these instances, Lester finds a way of avoiding the usual genre clichés and a direct comparison with Hill's film. Nevertheless, the characterisation had to link with what went on before, with Butch as thinker and Sundance as gun, and the dialogue has to have the same brittle humour ('You've nothing to fear from me,' says Butch in his first meeting with Sundance, to which the latter snaps back quickly, 'You noticed that too?'). Ironically, the earlier film might have owed something to Lester, with its jazzy Oscar-winning Burt Bacharach music (*It's Trad, Dad* had featured Bacharach's first hit song) and a colour-supplement style that would seem more suitable to a subject like *Help!* than to a western. But one feels Lester would rather have started from scratch than work against the very distinctive image of a successful original. Lester's 'prequel' has the additional burden of showing not only how Robert LeRoy Parker and Harry Longbaugh became Butch Cassidy and the

Sundance Kid, but how they became Paul Newman and Robert Redford as well.

The plot of the film is slight. It recounts the meeting and eventual partnership of Butch and Sundance and their erratic road to fame. Structurally speaking, their outlaw trail has two major diversions. There is a passage where they attempt the philanthropic road to heroism by transporting diptheria vaccine to a striken community, an abortive journey which saves no one and almost kills Butch; and an episode in which Butch is temporarily united with his wife and children. The road is darkened by two pursuing shadows: that of O.C. Hanks (Brian Dennehy) who mistakenly believes Butch has betrayed his hideout to the law in return for early parole; and that of Joe Le Fors (Peter Weller) whose attempt to capture Sundance earlier has been thwarted by the timidity of his posse and whose continuing obsession provides the finale with much of its vigour. Hanks and Le Fors are punctuations in the narrative more than active protagonists. They are omens of the future, nightmares on the fringe of the heroes' consciousness, a premonition that the 'fun' they seek is going to be bought at disproportionate cost.

Despite the individualist implications of the title, the film is about a society in transition in which people are having to re-define their roles and where the needs of character are being subordinated to the needs of community. The look of the country is changing at the onset of the modern age, and this is putting obstacles in front of Butch and Sundance's spirit of adventure. Banks have gleaming new safes called 'Non-Pareil Bank-Master' that are 'guaranteed pilfer-proof'. When Butch and Sundance visit the former's hero, Mike Cassidy, in jail (and the dissolve from a shot of the trees through which Butch and Sundance ride to the bars of Cassidy's cell is a sinister premonition of their constriction), they discover that the jails are now mechanically operated. This equation between law enforcement and automation means the end of the kind of pragmatic justice which Butch has wheedled out of the Governor at the beginning of the film, and which the ageing Sheriff Bledsoe (appropriately posed next to a dinosaur near the end) has belatedly represented. (This character, played by Jeff Corey, is the only remnant from George Roy Hill's original film.)

In this changing society, there is even the growth of billboard advertising and street theatre (a tightrope act, framed against an advertisement for Groves' Tasteless Chill Tonic), which suggests that not only the law is being institutionalised but entertainment too. Subliminally here, Lester and writer Allan Burns are picking up an intuition that informed the whole of Altman's *Buffalo Bill and the Indians* (1976): that the West represents not the heart of American adventurism but the origins of American showbusiness. Ironically, the now popular 'media' are gearing themselves up for Butch and Sundance's 'stardom' at precisely the time that the society is rejecting it. An early scene shows Butch having his photograph taken, an obligatory scene for the modern western that is concerned with the establishment, the processes and the ironies of legend (compare, for example, such moments in Arthur Penn's 1958 film *The Left-Handed Gun* or Kirk Douglas's *Posse* of 1975). Butch self-consciously poses against a backdrop of mythical heroes, and we are given an inverted shot of Butch from the photographer's viewpoint as he looks through his lens. But it is also Lester's view as he looks through *his* lens: a signifier of the way in which the director is to turn traditional western heroism on its head, and the search for mythical status is to up-end Butch before his time.

The film follows the crazy progress by which legend is created. Butch and Sundance achieve this partly by crude calculation, which includes selecting evocative names, and ensuring good public relations by monetary gifts to people in danger of eviction from their homes. No financial risk is involved, since they steal the money straight back from the villainous creditor — an incident lifted directly from Nicholas Ray's 1958 film, *The James Brothers* — but there is some risk of distortion: the old man whom Butch helps insists on calling him 'Dutch' and says, 'I believe I do remember you, Mr . . . er . . .' This status is also achieved partly by accident. Whilst recovering from a gunshot wound, Sundance at last succeeds in growing the moustache he wanted to complete his image, discovering the precious facial growth when he awakens in a golden light.

Tom Berenger as Butch and William Katt as Sundance were selected for their physical resemblance to Newman and Redford as well as their acting skill. In fact, their fresh lightweight performances are appropriate for characters who are as yet embryonic legendary figures. Indeed, it could be argued that they provide a superior spectacle to that of seasoned professionals like Newman and Redford behaving like adolescents, because at least in Lester's film, Butch and Sundance are meant to be a little adolescent. Butch petulantly tosses a stone after a train that he cannot rob because of his empty holster, and other characters get caught up in the heroes' infectious enthusiasm (such as the people at the Casino who behave like collaborators even though their place is being robbed, or the guard on the train, who declares that 'this is a lot of fun . . . have you any idea how boring it is riding the express car?'). The film is drawn to their child-like clowning and indeed some of the imagery used to reinforce that, notably the skiing in the snow, is reminiscent of the Beatles in *Help!* Butch is rather like d'Artagnan in *The Three Musketeers*, charming, enthusiastic but foolhardy, forever making lofty gestures only to find himself in a location which obstructs a dramatically effective exit. 'How do I get out of here?' he says after a ringing speech to Sundance, his exit line thwarted by a rock that suddenly reveals a sheer drop. (D'Artagnan similarly sweeps out of Buckingham's room after a ringing loyalist speech in *The Three Musketeers*, only to return sheepishly a moment later to say he cannot find his way out.) But it is a playfulness that must end. The crucial moment is conveyed typically by a deep red patch of blood staining a white shirt (similar imagery occurs in *Petulia*, *The Three Musketeers* and *Cuba*) which marks the moment when the games have to stop and the violence becomes real. It is the moment when Sundance commits his first killing and significantly, it is Sundance's shirt that is stained. He has embarked on a life-style that is as murderous to him as it is to other people.

It is a life-style also that is anachronistic before it has even begun. Society is now putting up paintings to the 'glorious heroes of the savage Indian battles' in the courthouse, in other words, commemorating a heritage that the two outlaws are set on extending. Butch and Sundance belong to the past, even as they ride towards the future. The film suggests this in a number of ways: through the passage of the seasons, which emphasises the relentlessness of change; and through aspects of the characterisation, notably the sorrowful collection of humanity that now makes up the once legendary Hole-in-the-Wall gang. The erosion of Butch and Sundance's ideal is emphasised with particular forcefulness through the characterisation of Mike Cassidy (A lovely performance, eloquently shabby, from Michael C. Gwynne). Cassidy is Butch's mentor and has been the inspiration for his future banditry, but when we see Cassidy, he is a tired washed-out character. Ironically, when Butch and Sundance come disguised as lawyers to Cassidy's cell, the old outlaw initially assumes that they are genuine and is delighted rather than dismayed: Butch has not sold out in his eyes, but is succeeding in the new square world. Cassidy is not an unsympathetic character ('Greatest country in the world. Guilty as hell, free as a bird,' he clucks contentedly, after being cleared by an expensive lawyer whom Butch has paid for by robbing a bank). But he is certainly a pathetic one, and a dubious model for an impending legendary life of crime. The consequences of Butch's indebtedness to Cassidy here are to be calamitous. In pulling the bank job for Cassidy, Butch has jeopardised the amnesty deal he negotiated with the governor ('if he does one more job, it's all off,' Bledsoe tells Cassidy). In getting Cassidy out, he inadvertently looses Le Fors on them. When Cassidy goes to warn Butch about the amnesty, Le Fors follows, just in the way that he has led Butch to Sundance earlier in the film. When threatened by Le Fors, Cassidy betrays Butch. It is an interesting contrast to the despised O.C. Hanks. Hanks does genuinely, if mistakenly, believe Butch betrayed him. Butch mistakenly hero-worships a man who is actually to betray him.

The outmoded progress of Butch and Sundance is also reinforced by a clever dramatic structure which keeps back-tracking on itself. The film's episodic nature and its seeming inability to sustain narrative momentum is a correlative to characters uncertain of their true destination and whose rootlessness and erratic ambition are driving them outside the limits of a new society. Butch and Sundance strive to push themselves to the forefront of the frame, but Lester mocks their aspirations by frequently framing them in long shot, as if they are being swallowed up by the landscape. They rarely seem to be going as quickly as they want, and are often driven backwards when they need to be going forwards: an ingenious motif for young men — like the kids in the Hole-in-the-Wall — attaching their future to a dream that has already passed them by. So Butch's first act on leaving prison is to go back to Hole-in-the-Wall; Butch and Sundance's first job together is to go back to the Casino from which Sundance originally made his spectacular escape (when they return, someone is fixing the window that Sundance originally broke). Butch goes back to his family for a while; Sundance goes back into the town when he learns that O.C. Hanks, who winged him earlier, is there; even the train in the final daring robbery goes backwards to the water tank. Every movement forward (their step towards fame) is simultaneously a step backwards (bringing their deaths nearer), which makes the ostensible celebratory finale especially bittersweet. The robbery is successful, but this effectively puts an end to the amnesty and makes them hunted men. Sundance cries delightedly, 'We're gonna be famous!' as they ride towards the camera, at which point the film does not simply stop but freezes, marking the moment indelibly as the end of their freedom.

For all their romanticism, Butch and Sundance are operating in a society that has lost its need for heroes. Putting themselves forward as the dramatic leads, they are in fact the Rosencrantz and Guildenstern of the American West (like Rosencrantz and Guildenstern, people mix them up and feel they are interchangeable). They are inconsequential adventurers labouring belatedly to fire the imagination of a tamed, authoritarian society increasingly indifferent to the calls of pioneering individualism. This is crystallised particularly by the magnificent scene in which Sundance has his showdown with O.C. Hanks. The earnest confrontation is undercut anyway by eccentric detail: for example, Hanks pulls his gun on Sundance early, not because he is the villain, but because he is deaf in one ear and cannot count as far as five. The seriousness of the encounter is undermined still further by the attitude of the townspeople — very different from the response of the town in *Shane* (1953) to a similar gunfight on a water-logged street — who are busying themselves with their work and noticing out of the corner of their eye a quaint and irrelevant contest between two anachronisms. The use of a mirror in this scene, fragmenting the confrontation and giving the sense of an unreal illusory encounter on a silver screen, is visually stunning.

The killing of O.C. Hanks is the point of 'no return' for both Sundance and Butch. It is the point at which Sundance is blooded, and the point at which the concept of 'home' finally disappears for Butch as a refuge, or alternative to his life as an outlaw. Oddly, when we are first introduced to Butch playing a harmonica in the dark, the shot has a momentary cosiness about it, a feeling of 'home on the range' — until the camera pulls back to reveal that Butch is in prison. It is a small but significant moment, the polarity between 'home' and 'prison' elaborated later when it is Butch's life of crime that prevents him from settling down. His harmonica is the only thing he can leave to his sons when he leaves home, presumably for the last time; and their only other souvenir is the picture taken by the photographer earlier which is on the sideboard when Butch has come back. The episode with his wife Mary (Jill Eikenberry) and the children only reinforces 'home' and 'security' as a possibility which Butch has forfeited in his search for fame and his inability to reconcile a sense of adventure with loyalty to wife and family.

'Goodbye, Robert,' says Mary to him when they part for the last time, pointedly calling him by his former name. Lester's films are often structured around a romantic relationship revisited, a relationship particularly recalled by the use of pet names (Petulia jokingly calling Archie 'Arnold' at the end of *Petulia*; Dapes's stuborn insistence on calling Alexandra 'Alex' in *Cuba*), and a relationship whose revival invariably leads to disillusionment or tragedy. *The Four Musketeers*, *Robin and Marian* and *Cuba* also have this pattern, and the sense of romantic loss in *Butch and Sundance* is further underlined by Patrick Williams's dark, hesitant love theme which contrasts so strikingly with the pastiche Irish jig he ingeniously composes to accompany Butch's wilder shenanigans. But Butch at home and the Butch of the tales are two different people and one notices, in the home scenes, how often Butch looks at himself in the mirror, as if trying to spy a correspondence between 'Robert' and 'Butch', husband and outlaw.

The film originally had an end-title which made explicit reference to the characters' deaths, and Lester was rather dismayed that the studio deleted it. In fact, the ending works very well on its own terms. The final train robbery recalls the last scene of *How the West Was Won* (1962), another western which searches relentlessly for a tone of affirmation and achieves only elegy and pessimism. It has some finely timed slapstick, notably an elaborately structured gag whereby the swinging pipe from the water tank misses Butch's head but knocks aside the gun placed on top of the train by the cavalry. (Butch's alertness to the dangers of swinging objects has been cleverly anticipated earlier when he ducks under a similarly dangerous piece of equipment from the photographer.) There is also some highly relevant detail, such as Sundance's dance on the top of the train — a dance in the sun — to simulate the presence of many outlaws, which actually captures the attempt of the two throughout the film to expand their own significance; or the moment when Le Fors tosses his boater after the fleeing outlaws as a reminder of his indomitable pursuit. Given the film's formal fluidity to express the restless progress of the heroes, the audience's foreknowledge of what is to happen to them and the film's brilliantly timed final freeze, it would be hard to respond to the film's end-titles on a level other than that of elegiac irony. It is a landscape of scrub and dust, with echoes of Monument Valley, the quintessential image to evoke what Butch and Sundance pursue — a dream of impossible western heroism which the film has progressively undermined.

The film has many of the characteristics that mark the development of the western in the 1970s. It has a sense of irony and comic deflation about people who pursue an outmoded adventurism; a realism about social details that undercuts the gloss of the classic western; and an impudent New World imagery (notably a butcher's window display with an American flag protruding glumly from a pig's rump) in which one feels that the film's presentation and evaluation of the American past are being influenced by the traumas of the American present.

If the overall effect is somewhat muted, the reason is partly that Butch and Sundance are rather nebulously presented (perhaps inevitably so, given their search for identity). Also Lester's ambivalent feelings about the western genre seem to result in a certain timidity in coming to grips with some of its fundamental issues, such as the concept of legitimised violence in the American psyche; the celebration of the outlaw (recalling Oscar Wilde's: 'The Americans are certainly great hero-worshippers and always take their heroes from the criminal classes . . . Perhaps, after all, America has never been discovered. I myself would say it had merely been detected'); and the secondary role of women in a society given over to romanticising 'buddy' relationships. In fact, Lester gives the buddy relationship between Fallon and Braddock in *Juggernaut* more resonance than that of Butch and Sundance, and that film is much better at picking up incidental but relevant detail — for example, the antagonism between the policeman and schoolboys outside the playground in *Juggernaut*, a quick miniature of the film's anti-authoritarian theme — without obstructing the flow of the narrative. *Butch and Sundance* moves somewhat uneasily between burlesque, nostalgia and demythology. It hesitates between romanticism and critical astringency. There seems insufficient interaction between content and context, characterisation and genre expectation to cause the friction necessary for gripping drama. The cost of the film's dynamic detail (like the Viscontian setting of the saloon in Telluride, with 'Für Elise' being heard on the piano) is a languishing narrative.

It is an attractive film nevertheless in its observation and restraint. There is bleakness and lyricism under the film's frivolity and a sense of sadness under its sense of play. It substitutes ironic melancholy for the usual western drive and excitement. Such a tone is not inappropriate to a film reflecting characters, a period and a genre that are all in the inevitable process of losing their innocence.

Notes

1. George MacDonald Fraser, *Royal Flash* (Pan, 1971), p. 73.
2. D.H. Lawrence, 'Pornography and Obscenity', *This Quarter*, July-September 1929.
3. George C. Scott's opening speech of Patton is also to be parodied by Richard Pryor in *Superman III*, as Gus Gorman disguises himself as an Army General and gives Superman a lethal slab of Kryptonite.
4. Quoted in Kenneth Graham, *English Criticism of the Novel 1865-1900* (Oxford University Press, 1965), p. 70.
5. Oscar Wilde, *The Importance of Being Earnest*, Act IV.
6. *Films and Filming*, September 1975.
7. Fraser, *Royal Flash*, p. 73.
8. For example, Leslie Halliwell, *Filmgoers Companion* 6th, edn (Granada, 1979), David Thomson's *Biographical Dictionary of the Cinema* (Secker & Warburg, 1975), Ephraim Katz's *Encyclopedia of the Cinema* (Macmillan, 1980) and Roy Armes' *A Critical History of the British Cinema* (Secker & Warburg, 1978).
9. The intensity of the violence is a measure of Lester's seriousness in dealing with the material. In television showings of the film, the moment when Robin slits a soldier's throat during the fight at Nottingham is sometimes deleted. An even more disturbing event is the moment when Sir Ranulf and his men follow Robin into the forest, and one of the men, lifting his visor, is hit by an arrow in the mouth. Lester told me: 'The arrow in the mouth in *Robin and Marian* was cut by Columbia by about four frames, which was crucial. It was cut because they felt they would have trouble with it . . . When we did the shot, we had the sequence worked out. The man would lift his visor: the arrow would be fired, it left the frame. I had an arrow stuck in a small apple in the man's mouth and we said "Action!" and he fell off his horse. The first four frames of that were cut out because if you put the two shots together and that jerk is sudden and there's a slight bit of camera movement, it does look to an audience that they see an arrow go into a man's mouth and throat, it's tremendously effective. I hate films that have violence in them, I'm not good at them and I try to avoid them. But if I do it and it's serious violence, let's do it as harshly, as unerotically as possible.'
10. What happened with Robert Shaw's performance as the Sheriff is very interesting. Lester told me that he was dissatisfied with the performance at the end of the film, and that, vocally, Shaw had been very poor.
   'He has wonderful eyes and he knows how to turn up for a film but he mumbled his way through the words. When we finished the film, I brought him in and he post-synched every line in the film, every single line. He came in at nine in the morning and we put it up shot by shot, he apologised every time he saw the performance. He gave a sparkling verbal performance which was in sync . . . Now you've got this very cool, rather disenchanted quality in the face with a very vibrant and emotionally intelligent and controlled voice. The combination is sensational.'
11. D.H. Lawrence, *Lady Chatterley's Lover* (Penguin, 1960), pp. 122-3.
12. Lester was unhappy with the way Columbia tried to sell *Robin and Marian* as a sentimental love story. ' "Love is the greatest adventure of all," the posters say,' comments Lester, 'and the film ends with a murder and a suicide'. He was also disappointed with the soupy score of John Barry (who had, in the past for Lester provided an appropriately bouncy score for *The Knack* and a suitably chilling one for *Petulia*). During the editing of *Robin and Marian*, Lester's temporary score for his guidance consisted of Tippett and Shostakovich (his favourite film composer), which gives an indication of the classical, austere and harsh sound he had in mind. Michel Legrand had written what Lester thought was a wonderful score for the film, for violin, cello and double string orchestra, but it was thrown out by executive producer

Ray Stark, who organised a competition amongst composers for best theme and chose John Barry. There are some attractive lyrical passages in the score (for Robin and Marian's first scene in the forest, for example), but there are also moments where it seems to be blasting against the tone of the film (as in Robin and John's return to England, and in their escape from Nottingham) and throughout the music is not very well recorded or played.

Chapter EIGHT

MIXED BATHING

The Ritz

Although he liked the script, which he felt to be unusually funny and affectionate towards its characters, Lester's immediate attraction to *The Ritz* might be described as logistic more than thematic. After a period of complicated and expensive co-productions which had culminated in a disillusioning experience on *Robin and Marian* over the vagaries of film financing and publicity, this new film gave him the opportunity to operate within a modest framework and with relatively little interference. The action of *The Ritz* is contained essentially within a single set (to judge from the reviews of the original stage production, the set was the star of the show), and, unlike the adaptations of *The Knack* and *A Funny Thing Happened on the Way to the Forum*, there is a minimal attempt to open it out from its theatrical origins. Lester had a three-week shooting schedule and a million-dollar budget, and the film was shot in continuity, for the most part using the same cast who had played the roles on the New York stage.

Rather in the way that *A Funny Thing Happened on the Way to the Forum* looks somewhat anomalous when viewed in the context of Lester's other sixties' work, *The Ritz* is the odd man out of the seventies. It shares none of the concerns with heroes, history and societies in transition that mark Lester's other films of the decade. In fact, it seems somewhat exceptional in seventies' cinema generally ('the less said about *The Ritz*, the better,' is the comment of one of Lester's generally most generous critics, James Monaco). The plot concerns a leading character on the run from a Mafia contract (fingered by his dying father-in-law and pursued by the Don's son) who inadvertently stumbles into a homosexual bath-house called the Ritz. It might seem like a cross between *The Boys in the Band* and *The Godfather*: one could even re-title it *The Boys in the Baths*. But the issue of homosexuality is so tangential to *The Ritz* that a fairly exhaustive booklet on the subject from the British Film Institute, *Gays in Film* (published in 1977) could survey the scene without even mentioning this film. *The Godfather* (1972) is alluded to in the film's very funny prologue, with its gold lighting and air of ceremony and claustrophobia as the family of mourners pay their final respects to the dying patriarch. But that is as far as it goes. Once inside the bathhouse, the film occupies a world of its own. Even a window turns out to be a brick wall.

What is there about this world that fires Lester's interest? To begin with, there is the plight of the hapless fugitive, Proclo, who offers comic opportunities through being a 'straight' figure in a 'bent' world. His entry into this alternative society (like Archie's in *Petulia*, even like Major Dapes in the later *Cuba*) is at first disorientating but is to lead to a revaluation both of himself and this society. Like the two leading characters in *Some Like it Hot*, he must decide whether his life is more important to him than his 'manhood' and, after a degree of internal struggle, he decides that it is. His transparent disguise (dark glasses and a hair-piece like a black dish-cloth) and his production of infinite identity cards only underline the character's insecure sense of self. Jack Weston (Lester's transatlantic Roy Kinnear) conveys the man's vulnerability and shock with infinite comic resource. He soundlessly mouths the name 'Claude Perkins' in horror at recognising that the man pursuing him around the Ritz is an old army acquaintance (a brilliant variation on the theme of the 'love that dare not speak its name'). Warned against entering the Steam Room, Weston turns and looks at the camera with an expression of alternating bravado and resignation worthy of Oliver Hardy.

A similar affection emerges from Rita Moreno's sparkling performance as Googie Gomez, the club's resident singer. 'She has this superb gift of getting a laugh on a straight line by doing it an octave above or below where you expect it to be,' Lester enthused. 'It's something really to think about, a gift a lot of actors today don't have, especially if they've grown up in TV and not on the stage.' Googie's linguistic perversions border on the surreal, recalling Lester's perennial fascination with the richness and ambiguity of language which his adaptations with Charles Wood had particularly elaborated. The delicate lyrical gift of Stephen Sondheim is ground between Googie's teeth as she inimitably mouths her way through 'Everytin's comming up *rosses*' (her shoe flying off and landing on the accountant's desk). She has an inadvertent way of using language as a form of instant self-denigration. Demanding silence, she says, 'Don't *spik*'. Trying to get Proclo (whom she has mistaken for a wealthy theatrical producer) into a romantic mood by conjuring up images of South Sea Islands she begins: 'Think of a *bitch* . . .' She is a character who is sometimes 'down in the dump' and whose colloquial phrase for wet weather is: 'It's pissing dogs and cats'. It is a *tour de force* of writing and performance and Lester assists with a concentration of imagery that correlates to the verbal confusion: eyelashes in the fridge; several electric plugs stuck in one socket and in danger, like the character, of short-circuiting; a dressing room for the star which is actually a converted boiler room (the boiler itself is shaking). 'My career is no yoke,' says Miss Gomez and Lester shows a fondness for the unglamorous end of show business that is present in Roy Kinnear's strenuous clowning in *Juggernaut* and is also to surface in his handling of Miss Wonderly in *Cuba*. Having failed to land a part in *The Sound of Music* (as 'one of those fuckin' Trapp children') Miss Gomez has clearly felt the blows, but her entrance in the film is indicative: coming in out of the rain with a drenched copy of *Variety* over her head, protected, as ever, by her illusions.

In *The Ritz*, there is a sadness under the gaiety, which, for a director who likes infusing humour with subterranean particles of seriousness, would be very congenial. The rain and darkness outside emphasise the Ritz as a retreat from an oppressive outside world. The film is careful to catch people on their own in the act of feeding their fantasies. The intensity of their illusions is occasionally highlighted (literally so when Claude sees the deliciously chubby Proclo, the music surges, 'Till . . .' as the fountain goes on, the lights come up, and Claude goes in search of eclairs and chocolate gateau to court his fat friend). More often, though, one is more aware of the vulnerability under the façade, when the wigs come off and the illusion of glamour and gaiety is stripped bare. In this respect, the interior of the Ritz, resembling an ocean liner that has seen better days, is very expressive. Its oppressive reds and peeling wallpaper reflect a world whose occupants are living the remnants of a dream that could, as Proclo says, turn at any moment into nightmare. Significantly, the star portraits on the walls — Monroe, Harlow, Presley, James Dean, W.C. Fields — are of stars who either died young or who were notoriously self-destructive, or both, and one of the films showing in the cinema is *A Star is Born*, one of the Dream Factory's most penetrating exposures of the truth beneath the tinsel.

On stage, apparently, the efficient mechanism of the plot was particularly facilitated by an elaborate set, with each room like a rabbit-warren from which the characters peered out, and which permitted the audience to see different stages of the action taking place simultaneously. In the film, although the original is fairly faithfully transposed, a feeling of fragmentation is not entirely avoided. As with *A Funny Thing*, Lester once again has some difficulty in finding the appropriate visual style for farce. Because he cannot approximate the consistent long shot of the theatre audience, the simultaneous interaction of the disparate elements does not happen on the screen, and the film tends to proceed in discrete short episodes. The humour accumulates more than develops. Lester's comic style does not lend itself to theatrical farce. Quite apart from the fact that it draws on social observation rather than comic mechanism, Lester's method is rooted in montage whereas farce requires *mise en scène*. The tension between Lester's shooting style and the theatrical nature of the original makes for a somewhat lethargically paced film.

The film's irreverent attitude to the theme of homosexuality — its refusal to search for 'redeeming social values' in its handling of the subject — eliminates any offensiveness from the material. The general strategy seems to be to poke fun at the reactions to homosexuality of the 'straight' characters (Proclo and his murderous brother-in-law Carmine) rather than at homosexuality itself. It merely gives an extra spice to the Mafia-style kiss between two men that concludes the conciliatory finale, and to the impersonation of the Andrews sisters by Proclo and his two friends, Claude and Chris, which manages to give a whole new dimension to the lyric of 'The Three Caballeros' ('we're three caballeros/three *gay* caballeros'). Actually, the 'straight' characters are weirder than the so-called 'bent' ones. Quite apart from Proclo, Googie and Carmine as representatives of normality, there is also the detective with the soprano voice (Treat Williams). He is hit by a slammed door which turns up the brim of his fedora, and he adopts a falsetto that serves as a sudden and startling reminiscence of Humphrey Bogart as he feigns effeminacy in the famous bookshop scene of *The Big Sleep* (1946).

'It was a slight film,' says Lester, 'and it did . . . slightly.' Fair enough. It still has its moments, like that incident when Carmine orders everyone into the pool and the water slowly turns black with mascara; or that entrance of a character who looks like a gangster but turns out to be one of the band, the ominous double-bass music over the soundtrack not conjuring up a mood but letting one know what instrument he plays. As a safe and sound rendering of a risqué play, *The Ritz* is amusing and amiable. As a film farce from one of the modern cinema's foremost handlers of physical comedy, it is frankly disappointing. There is a suspicion of tiredness about it, as if he did not quite have the energy to re-think the material from scratch and, as in the past, to explode it out from its theatrical base. Momentarily, Lester had lost the knack.

Chapter NINE

ROMANCE AND REVOLUTION

Cuba

Although artistically one of the worst-received films of Lester's
career, *Cuba* is amongst his very finest works and a stunning return
to form after the tentative cinematics of *The Ritz* and *Butch and
Sundance: The Early Days.* Part of the film's exhilaration might
come from the reunion with writer Charles Wood and cameraman
David Watkin who have proved such stimulating and creative collaborators with Lester over the years. Part of its freshness and
interest could also stem from the fact that *Cuba* developed originally
out of an idea of Lester's own, inspired by a conversation with a
friend about the absence of leadership in contemporary society and
a debate about great modern leaders. From there Lester's thoughts
began to formulate in complex ways around Castro and *Casablanca*,
and out of that audaciously bizarre combination comes *Cuba*.

The film is set in Havana in 1959 during the last days of the Batista
regime. The central character is Major Robert Dapes (Sean
Connery) who has been hired as security adviser to one of Batista's
chief military officers, General Bello (Martin Balsam). During the
course of the film, he encounters Alexandra (Brooke Adams), who
is married to a member of one of the wealthiest Cuban families,
Juan Pulido (Chris Sarandon), and with whom some years ago he
has had an affair. Their romance revives against the background of
revolution, but Lester's treatment of it is to be typically ironic,
emotional involvement spluttering nervously against traumatic
social change.

Cutting across this major narrative thread are a number of
equally significant minor developments, which considerably deepen
the texture of the film. A portly American businessman, Gutman
(Jack Weston), is dealing with the Pulidos in an endeavour to make
a quick financial killing. Two undistinguished and indistinguishable
accountants are attempting to balance Batista's books, seemingly

unaware that the political ground is shifting beneath their feet. It is a nice metaphor for the way Americans are blind to the politics of Cuba but keep their eyes on the money. A naive entrepreneur (Dave King) is importing a bit of traditional showbiz into this territory with his stripper, Miss Wonderly. Against this undercurrent of ugly American enterprise, intimations of revolution are stirring. A student, Julio (Danny De La Paz), has escaped from the police at the beginning of the film. The old order is represented by Pulido Sr (Walter Gotell) who presides, Godfather-like, over a baptism with a churchman standing meekly alongside and the peasants politely applauding — an epitome of the kind of society that is to be overthrown. Meanwhile, by the pool, the prostitutes read Hollywood fan magazines and are assigned to entertain Gutman and Dapes by Bello's aide, Ramirez (Hector Elizondo), performing the role of procurer with scarcely suppressed distaste.

What is remarkable is that all these characters, and more, are introduced in the first few minutes of the film. 'Somebody should teach a course in film openings, from the beginning until the end of the titles,' Lester said to me, 'because, in most cases, that is the time when the director is most free. It comes out of one's instinct and is often pure cinema, images that are unrelated, as in the opening of *Robin and Marian*, but give the mood of what's to come.' In *Cuba*, as well as being extraordinarily economical (with hardly any dialogue, the main characters and situation are indelibly established), it is also engagingly eccentric: a man who seems to be reaching for a gun is actually feeling an ink-stain from his leaky pen; another man in handcuffs is actually chained to his own briefcase. It is a kaleidoscopic whirl of colour, image and soundtrack that ostensibly throws one into an exhilarating, tourist view of Cuba, except that the weather is noticeably overcast and the quirkiness of the detail gives a jumpy, uneasy sensation. As Fritz Lang said, the distinctive directorial contribution of every decent film is in that film's rhythm, and it is in the rhythm of that opening that one feels Lester's presence: the quickness of his wit and of his eye; his perception of a society through a pointillistic accumulation of significant detail; a style that gives the impression of a mind in action, of thinking as a dynamic process. Conflict and dialectic are rooted in the method, and montage, pre-eminently, is the style of revolution.

Lester enriches the opening still further by disrupting linear narrative development and instead mixing together all these elements like a cocktail. It is a witty effect since drinks are very important in this section of the film. Elaborate conconctions reflect the luxurious social position of the Pulidos and General Bello, whilst the frothy mixture of beer and sugar drunk by the rebel photographer at the airport both indicate his modest status and suggest a society about to fizz and explode, like the blender which explodes in a scene between Dapes and Alexandra. (They laugh, but that kind of *social* explosion is truly to blow them apart.) Huge Coca-Cola hoardings characterise Cuba as an American colony, a sense reinforced by westerns on the television and pop-music over the radio; whilst there is a marvellous shot in the early part of the film of Pulido's bottles of rum on an assembly line, the principal source of his wealth and which are clinking together and beating out the rhythm of the country's economy, the sweet music of money. Significantly, the eruption of Castro's revolution is signalled by the sound of breaking glass, as these same bottles smash helplessly to the ground, and society, relationships and narrative fragment into little pieces.

As well as being a highly typical way of testing and teasing an audience's visual perception as he leads them gradually into a narrative, Lester's filmic mosaic in this opening is appropriate to his purpose in another way. The juxtaposition of people and events that seem separated in space is an early suggestion of the way in which their lives are to collide, at times violently. The percussive editing implies a connection between them of which they are as yet unaware and suggests a whole society in a state of tension, people from different walks of life about to be thrown uncomfortably together. As an extreme example of this tendency, the main strategy of the plot is to confront Fidel Castro with Colonel Blimp.

The Blimpish Major Dapes in *Cuba* is a man out of his time, demoralised and discomfited by youth, and fighting the kind of 'fair war' that can no longer be won by honourable means. He is an interesting example of the Lester hero, since he contains all the contradictions of heroism in the Lester world, contradictions which render him impotent as his confusions grow about where his military prowess should most fruitfully be applied. He is a mercenary but also a man of principle, fighting to preserve an 'elected' government whilst coming to recognise that this government and its election are corrupt. At one stage in the film he passes a picture of Ernest Hemingway on a wall, and one feels his conception of himself is as a sort of Hemingway figure; a feedom fighter in a foreign land. But a yawning chasm begins to open up between his soldiering expertise and his political alliances. He is, in effect, a Musketeer at loose in the twentieth century, the professional man of action behaving according to a gentlemanly code learnt from old skirmishes and old movies that seems absurd and incongruous, both in terms of his own mercenary values and in the theatre of modern warfare. He might see himself as 'Mr Kleen' (amusingly alluded to in a TV commercial when Dapes comes into a room, prior to his meeting with General Bello), but, as he comments, 'Soldiering has changed. It's not as clean as it was.' In the second part of the film, he has a tiny blood-spot on his white collar to denote his blemished values, a red-on-white motif which also occurs in *The Four Musketeers* and *Butch and Sundance: The Early Days* as disillusionment begins to cloud the heroes' sense of life as romantic adventure. Sean Connery's performance has a beautiful sense of integrity baffled by events, that is eloquently amplified by the director's always presenting Dapes's crucial revelations in long shot, as if the man is balefully staring out at a truth he can barely perceive. The events in *Cuba* form Dapes's political education. He is the man who came 'too late' — for Cuba and for Alexandra. He even arrives late for General Bello's dinner party where half the guests are massacred by the rebels — a date which he, as a military man, ought to have kept.

In a crucial exchange, Dapes tells General Bello that 'you will only defeat someone like Castro if you are right'. Implying that Dapes seems prepared to fight the Cuban revolution as if it were an unsophisticated version of World War Two, the statement does show his recognition that the will to fight is closely bound up with a conviction that what one is fighting for is worthwhile. (One thinks of that telling moment in the Cuba section of Coppola's *Godfather II* when Michael Corleone sees a 'terrorist' commit a successful but suicidal act of political assassination, and senses that, with that kind of selfless dedication, the revolution must succeed.) This in turn emphasises Lester's skilful contrast between the two armies, which is built up through the film by an accumulation of unemphatic and tangential detail. Whereas the rebels are always seen actively at their work and sharing roles in a measure of the social equality for which they are fighting (the women at the radio or the duplicating machine, the men baking bread), Bello's soldiers are variously seen as procurers, caddies, guards, gardeners, waiters and parking meter attendants. The 'parking meter detail' is Bello's main pride and joy: the smashing of the parking meters is practically the first sound we hear of the revolution. The rebels may not be soldiers but they are fighters with a cause, whereas Bello's men are bored professionals under the command of a pragmatic incompetent.

The General's vain and jovial ingenuousness is smoothly pene-
trated by Dapes in a witty and quite beautifully acted scene (by
Connery and Balsam) in a room whose swords, guns and miniature
toy cannon expose Bello's front of military statesmanship as an
artificial game. Martin Balsam's idiot commander might be seen as
a close relation of Michael Hordern's Lieutenant Grapple in *How I
Won the War*, and, with Charles Wood forging the screenplay, it is
not surprising that *Cuba* has some of the anguished satire and ferocious farce of the earlier film. As in *How I Won the War*, an untried
man has to learn how to drive a tank and winds up shooting at a
plane that is coming to his assistance, and there is a similarly wry
comment on an army which takes care of its soldiers' feet better than
it takes care of its soldiers.

The true state of Bello's wilting army is most powerfully conveyed
by his aide, Captain Ramirez, one of those small parts in a Lester
film which invariably carry a wealth of implication and in which
Hector Elizondo gives a performance of suppressed despair that
adds a haunting poignancy to the film. Progressively degraded by
the ignoble sexual and military roles he is called upon to play,
Ramirez has resignation and defeat written all over his face. He
strikes up a bond with Dapes because both cling to a sense of soldiering as a worthy calling and become progressively confused and
embarrassed by a situation which unpicks all the rules. Horrified
when he sees government soldiers opening fire on what seem to be
frightened civilians, Dapes demands to know from Ramirez why the
people were shot:

Ramirez: Perhaps they tried to escape.
Dapes: From what?
Ramirez: From being shot.
Dapes: How do you know they were rebels?
Ramirez: Because they tried to escape.
Dapes: Wouldn't you try?
Ramirez: Yes.
Dapes: Are you a rebel?
Ramirez: If I try to escape, I am.

The logic baffles Dapes, blurring the line between friend and enemy,
rebel and innocent bystander, between people you should shoot at
and folk who simply get caught in the crossfire. The conversation is

abruptly cut short when Ramirez himself is shot by a bullet aimed at Dapes. It is the most sickening emotional blow in the film. Dapes's stunned reaction to it is accompanied by the film's most noticeable camera movement, as Lester tracks from a character who is being progressively diminished by the complexity and irrationality of events. This still point of contemplation — the quietest moment of an exceptionally rich and turbulent soundtrack — marks the point where Dapes's commitment to the government trails away, and the point where we are allowed to ponder a man at sea in a world with which he has lost contact.

Anachronistic in his view of modern warfare, Dapes is even more antiquated in his view of women. He is startled to find that one of the guerillas is a woman, and only just manages to deflect her grenade, tossing it recklessly in the direction of his own side in an instinctive gesture which seems unwittingly to anticipate the ultimate twisting around of his values. 'Women!' he exclaims, as if tossing a hand-grenade is merely a symptom of their legendary impulsiveness. He gallantly drapes coats and jackets over the female victims of the rebel attack at Bello's party, in pointed contrast to Pulido Sr, who ignores Dapes's request for his coat to staunch the bleeding of a wounded girl ('You unfeeling bastard!' Dapes shouts after him) and sweeps out of the room. Pulido only sheds his coat in the final airport scene when it falls from his shoulders and retrieving it might mean his missing his getaway plane. It is a detail that is very suggestive about the people who will cling to what they have until the very moment that their own skin is involved.

Dapes's old-world courtesy — both noble and ridiculous — is particularly pronounced when he renews his affair with Alexandra. He first catches sight of her through some blinds and the motif of blindness runs through their relationship: he turning a blind eye to what has happened to her; she turning a blind eye to what is happening in the country. Her impulse to resume their former affair is triggered by her fury and exasperation at the infidelities and social crudities of her husband Juan. The former relationship between Dapes and Alexandra is recollected by her not in an actual flashback scene but in the form of a brief sequence of photographs, which is a revealing device to convey how she recalls the relationship — not as something she lived through but as something from which she has brought back trophies. This idea of trophy oddly links her to that Captain in Bello's army, introduced comically but gradually revealed as brutish (characteristic of Lester to reveal the savagery under the farce, the whole procedural method of *How I Won the War*). Her main trophy is a locket from Dapes which Juan has thoughtlessly given to his mistress and which Alexandra snatches back in an angry anticipation of her own adultery. The Captain's trophies are the ears of dead revolutionaries. The link would explain that remarkable cut from the Captain's severing of the ears of a dead rebel to a shot of Alexandra as she carefully fastens on one of her diamond ear-rings. It is that polarity between capitalist luxuriance and revolutionary sacrifice that is at the thematic heart of the film.

Alexandra is the most interesting heroine yet in Lester's films. In the past, if one has had any serious reservations about Lester, it concerned his treatment of women, who tended to be dealt with very cursorily. *Cuba* is a massive leap forward in this regard, since the women here, whether they be workers, prostitutes or revolutionaries, are involved and alert. (When Gutman is complaining about administrative inefficiency and grumbles, 'Don't you Cubans realise that time is money?' his prostitute companion has the sharpness to reply brightly, '*I* do'.) Alexandra is clear-headed and materialistic, and indeed patronising towards her menfolk, smiling with ineffable condescension when she sees Dapes gallantly covering the exposed Miss Wonderly with his coat when there has been a shooting at the Flamingo hotel. She is often caught in a position where she is looking down on people, loftily detaching herself from their obsessions and moving them like chess pieces in her own personal power game. This motif of lofty withdrawal is brilliantly crystallised in a shot of her after making love to Dapes where she stands awake by the bed and looks down at the slumbering man (in a love scene of lurking dissatisfaction and visual separation that recalls the filming of the Archie/Petulia love scene in *Petulia*). The shot looks momentarily as if filmed through a soft, atmospheric gauze only for the material between us and the heroine to be revealed as a severely practical mosquito net. There is invariably a sting to Lester's romanticism. Alexandra is like Lester in that she is reluctant to indulge romanticism for fear of looking foolish in a cynical world, so the romantic idealist always ends up being overtaken by the rational realist. During her walk with Dapes, they stop in front of a huge poster advertising Pulido cigars and rum; and it is Alexandra's reluctance to detach herself from such practical luxuriance at the call of an incongruous emotional whim that will eventually call a halt to their relationship.

We learn that Dapes and Alexandra met during World War Two

in North Africa — possibly in 1942 in Casablanca. (It is, incidentally, strange that so many critics queried Alexandra's age in the film, as if Wood and Lester had miscalculated. The film makes the point that the sexual liaison between Dapes and Alexandra was conducted while, unknown to Dapes, the girl was under the age of consent: it is another blow to Dapes's misplaced romantic illusions about the past.) References to Michael Curtiz's 1942 classic, *Casablanca*, abound, as do references to other film classics (for example, the names of Gutman and Miss Wonderly, borrowed from *The Maltese Falcon*). Dapes is playing a sort of Bogart role, a freewheeling soldier of fortune whose political allegiances gradually shift under the pressure of events. Martin Balsam's General Bello might be the decadent equivalent of Claude Rains, oozing suave corruptibility, and there is even a black servant like Sam (whose only line, however, is an abrupt 'Mind your own business, señor,' when Dapes asks him what he will do, come the revolution). Interestingly, the character of General Batista is established through allusion to a different film tradition, in the scene where he watches Terence Fisher's *Dracula* on television: analogous to Batista as monster, and Cuba as a society sucking the blood of its people perhaps, but, in the scene we see, Dracula's crumbling under the pressure of righteousness and the sun seems also to anticipate the imminent disintegration of Batista's world.

The love of Dapes's life, whom he has tried but failed to forget, has returned (like Rick's in *Casablanca*). Unfortunately, as often in Lester, whose characters' revival of a romantic relationship ends in destruction, the situation fails to live up to expectations. In fact, unlike 'As Time Goes By', Patrick Williams's love theme for *Cuba* obstinately refuses to develop — like the relationship. Lester feels that Williams's theme was perhaps a little too heavy for these scenes, making them seem more emphatic and longer than they were, but I have never found that. It is intriguing, though, that the musical style Lester had in mind for this relationship was something like the cool love theme of *Black Orpheus*. Like Orpheus, Dapes makes the mistake of looking back, and descends into the underworld.

Dapes keeps his illusions as long as he can, staring and even talking for some time at Alexandra's mirror image when she returns to him at the Flamingo; repeatedly calling her by her pet name from the past 'Alex' (everyone else calls her 'Alexandra'); and adopting a protective tone as towards an innocent. (In fact, she is well able to look after herself and seems sexually very experienced, the implication being at one stage that she has married Juan after being the mistress of his father.) All this breaks down when he says, 'Come away with me,' and she has the alarming practicality to ask 'Where?', implying that what she has is infinitely superior to anything he can provide. Their final airport scene overturns that of *Casablanca*, in that Lester's is one of unheroic selfishness, separation and confusion, where Dapes has to depart along with other disreputables, fleeing with their goods from a liberated country. Unlike Ingrid Bergman, Alexandra sheds salty tears behind a wire fence, wholly unprepared to cross the barrier separating romantic sacrifice from capitalistic comfort.

To compound the undermining of the lovers, Lester has them finally upstaged by Castro, giving the revolution and not the lovers the last word. He also has Alexandra's husband, Juan, meet the final, fatal consequences of his actions in the very symbol of the Pulido's affluence, the swimming pool, to which Juan has often petulantly retreated as escape from distasteful social responsibilities and to wash away his feelings of adulterous guilt, tossing off his clothes in a gesture, like that of Buckingham in *The Three Musketeers*, that reeks of careless affluence. Elsewhere in the film, the montage has flipped between the swimming pools of the upper classes and the mud of the impoverished quarters of Havana, and the imminence of Juan's death is signalled by the garden sprinkler's being turned off, a simple but, in its context, sinister portent of a changing social situation. The blood-stained pool in which he dies — which represents the death of a way of life — evokes subliminally in one's mind a comparison with one of the most extraordinary shots of the film, a brief glimpse of a blood-red sunrise after Alexandra has met Dapes outside the prison. At first sight, it seems simply to signify a passage of time. In retrospect, it becomes a vivid symbol of a revolutionary dawn.

When Bogart in *Casablanca* talked about the problems of two people not amounting to a hill of beans in this crazy world, no one believed him, since his actions bespoke the very epitome of heroic idealism. *Cuba*, despairingly, takes the words at their face value. Life is cheap. Even given the film's rebel sympathies, the massacre at General Bello's party is a sizeable shock, a blur of white dinner jackets and red dresses interrupted by the green uniform of a Fidelista, the mirrors multiplying the confusion and terror. From the massacre, Lester cuts directly to a 'hill of beans', the paltry meal of Julio's sister as she watches a western on the television in her room, which is part of a shabby apartment block ironically called 'Hollywood Hotel'. People are not taken much into account, being shot indiscriminately, left to rot in prisons, victims of an impersonal social brutality that at one stage horrifies Dapes sufficiently for him to refuse to finger Julio when looking at police photographs that might identify the gunman at the Flamingo. The trigger-happy Julio is the negative and most menacing side of the revolution, but mostly the film has the courage (like Roger Spottiswoode's remarkable 1983 film, *Under Fire*, which shares many features with *Cuba*) to expose the horrendous social and political conditions which America and Britain were tacitly endorsing. The society of *Cuba* is essentially one of mercenaries and prostitutes. People are for sale. Life is a lottery, and the survivors are those who can fix the game, like a British exile, Skinner, brilliantly played by Denholm Elliot. He is our man in Havana, one might say, a figure worthy of Graham Greene in his seedy obsequious cunning. He is quick to flatter Bello at the golf course, but does not pander so much to the less significant players ('Your bash, vicar'). You get by in that society by 'greasing people's palms', Skinner says. There is a lovely moment where Dapes pointedly tips a particularly avaricious policeman who only later discovers that he has been paid in Monopoly money: a neat comment on that policeman's habit of taking without looking; on Dapes's evolving disillusionment with the value of what he is doing in Cuba; and on the rapid devaluation of the old currency in a country in Cuba's changing situation. One might add that the currency of words like 'honour' and 'love' are also devalued in the course of the film. The most loving conversation is that between Alexandra and Juan. 'It's not like you to be so unselfish', Juan says appreciatively to her, to which she replies, with equal sincerity: 'It's not like you to notice'. It is the last conversation they have in the film.

Because it was an unhappy film to make (details of some of Lester's dissatisfactions with the script and difficulties during the shooting are given in his interview in the Summer 1983 edition of *Sight and Sound*), Lester has tended to dismiss the film as unsatisfactory. It seems to me one of his most durable works, evidence, perhaps, like *Juggernaut* (another film with a tight time-structure and centrally concerned with bombs and brains), that Lester seems to work best when under the greatest pressure. Several key characteristics and concerns have rarely come together so felicitously: the jostling together of real and imagined characters, as in a number of Lester's films, so that fiction becomes a kind of history and history becomes a sort of fiction; the narrative ingenuity that bounces a variety of human flotsam — revolutionaries and reactionaries, renegades and romantics — on a wave of social convulsion like corks on a tide. Ironic, incisive and intelligent, *Cuba* is one of Lester's most unflinching examinations of the Human Comedy through the wintry imagery of warfare, and perhaps his definitive vision of life as absurdist battle.

Chapter TEN

MEN AND SUPERMEN

Superman II; Superman III

Richard Lester has been in on the 'Superman' saga from the start.[1] On *Superman: The Movie*, after having turned down the offer of directing the film, he acted mainly as an uncredited go-between for the director (Richard Donner) and the producers (the Salkinds), who by that time were not on speaking terms. He also recommended that all ideas for a sequel be forgotten until the first one had succeeded, ironic advice since, after relations between Donner and the Salkinds had irrevocably broken down, Lester was hired to take over the second part. On *Superman II,* he incorporated approximately 20 per cent of existing material with 80 per cent of new material of his own, integrating the pre-existing footage with his own concept by ingenious doubling, dubbing and disguise. *Superman III* is Lester's concept from beginning to end.

Whilst Lester was making his way to the 'Superman' controls, the trilogy itself was assuming an intriguing and varied shape. *Superman: The Movie* is the exposition of the myth: an epic ennobling statement of the Superman theme. *Superman II* offers a darker counterpoint, exploring some of the negative Nietzschean implications of superheroism, and complicating the love interest by revealing Superman's Clark Kent identity to Lois Lane. *Superman III* restates the major themes of its two precedents but in a different key and towards a different goal.

Superman II

Superman II is *Superman* as seen from the dark side of the moon. It is a sombrely photographed, predominantly nocturnal film in which evil gives a formidable account of itself and good is shown to have its blemishes. The world it inhabits is deliberately harsher than that of the original, displacing the former's innocent pastoral with desert aridity. America is represented as a despoiled Eden, in which visitors from another planet are greeted almost immediately by a snake. The world here is more volatile and *Superman II* is less concerned with celebrating magic in the air than lamenting treachery on the ground.

The special effects are still tremendous but placed in a context stressing an awareness of the limitations as well as the glories of superpower. Religious awe is not in Lester's nature and it is important that *Superman II* has a director who is not swept away by his protagonist's mythical potency. Superman's progress through the film is to be a prolonged trial of temptation in which his supernatural powers are to be imperilled by the urgency of his earthbound emotions. The narrative is structured around two major events: Lois Lane's early discovery that Superman and Clark Kent are one and the same; and the invasion of America by three super-rebels who are the traitors originally expelled from Krypton in Part One by Superman's father. The working out of the two elements is ingenious, *Superman II* having an emotional and political maturity that takes it well beyond the usual boundaries of comic strip.

If all this sounds a bit forbidding it should be insisted that the film is stylish, exciting and fun. Yet it would be a mistake to approach the film too readily as a return by Lester to the world of his early films, with their two-dimensional characterisation, their visual fireworks and the comic-strip format of a film like *Help!*, in which Paul McCartney even had a Superman comic on his music stand. *Superman II* is much more evocative of the films of Lester's maturity, particularly those which offer a radical revision of the conventional screen hero's power and prowess or cast an ironic eye at the idols a society revealingly chooses to worship. In Lester's hands Superman is a figure not unlike d'Artagnan in *The Four Musketeers* or the Sean Connery hero of *Cuba*, heroic men who are often made to look incongruous and foolish in the cynical world in which they operate and whose well-meant actions have an effect which can lurch between the unfortunate and the tragic. Superman is also like other Lester superheroes (The Beatles in *A Hard Day's Night*, Robin Hood in *Robin and Marian*, even Flashman in *Royal Flash*) who find that their status forces them into a role which prevents them from leading a normal life. The emotional consequence of this in *Superman II* is the gathering confusion in the hero's mind about whether he wants to be Superman or Clark Kent.

It is characteristic of Lester that the film's best jokes are not diversions from his main theme but serve to intensify it. For example, rushing to Lois's assistance at one stage Clark Kent tears open his jacket to reveal his familiar Superman costume lurking incongruously underneath. The humour is felt, but also the underlying tension — the hero's increasing difficulty in keeping his twin identities separate and in choosing between them. It is almost like Dr Jekyll's gradual inability to control the shift of personality between Jekyll and Mr Hyde.

Lois's response to the dilemma is handled very sympathetically. Like a number of Lester heroines (most notably Petulia and the Brooke Adams character in *Cuba*), she finds herself having to choose between two men and between the rival claims of worldly ambition and idealistic love. Lester has developed considerably as a director of actresses in recent years as his films have become more sensitive to feminist problems. Margot Kidder's lively dark-haired career girl in *Superman II* is a close relation of Brooke Adams's in *Cuba*, two tough and resourceful women who wish to remain in charge of their own destinies and whose clear-headed professionalism makes them less prone to romantic whims than their menfolk. Nevertheless, neuroticism is the price they pay for their independence and Lester makes a neat visual contrast between Lois's health fanaticism over orange juice and the state of her congested ash-tray.

In the meantime, the hero (deftly played by Christopher Reeve) is being compelled to compete with himself — between the superhero the heroine wants and the ordinary fellow that is all she can have. Lester has said that the situation of the hero's competing with himself over the girl was one of the things that most interested him about the film. The reason for this is probably that variations of this kind of character have appeared before very powerfully in Lester's films. I am thinking particularly of the character of Petulia's husband, David (Richard Chamberlain) in *Petulia*. 'Don't say that . . . I'll never be able to compete with myself,' says David to his wife during one of Petulia's more fulsome tributes. He is the pure-white vision of the beautiful American superhero, slowly frustrated and emasculated by this steady drip of adulation and expectation, which makes demands on him he knows he cannot fulfil and induces an impotence that, in his case, leads to violence. David is an ordinary man whose endeavour to sustain a superimage cracks his self-confidence, just as Superman is to discover that he has more Clark Kent in him than he realises. Both characterise a glossy idealised America and both sooner or later have to reveal their human frailties, becoming painfully aware of the limitations of their powers.

Petulia might seem an odd film to invoke in the context of *Super-*

man II, but the link is provided by Lester's similar vision of the two heroes and the unflattering image both pictures project of America. Lester offered *Petulia* as a picture of America in a state of incipient crisis, as the 1967 'summer of love' began to collapse, liberation gave way to frustration, and Vietnam became an ever more insistent presence on the American conscience. *Superman II* is a picture of America in a state of near-paralysis. This paralysis, it is implied, is brought about by decling moral leadership. The President is a geriatric pretending to be a juvenile, judging from the token toupée splayed across his head in a forlorn and totally unavailing attempt to disguise devitalisation and suggest eternal youth. I will resist making any speculations about possible modern parallels and merely say that the character is mournfully impersonated by E.G. Marshall at his most earnestly ineffectual.

The lid is taken off the White House (literally) when the trio of super-rebels burst through the roof. Their leader Zod (Terence Stamp at his most effectively stone-faced) rapidly has the weak President kneeling at his feet. These three Krypton rebels have the same powers as the hero and represent the Nietzschean side of the Superman potential. (Arranger Ken Thorne at the beginning inverts one of John Williams's musical motifs and turns it ingeniously into a direct quote from Richard Strauss's *Also Sprach Zarathustra*. Throughout, Thorne's orchestrations are brassier, more secular than Williams's and his theme for Zod is simply a negation of the hero's theme, like the theme for Mephistopheles in Liszt's *Faust* symphony.) Significantly, these rebels have unknowingly been released from their bondage by Superman himself who, in saving Lois at the beginning from some terrorists in Paris, has dispatched a bomb into the atmosphere that has exploded the rebels free from their confines. This event has tantalising implications, inviting an interpretation of it as an allegory of American global interference, noble in intention but which actually unleashes an alarming situation that leads to ignominious American surrender.

Needless to say, Superman returns to the fray to confront Zod's unholy trio, and the stage is set for the film's most spectacular battle scenes and special effects, a delicious cross between the sprightly contest of magic powers that concludes Corman's *The Raven* (1962) and an agnostic rendering of *War of the Worlds* (1952). For all the incidental humour, the conflict is fundamentally serious. The battle in *Superman II* has to be concluded in Superman's domain, for, on earth, the confrontation between the superpowers results only in a duplication of each other's effectiveness — perhaps a bleak comment on the nuclear stalemate of modern superpowers, as in *The Bed-Sitting Room*. The recurrence of battle in Lester's work is further evidence to confound those who associate Lester with frivolous comedy and to suggest instead a man whose films are suffused with an anarchic spirit and who sees society as violent, unstable and irrational.

There is a peculiar combination of wit and ferocity in Lester. Part of him is amused at the gap between human potential and fulfilment; part of him is appalled at human cruelty and stupidity. He is at once comic and misanthrope, poised between a humour that celebrates human resilience or castigates human ridiculousness. *Superman II* is Lester in generally genial mood, but still mockingly irreverent about earthly aspirations and achievements. On their way to earth Zod and the others nonchalantly deflate the combined American-Soviet space programme (encapsulating in one scene the comic thrust of Lester's earlier satire on the space race, *The Mouse on the Moon*). On earth, they discover human resource and resistance to be so puny that for a while their greatest enemy is sheer boredom. In fact, in *Superman II*, the humans are noticeably more mean-spirited and aggressive than in *Superman*. In some ways the spokesman for their values in this film is Lex Luthor (Gene Hackman) who has been cleverly transformed from the facetious adversary of Part One to a cynical chorus figure, a man of sycophantic cunning (addressing Zod variously as 'Magnificent One', 'Your Grace', My Fullness'), playing off one faction against the other, and preparing to exploit whatever he can salvage from the debris.

In this film, then, Superman is felt to be more of an outsider than in the original ('Freak!' cries a cab-driver after him early in the film). This is ironic in one sense since his status as deity is to be undermined. On the other hand, it is inevitable since his values are at odds with the godless universe he inhabits and cares for, a point emphasised by the film's sustained verbal and visual assault of impudent blasphemy (of which Zod's walking on the water is probably the most striking example). In this context, Superman's goodness looks incongruous. Unlike the original, the only innocent left in the world is Superman himself — and even this is not to last.

The film is at pains to point out that Zod in America is in the process of destroying something that might not actually be worth preserving. It is striking that the rebels rarely initiate violence. What they do is turn earthly aggression against itself with redoubled force, exposing (in the demolition of the militia) the absurdity of modern weaponry and (in the repulsing of the angry crowd) the self-destructiveness of vigilantism, where the people — as in *The Mouse on the Moon* and *The Bed-Sitting Room* — are assailed by their own garbage. Both Superman and Zod have to come to terms with an unpleasant vision of the New World. Zod's initial encounters are with familiar stereotypes of redneck America — the uncouth sheriff and his deputy, the undisciplined soldiers, the bar-room bullies testing their strength (a small-scale version of the film's main theme) — who symbolise loutishness, bigotry and misogyny: in other words the values celebrated by such modern films as *Any Which Way You Can* (1980) and *Smokey and the Bandit Ride Again* (1980). Clark Kent is to be savagely beaten by an unkempt cowboy ('Mr Wonderful') in a diner, discovering the hard way that ordinary mortality is often both humiliating and painful ('Blood . . . That's my blood,' he says: it is the first time he has seen it). The incident is an example of the American capacity for casual violence that Lester criticised so severely in *Petulia*. When the apparatus of the rednecks is blown back in their faces, Lester clearly enjoys their annihilation, whether it be performed by Superman or Zod.

Indeed, Zod is treated with some respect by Lester, rather like the eponymous Juggernaut or the Sheriff of Nottingham in *Robin and Marian*, who is less a villain than an adversary worthy enough to justify and vindicate the hero. Without Zod, Superman would be irrelevant in *Superman II*, reduced merely to rescuing humans from the consequences of their own foolishness — like the child playing by the Niagara Falls, or Lois clambering absurdly up the Eiffel Tower for her exclusive story and her possible Pulitzer Prize. If society should not need recourse to magical figures to solve its man-made problems, thinks Lester, it is equally true that its seemingly limitless selfishness and vanity make it unworthy of supermen anyway.

In *Superman II*, the hero loses his innocence, becoming himself embroiled in a catalogue of human and political folly. His emotional vulnerability and his carelessness with a bomb temporarily conspire to bring to its knees the country whose values he is supposed to embody. His ingenuous desire to travel any distance and bear any burden for 'truth, justice and the American way' gathers post-Kennedy accretions of self-doubt and disillusionment. If the fantasy of this version is subdued, the intelligence is probing. If its narrative line is more fragmented than the original (Otis and Miss Teschmacher disappear rather abruptly from the narrative), it builds to a more satisfying denouement. If Lester's witty iconoclasm takes something away from the hero's stature, it transforms *Superman II* from period escapism to brilliantly contemporary political satire. The American superhero has been brought into the modern age. It is an age where nuclear annihilation might be its ultimate special effect.

Superman III

Superman III gently satirises the Americana that was seen so lovingly in *Superman: The Movie*, and offers entertaining variations on that first film's essentially comic villainy. The double life of Clark Kent and Superman, which was the romantic complication of *Superman II*, is now given the dimension of a Dostoevskian duality raging within the hero himself. This is about as far as you can take the idea of Superman without breaking it completely, and *Superman III* is quite consciously designed as the Superman movie to end all Superman movies. Lester, as always, is intent on cutting his superheroes down to size (even the plot of *Superman III* is launched, so to speak, from the cover of a matchbox, which is where Gorman sees the advertisement for the computer firm which will begin his criminal career). You'll still believe a man can fly. You might not believe that it will do him, or anyone else, much good.

The credit scene is superb in the way it lays the groundwork for many aspects of the film's plot, themes and style. It is Lester's finest piece of visual slapstick for some time, vindicating I.A.L. Diamond's recently expressed opinion that only Lester and Blake Edwards these days can handle physical comedy.[2] A gorgeous blonde, Lorelei Ambrosia (Pamela Stephenson), strolling through the streets of Metropolis, sets off a chain of sight gags which include three passing references to Lester's 1965 film, *The Knack* (jokes around a photo-booth, a manhole and a painting). 'Back to 1965' is going to be an important motif of the film, since Clark returns to Smallville for a reunion with his Class of '65 and meets an old flame, Lana (Annette O'Toole). Their meeting is nicely introduced by the song, 'Roll Over Beethoven' sung by the Beatles, which not only evokes the period, but Lester's own past association with the Beatles on *A Hard Day's Night* and *Help*! The sentiments of the song — the displacement of great men, whether it be Beethoven or Superman, in the face of modern trends — become highly relevant to the film.

Unlike Lois, Lana is to prefer Clark to Superman: the song we hear when their romance is flourishing is, appropriately, '*Earth* Angel'. (The meeting at the end between Lana and Lois has an amusingly bitchy edge to it: no two women have ever got on in a Lester film). As well as romantically, Superman must also 'roll over' in terms of strength and brain-power. He is to be upstaged by a giant, villainous computer.

This development is also prepared for in that credit sequence. Lorelei's walk, which precipitates such chaos, is towards the office of her boss, Ross Webster (Robert Vaughn), who, with the aid of his sister Vera (Annie Ross) and computer wizard Gus Gorman (Richard Pryor), will devise this computer as part of his plan to corner the world market in oil. Whether quoting 'that great man' Attilla the Hun or silencing a row not by raising his voice but by closing his eyes, Vaughn plays Webster with consummate timing and the right amount of solemnity and relish. Richard Pryor also does one wonderful double-take when he receives his pay check which, due to his computer wizardry, has revised his salary from 200 dollars to 85,000 dollars per week. Later the performances are to be upstaged by the film's technology, which might be dramatically an anti-climax but is thematically crucial. For in a push-button society, where computers and even traffic signals can behave violently, the individual — even the superman — becomes increasingly insignificant.

This is another dimension of the film anticipated by the credit sequence. Superman can rescue a man from being drowned in his own car, after crashing into a fire hydrant, but he is not around whilst a robbery is being committed, and the context is already being prepared for a less awesome presentation of the hero. The clue is in the style: The comedy of this opening scene is observed with a deadpan gravity that evokes the poker-faced humour of Tati. In *Superman III*, Superman is Lester's Monsieur Hulot, kindly wanting to help but rather struggling to come to terms with the havoc of a technological world. Like the Beatles in *Help!*, he seems an extra in his own film: like Hulot in *Traffic*, he is shunted off into a supporting role.

What is more, affected by some imperfect Kryptonite which Gorman has contrived to keep him out of the way, Superman starts using his power for peevish ends: blowing out the Olympic torch; straightening the Leaning Tower of Pisa. He also comes on very macho with Lorelei astride the Statue of Liberty; his costume begins to get dirty; and he starts acting drunk and difficult, that is, normally. Two things are involved here: a satirical put-down of American superpower, the myth that their behaviour is spotlessly motivated and unfailingly beneficial; and a characteristic Lester ploy in getting behind the façade of his superheroes to the grubbier reality (like the lice in the hair of the Musketeers, or the modification of Sean Connery's Mr Kleen as he becomes more embroiled in events in *Cuba*).

The subsequent fight between Clark Kent and Superman in a modern waste land is a struggle between the Jekyll and Hyde sides of his personality and played quite without comic diversion, like the final fight of *The Four Musketeers*. Violence is never taken lightly in Lester's films. The struggle picks up the motif of the double that runs right through the film. Lorelei is a 'dumb blonde' who secretly reads Kant; Webster has a 'Humanitarian of the Year' award but is a devious egomaniac; Gorman sides with the villains but is secretly in tune with Superman. People project different images to themselves and to each other (Gorman is even startled by his own reflection at one stage), and everything has a dual potential for good and evil. The force that enables Clark to smash the skittles to save Lana's little boy from total humiliation in the bowling alley is the same force that Superman petulantly unleashes when he smashes the bottles at the bar by flicking peanuts at them. Lester characteristically gives an interestingly ambivalent perspective to the concept of super-manhood, without making Superman an anti-hero, but without swallowing his glutinous goodness either.

The final part of the film is all destruction and special effects. If the giant computer is to die of 'acid indigestion', as Superman puts it, the film itself at this juncture suffers from metal fatigue. There is nevertheless sufficient deflating detail (a paper cup and Coke tin left as incongruous evidence of human rubbish amid the gleaming controls of the superhuman computer) to suggest the continuing sharpness of Lester's satirical eye. Metropolis has got used to Superman. When he flies in to help fight a fire, the fire chief says, unconcernedly, 'Oh, it's you'. They are beginning to find him a bit boring, as virtue itself becomes tiresome after a while. He can fly up and down — but Gus Gorman's yo-yo can do that, and Gorman can even fall off the top of a skyscraper and survive without Superman's help. In fact, the films have gradually become aware of the problems Superman *cannot* solve: such as unemployment, for example. What *Superman III* does is to demonstrate Superman as an irrelevance.

'You're just in a slump, you'll be great again,' cries Lana's boy after the tarnished angel, Superman, who is now drunk and unshaven. It is rather like the hollow shout of the boy at the end of *Shane* (1953) after his departing superhero. It was also Reagan's message to America in the 1980 election, but in the context of *Superman III*, that does not make the message any the less anachronistic and even makes it dangerous. The Superman theme has turned itself inside out: from the expansive self-confidence of Part One to burlesque and self-parody. Lester's perception in this film is that Superman might be a diverting idea for a video game perhaps but he does not represent a mature perception of national identity.

All credit is due to the writers, particularly David and Leslie Newman, for developing the idea with such unexpected irony and intelligence; and there should be particular praise for Christopher Reeve, for sustaining and indeed refining a central performance which has given the series a rock-solid foundation. For Richard Lester, it has been a technical adventure, a consummation of craftsmanship, and a way back into the very heart of commercial cinema. If it eases the way for more personal projects in the 1980s, I, for one, can hardly wait.

Notes

1. For a controversial account of the complex and sometimes stormy background to the Superman films, see David Pirie's article, 'The Truth about Superman' in *Time Out*, April 10–16, 1981. The producers of the Superman films, Alexander and Ilya Salkind had produced the *Musketeers* films, which began their association with Lester.

2. See the excellent interview with Diamond by Adrian Turner in *Films and Filming*, May 1982.

FILMOGRAPHY

1959 *The Running, Jumping & Standing Still Film*. Columbia. Directed by Richard Lester. Produced by Peter Sellers. Photographed and edited by Richard Lester, Peter Sellers. Shot in 16mm. Printed in sepia, 35mm. 11 minutes. With Peter Sellers, Spike Milligan, Mario Fabrizi, Leo McKern.

1962 *It's Trad, Dad* (US title *Ring-a-Ding Rhythm*). Columbia. Directed by Richard Lester. Executive Producer: Milton Subotsky. Screenplay by Milton Subotsky. Photographed by Gilbert Taylor. Art Director: Maurice Carter. Musical supervision by Norrie Paramor. Incidental music by Ken Thorne. Edited by Bill Lenny. 73 minutes.

With Helen Shapiro (Helen), Craig Douglas (Craig), Frank Thornton (TV director), Bruce Lacey (Gardener), Hugh Lloyd (Usher), Deryck Guyler (Narrator), David Jacobs, Pete Murray, Alan Freeman.

1963 *The Mouse on the Moon*. United Artists. Directed by Richard Lester. Produced by Walter Shenson. Screenplay by Michael Pertwee from the novel by Leonard Wibberley. Photographed in Eastmancolor by Wilkie Cooper. Production designer: John Howell. Music by Ron Grainer. Edited by Bill Lenny. 85½ minutes.

With Margaret Rutherford (Gloriana), Bernard Cribbins (Vincent), Ron Moody (Mountjoy), David Kossoff (Kokintz), Terry Thomas (Spender), June Ritchie (Cynthia).

1964 *A Hard Day's Night*. United Artists. Directed by Richard Lester. Produced by Walter Shenson. Screenplay by Alun Owen. Photographed by Gilbert Taylor. Art director: Ray Simm. Songs by John Lennon, Paul McCartney. Musical director: George Martin. Edited by John Jympson. 87 minutes.

With John Lennon (John), Paul McCartney (Paul), George

164

Harrison (George), Ringo Starr (Ringo), Wilfrid Brambell (Grandfather), Norman Rossington (Road manager, Norm), Victor
Spinetti (TV director), John Junkin (Shake).

1965 *The Knack.* United Artists. Directed by Richard Lester. Produced by Oscar Lewenstein. Screenplay by Charles Wood, based on
a play by Ann Jellicoe. Photographed by David Watkin. Art director: Assheton Gorton. Music by John Barry. Edited by Antony
Gibbs. 86 minutes.
  With Rita Tushingham (Nancy), Ray Brooks (Tolen), Michael
Crawford (Colin), Donal Donnelly (Tom).

1965 *Help!* United Artists. Directed by Richard Lester. Produced by
Walter Shenson. Screenplay by Marc Behm, Charles Wood. Story
by Marc Behm. Photographed in Eastmancolor by David Watkin.
Art Director: Ray Simm. 92 minutes.
  With John Lennon (John), Paul McCartney (Paul), Ringo Starr
(Ringo), George Harrison (George), Leo McKern (Clang), Eleanor
Bron (Ahme), Victor Spinetti (Foot), Roy Kinnear (Algernon).

1966 *A Funny Thing Happened on the Way to the Forum.* United
Artists. Directed by Richard Lester. Produced by Melvin Frank.
Screenplay by Melvin Frank, Michael Pertwee, based on the musical
comedy from book by Burt Shevelove, Larry Gelbart. Photo-
graphed in DeLuxe colour by Nicolas Roeg. Production designer:
Tony Walton. Music and lyrics by Stephen Sondheim. Musical
director: Ken Thorne. Edited by John Victor Smith. 99 minutes.
  With Zero Mostel (Pseudolus), Phil Silvers (Lycus), Jack Gilford
(Hysterium), Buster Keaton (Erronius), Michael Crawford (Hero),
Annette Andre (Philia), Michael Hordern (Senex), Leon Greene
(Miles).

1967 *How I Won the War.* United Artists. Directed and produced by
Richard Lester. Screenplay by Charles Wood, from the novel by
Patrick Ryan. Photographed in Eastmancolor by David Watkin.
Art directors: Philip Harrison, John Stoll. Music by Ken Thorne.
Edited by John Victor Smith. 110 minutes.
  With Michael Crawford (Goodbody), John Lennon (Gripweed),
Roy Kinnear (Clapper), Lee Montague (Transom), Jack
MacGowran (Juniper), Michael Hordern (Grapple), Jack Hedley
(Melancholoy Musketeer).

1968 *Petulia*. Warner-Seven Arts. Directed by Richard Lester. Produced by Raymond Wagner. Screenplay by Lawrence B. Marcus. Adapted by Barbara Turner from the novel *Me and the Arch Kook Petulia* by John Haase. Photographed in Technicolor by Nicolas Roeg. Production designer: Tony Walton. Music composed and conducted by John Barry. Edited by Antony Gibbs. 105 minutes.

With Julie Christie (Petulia Danner), George C. Scott (Archie Bonner), Richard Chamberlain (David Danner), Arthur Hill (Barney), Shirley Knight (Polo), Pippa Scott (May), Joseph Cotten (Mr Danner), Kathleen Widdoes (Wilma).

1969 *The Bed-Sitting Room*. United Artists. Directed by Richard Lester. Produced by Richard Lester, Oscar Lewenstein. Screenplay by John Antrobus. Adapted by Charles Wood from the play by Spike Milligan, John Antrobus. Photographed in Eastmancolor by David Watkin. Production designer: Assheton Gorton. Edited by John Victor Smith. Music by Ken Thorne. 91 minutes.

With Rita Tushingham (Penelope), Ralph Richardson (Lord Fortnum, the Bed-Sitting Room), Peter Cook (Inspector), Dudley Moore (Sergeant), Spike Milligan (Mate), Michael Hordern (Bules Martin), Roy Kinnear (Plastic Mac man), Arthur Lowe (Father), Mona Wasbourne (Mother).

1973 *The Three Musketeers (The Queen's Diamonds)*. Twentieth Century-Fox. Directed by Richard Lester. Produced by Alexander Salkind, Ilya Salkind, Pierre Spengler. Screenplay by George MacDonald Fraser. Based on the novel by Alexandre Dumas Sr. Photographed by David Watkin. Music by Michael Legrand. Production design by Brian Eatwell. Edited by John Victor Smith. 107 minutes.

With Michael York (d'Artagnan), Oliver Reed (Athos), Raquel Welch (Constance Bonancieux), Richard Chamberlain (Aramis), Frank Finlay (Porthos/O'Reilly), Charlton Heston (Cardinal Richelieu), Faye Dunaway (Milady de Winter), Christopher Lee (Rochefort), Geraldine Chaplin (Anne of Austria), Jean-Pierre Cassel (Louis XIII), Spike Milligan (Bonancieux), Roy Kinnear (Planchet), Michael Gothard (Felton), Simon Ward (Duke of Buckingham).

1974 *The Four Musketeers (The Revenge of Milady)*. Credits as for *The Three Musketeers*, except: Music by Lalo Schifrin. 103 minutes.

1974 *Juggernaut*. United Artists. Directed by Richard Lester. Produced by Richard de Koker, David Picker, Denis O'Dell. Screenplay by Richard de Koker; additional dialogue by Alan Plater. Photographed in Panavision colour by Gerry Fisher. Music by Ken Thorne. Production design by Terence Marsh. Edited by Antony Gibbs. 110 minutes.

With Richard Harris (Fallon), Omar Sharif (Captain), David Hemmings (Charlie Braddock), Anthony Hopkins (Supt McCleod), Ian Holm (Nicholas Porter), Shirley Knight (Barbara), Roy Kinnear (Mr Curtain), Roshan Seth (Azad), Cyril Cusack (O'Neill), Freddie Jones (Sid Buckland), Clifton James (Corrigan), Mark Burns (First Officer Hollingsworth).

1975 *Royal Flash*. Fox-Rank. Directed by Richard Lester. Produced by David Picker, Denis O'Dell. Screenplay by George MacDonald Fraser, based on his own novel. Photographed in Technicolor by Geoffrey Unsworth. Edited by John Victor Smith. Production design by Terence Marsh. Musical director: Ken Thorne. 118 minutes (cut to 102 minutes).

With Malcolm McDowell (Captain Harry Flashman), Alan Bates (Rudi von Starnberg), Florinda Bolkan (Lola Montez), Britt Ekland (Duchess Irma of Strakenz), Oliver Reed (Otto von Bismark), Lionel Jeffries (Kraftstein), Tom Bell (De Gautet).

1976 *Robin and Marian*. Columbia. Directed by Richard Lester. Produced by Denis O'Dell. Screenplay by James Goldman. Photographed in Technicolor by David Watkin. Edited by John Victor Smith. Production designer: Michael Stringer. Music by John Barry. 107 minutes.

With Sean Connery (Robin Hood), Audrey Hepburn (Maid Marian), Robert Shaw (Sheriff of Nottingham), Richard Harris (King Richard), Nicol Williamson (Little John), Denholm Elliot (Will Scarlet), Kenneth Haigh (Sir Ranulf de Pudsey), Ronnie Barker (Friar Tuck), Ian Holm (King John).

1976 *The Ritz*. Warner Bros. Directed by Richard Lester. Produced by Denis O'Dell. Screenplay by Terrance McNally. Based on his own play. Photographed in Technicolor by Paul Wilson. Edited by John Bloom. Production designer: Philip Harrison. Music/musical director/arranger: Ken Thorne. 91 minutes.

With Jack Weston (Proclo), Rita Moreno (Googie Gomez), Jerry

Stiller (Carmine Vespucci), Kaye Ballard (Vivian Proclo), F. Murray Abraham (Chris), Paul B. Price (Claude), Treat Williams (Michael Brick).

1978 *Butch and Sundance: The Early Days*. Twentieth Century-Fox. Directed by Richard Lester. Produced by Gabriel Katzka, Steven Bach. Screenplay by Allan Burns. Based on characters created by William Goldman. Photographed in DeLuxe Colour by Laszlo Kovacs. Edited by George Trirogoff. Production designer: Brian Eatwell. Music by Patrick Williams. 112 minutes.

With William Katt (Harry Alonzo Longbaugh, known as 'The Sundance Kid'), Tom Berenger (Robert Leroy Parker, known as 'Butch Cassidy'), Jeff Corey (Sheriff Ray Bledsoe), John Schuck (Harvey Logan), Michael C. Gwynne (Mike Cassidy), Peter Weller (Joe Le Fors), Brian Dennehy (O.C. Hanks).

1979 *Cuba*. United Artists. Directed by Richard Lester. Produced by Alex Winitsky, Arlene Sellers. Screenplay Charles Wood. Photographed in Technicolor by David Watkin. Edited by John Victor Smith. Production designers: Gil Parrondo, Philip Harrison. 122 minutes.

With Sean Connery (Major Robert Dapes), Brooke Adams (Alexandra Pulido), Jack Weston (Gutman), Hector Elizondo (Ramirez), Denholm Elliot (Skinner), Martin Balsam (General Bello), Chris Sarandon (Juan Pulido), Danny De La Paz (Julio Mederos).

1981 *Superman II*. Columbia-EMI-Warner. Directed by Richard Lester. Produced by Pierre Spengler. Screenplay by Mario Puzo, David Newman, Leslie Newman. Based on the characters created by Jerry Siegel, Joe Shuster. Story by Mario Puzo. Photographed in Panavision Technicolor by Geoffrey Unsworth, Bob Paynter. Edited by John Victor Smith. Production designers: John Barry, Peter Murton. Music/music director: Ken Thorne. Music from original material composed by John Williams. 127 minutes.

With Gene Hackman (Lex Luthor), Christopher Reeve (Clark Kent, Superman), Ned Beatty (Otis), Jackie Cooper (Perry White), Sarah Douglas (Ursa), Margot Kidder (Lois Lane), Jack O'Halloran (Non), Valerie Perrine (Eva Teschmacher), Susannah York (Lara), Clifton James (Sheriff), E.G. Marshall (US President), Marc McClure (Jimmy Olsen), Terence Stamp (General Zod).

1983 *Superman III*. Columbia-EMI-Warner. Directed by Richard Lester. Produced by Pierre Spengler. Screenplay by David Newman, Leslie Newman. Based on the characters created by Jerry Siegel, Joe Shuster. Photographed in Panavision color by Robert Paynter. Edited by John Victor Smith. Production designer: Peter Murton. Music by Ken Thorne. Original Superman themes by John Williams. 125 minutes.

With Christopher Reeve (Clark Kent, Superman), Richard Pryor (Gus Gorman), Jackie Cooper (Perry White), Marc McClure (Jimmy Olsen), Annette O'Toole (Lana Lang), Annie Ross (Vera Webster), Pamela Stephenson (Lorelei Ambrosia), Robert Vaughn (Ross Webster), Margot Kidder (Lois Lane).

INDEX

Accident 57
Adams, Brooke 143, 156
Airport 1975 92
Alpert, Hollis 39
Also Sprach Zarathustra 157
Altman, Robert 54, 65, 127, 130
Anderson, Lindsay 21
Antrobus, John 73
Any Which Way You Can 159
Ariel 20, 38n15
Armes, Roy 9
Arnold, Jack 12
Attenborough, Richard 53

Bacharach, Burt 6, 128
Bad Timing 65
Balkan, Florinda 109, 115
Ball, Kenny 8
Balsam, Martin 143, 147, 150
Barker, Ronnie 117
Barry, John 136-7n12
Barry Lyndon 113
Bates, Alan 110, 113
Battleship Potemkin 27
Baxter, John 64
Bean, Robin 22
Beatles, The 4, 7, 19, 22-7, 32-7, 48,
  110, 155, 160
Bed-Sitting Room, The viii, 3, 8, 25,
  37, 49, 55, 66-75, 112, 158, 159, 166
Beethoven, Ludwig van 35,160
Bel Geddes, Barbara 60
Bell, Tom 107
Berenger, Tom 130
Bergman, Ingrid 151
Bewes, Rodney 87
Big Sleep, The 141
Bilk, Acker 5, 7, 11
Billington, Kevin 10
Billy Liar 30
Black Orpheus 150
Bob and Carol and Ted and Alice 65
Bogart, Humphrey 141, 151
Booker, Christopher 36
Boorman, John 5
Boys in the Band, The 138
Brambell, Wilfred 24
Brecht, Bertholt viii, 50, 54, 117
Bridge over the River Kwai, The 50, 51
Bron, Eleanor 34

Brook, Peter 49
Brook Brothers, The 6
Brooks, Ray 27
Browne, Sir Thomas 65
Bryden, Ronald 21
Buffalo Bill and the Indians 130
Buñuel, Luis 3
Burns, Allan 126
Burns, Mark 93
Butch Cassidy and the Sundance Kid
  128
Butch and Sundance: The Early Days
  vii, 72, 110, 125-35, 143, 146, 168

Cammell, Donald 36
Carabiniers, Les 49
Carlyle, Thomas 104n2
Casablanca 143, 150, 151
Cassell, Jean-Pierre 82, 84
Catch-22 49
Chabrol, Claude 101
Chamberlain, Richard 56, 156
Chaplin, Geraldine 82, 84
Charge of the Light Brigade, The 74
Checker, Chubby 5
Chekhov, Anton 63
Chisholm, George 12
Christie, Julie 56
Citizen Kane 19
Clockwork Orange, A 107, 108, 113
Cockleshell Heroes 51
Colditz Story, The 51
Collins, Wilkie 32
Colman, Ronald 107
Connery, Sean 117, 124, 143, 146, 147,
  155
Cook, Peter 72
Coppola, Francis Ford 65
Corey, Jeff 129
Cotten, Joseph 64
Crawford, Michael 27, 40, 41, 44, 48,
  54
Cribbins, Bernard 14
Criminal, The 6
Crowther, Bosley 53
Cuba vii, 34, 49, 86, 88, 110, 113, 131,
  134, 139, 140, 143-53, 155, 156, 162,
  169
Cusack, Cyril 104n1
Cutts, John 5

Dali, Salvador 68
Damned, The 74n5
Dankworth, John 6
Dean, James 140
De La Paz, Danny 144
Dennehy, Brian 129
Diamond, I.A.L. 160
Dr. Strangelove 49
Donnelly, Donal 27
Donner, Clive 6
Donner, Richard 154
Dostoevsky, Fyodor 160
Douglas, Craig 5, 8, 9, 11
Douglas, Kirk 51, 130
Dracula 150
Dumas, Alexandre vii, 76-9
Dunaway, Faye 78, 115
Dunn, Clive 16
Durgnat, Raymond 13, 17, 104n2

Earthquake 92
Easy Rider 65
Edwards, Blake 160
Edwards, Jimmy 72
Eikenberry, Jill 133
Ekland, Britt 114
El Dorado 118
Elgar, Edward 109, 113
Eliot, T.S. 67
Elizondo, Hector 144, 147
Elliot, Denholm 117, 152
Epstein, Brian 33

Fabrizi, Mario 1, 16
Fairbanks Jr, Douglas 107
Farber, Manny 9
Faust Symphony 157
Feiffer, Jules vii
Feldman, Marty 67
Femme Mariée, Une 20
Fields, W.C. 140
Finlay, Frank 81, 89
Finney, Albert 107
Fisher, Roy 37
Flynn, Errol 107
Forbes, Bryan 91
Fosse, Bob 116
Four Musketeers, The 49, 52, 76-90, 115, 117, 134, 146, 155, 162, 163, 166
Frank, Melvin 40-1
Fraser, George MacDonald 77, 106, 107, 112
Freeman, Alan 10
French, Philip 5, 7, 105n2

Front Page, The 41
Funny Thing Happened on the Way to the Forum, A vii, 16, 36, 39-47, 94, 122, 138, 141, 165
Furie, Sidney J. 5

Gaitskell, Hugh 36
Galileo Galilei ix
Genevieve 54
Georgy Girl 30
Gilford, Jack 44
Go-Between, The 75n5, 85
Godard, Jean-Luc 20, 49, 64
Godfather, The 65, 138, 139
Godfather II 146
Goldman, James 121
Gotell, Walter 144
Graduate, The 65
Gow, Gordon 112
Grainer, Ron 15
Greene, Graham 152
Greene, Leon 39, 42
Gunn, Thom 23
Guns of Navarone, The 51
Gwynne, Michael C. 131

Hackman, Gene 158
Haigh, Kenneth 25, 122
Halliwell, Leslie 9
Hard Day's Night, A vii, 4, 7, 10, 14, 18, 19, 22-7, 33, 34, 36, 48, 125, 155, 160, 164
Harlow, Jean 140
Harris, Richard 91, 108, 120
Harrison, George 25, 34, 35
Have Jazz, Will Travel 4
Hawks, Howard 118
Hayward, Louis 107
Heath, Edward 99, 100, 102
Hedley, Jack 50
Heller, Joseph 49
Help! 7, 9, 18, 19, 22, 32-7, 39, 128, 131, 155, 160, 161, 165
Hemingway, Ernest 145
Hemmings, David 91, 93
Hepburn, Audrey 117, 124
Heston, Charlton 67, 78, 82
Hill, Arthur 59
Hill, George Roy 128
Hitchcock, Alfred 37n14, 105n2
Hoggart, Richard 30
Holm, Ian 97, 122
Home, Lord 19
Homecoming, The 38n14
Hope, Anthony 106, 111

Hopkins, Anthony 96
Hopper, Dennis 65
Hordern, Michael 39, 42, 44, 49, 55, 69, 72, 91, 147
Howerd, Frankie 14
How I Won the War vii, 10, 25, 37, 48-56, 74n3, 94, 117, 147, 149, 165
How the West Was Won 134

Ibert, Jacques 73
If 113
Importance of being Earnest, The 111
It's Trad, Dad 2, 4-11, 23, 67, 128, 164

Jacobs, David 10
Jagger, Mick 36
James, Clifton 95
James Brothers, The 130
Jeffries, Lionel 107
Jellicoe, Ann 27, 28, 38n16
Johns, Jasper 32
Jones, Freddie 102
Joyce, James 62
Juggernaut vii, 24, 39, 91-105, 108, 109, 122, 123, 135, 140, 152, 167
Jules et Jim 20

Kael, Pauline 64
Katt, William 130
Keaton, Buster 39, 41, 44
Keaton, Diane 36
Kelly, Gene 26
Kennedy, John F. 36, 159
Kidder, Margot 156
King, Dave 144
King and Country 49
King Lear 69
Kinnear, Roy 35, 39, 50, 54, 77, 85, 91, 93, 95, 112, 139, 140
Knack, The vii, 2, 9, 14, 18, 19, 20, 22, 27-32, 37, 38nn14-15, 70, 103, 108, 125, 136n12, 138, 160, 165
Knight, Shirley 56, 58, 91, 95
Kossoff, David 12
Kubrick, Stanley 49, 50, 108, 113, 116
Kurosawa, Akira 121

Lacey, Bruce 1
Lady Chatterley's Lover 70, 123
Ladykillers, The 14
Lancelot and Guinevere 13
Lang, Fritz 144
Larkin, Philip 19
Lawrence, D.H. 106, 123
Lean, David 51

Lee, Christopher 78
Left-Handed Gun, The 130
Legrand, Michel 80, 136n12
Lennon, John 22, 23, 24, 26, 33, 34, 36, 37, 50
Lewenstein, Oscar 40
Leyton, John 6
Lightfoot, Terry 7
Liszt, Franz 157
Lloyd, Hugh 8
Lodge, David 1
Losey, Joseph 6, 20, 32, 49, 57, 74n5, 86, 104n2
Lotna 118
Lowe, Arthur 69, 72
Lynn, Vera 49

McCabe and Mrs Miller 127
McCartney, Paul 23, 24, 26, 33, 34, 155
McDaniels, Gene 6, 9
McDowell, Malcolm 107, 108, 113
McDowell, Paul 7
McGowran, Jack 49
Machiavelli 13
Mackendrick, Alexander 65
McKern, Leo 2, 34
Macmillan, Harold 13-14, 36
McQueen, Steve 93
Maltese Falcon, The 150
Man Who Would Be King, The 124
Marcus, Steven 106
Marshall, E.G. 157
Marx Brothers, The 25, 34
Masculin Feminin 64
*M*A*S*H* 54
Matthau, Walter 92
Mazursky, Paul 65
Melly, George 4, 17, 21, 31
Milligan, Spike viii, 1, 3, 67, 72, 73, 77
Mitchell, Adrian 49
Modesty Blaise 32
Monaco, James ix, 138
Monroe, Marilyn 140
Montague, Lee 50, 55
Moody, Ron 12, 13
Moonstone, The 32
Moore, Dudley 72
Moreno, Rita 113, 139
Mortimer, Caroline 95
Mostel, Zero 41, 44
Mouse on the Moon, The 3, 11-17, 23, 66, 158, 159, 164
Mouse that Roared, The 12
Murray, Pete 10

Nada 101
Neophiliacs, The 36
Newman, David 163
Newman, Leslie 163
Newman, Paul 93, 129, 130
Nichols, Mike 62, 65
Nielsen, Carl 34, 73-4
Nietzsche, Friedrich 154
Nimmo, Derek 26
North, Alex 43

O'Neal, Ryan 113
Orwell, George 30
Osborne, John 19
Other Victorians, The 106
O'Toole, Annette 160
Owen, Alun viii, 21, 23, 24, 27, 33
Owen, Wilfred 49
O What a Lovely War 53-4

Parker, Alan 36
Paths of Glory 50, 51
Patterson, Otillie 7
Patton 108, 136n3
Peeping Tom 31
Penn, Arthur 37, 130
Performance 36
Pertwee, Michael 12, 14
Petulia vii, 10, 24, 36, 37, 49, 55, 56-66, 72, 73, 88, 114, 131, 134, 136n12, 139, 149, 156, 157, 159, 166
Pinter, Harold 19, 38n14
Plater, Alan 91, 94, 105n3
Plath, Slyvia 20, 38n15
Polanski, Roman 20
Poseidon Adventure, The 92, 94
Posse 130
Pound, Ezra 20
Powell, Michael 31
Power, Tyrone 107
Presley, Elvis 140
Prisoner of Zenda, The 106, 111
Private Life of Sherlock Holmes, The 105n3
Profumo, John 18, 36
Pryor, Richard 161
Pulleine, Tim 34
Python, Monty 1, 54, 70

Quatre Cents Coups, Les 20

Rains, Claude 150
Rathbone, Basil 107
Raven, The 157
Redford, Robert 129, 130

Reed, Oliver 81, 82, 109, 113
Reeve, Christopher 156, 163
Religio Medici 65
Repulsion 20
Richardson, Ralph 68, 69, 72
Richardson, Tony 21, 74n1
Rio Lobo 118
Rise and Rise of Michael Rimmer, The 10
Ritchie, June 14
Ritz, The 113, 138-42, 143, 167
Robbins, Jerome 43
Robin and Marian vii, 5, 24, 86, 88, 117-25, 134, 136, 138, 144, 155, 159, 167
Robinson, David 5
Roeg, Nicolas 36, 40, 47, 65
Ross, Annie 161
Rossington, Norman 26
Royal Flash 2, 16, 24, 106-17, 155, 167
Running, Jumping & Standing Still Film, The vii, 1-4, 6, 7, 23, 73, 125, 164
Rutherford, Margaret 12-13

Salkind, Alexander and Ilya 154, 163n1
Sarandon, Chris 143
Schifrin, Lalo 80
Schlesinger, John 21
Scott, George C. 56, 57-8, 61, 136n3
Sellers, Peter viii, 1, 2, 12
Send Him Victorious 91
Servant, The 20, 104n2
Sellers, Peter viii, 1, 2, 12
Shakespeare, William 69, 116
Shane 133, 163
Shannon, Del 6, 9
Shapiro, Helen 5, 9, 11
Sharif, Omar 91, 93, 105n3
Shaw, Robert 121, 136n10
Shenson, Walter 16, 23, 40
Shoot the Moon 36
Shostakovich, Dmitri 136n12
Silvers, Phil 39, 40, 41, 44, 46
Simpson, N.F. 1
Sinatra, Frank 23
Smith, John Victor 125
Smokey and the Bandit Ride Again 159
Some Like it Hot 139
Some People 6
Sondheim, Stephen 43, 139
Sound of Music, The 71
Spartacus 43
Spinetti, Victor 26, 35

Spottiswoode, Roger 152
Stamp, Terence 157
Star is Born, A 140
Stark, Graham 2
Starr, Ringo 23, 24, 26, 34, 35, 36, 39, 48
Stephenson, Pamela 160
Stride, John 97
Strauss, Richard 157
Subotsky, Milton 4
Superman: the Movie 154, 155
Superman II vii, 3, 4, 15, 22, 24, 113, 154-60, 168
Superman III 4, 136n3, 154, 160-3, 169
Sweet Smell of Success 65
Swift, Jonathan 13
Sylvester, David 22

Taking of Pelham 123, The 92
Tati, Jacques 161
Taylor, Don 91
Taylor, Gilbert 33
Tchaikovsky, Peter 115
Temperance Seven, The 7
Third Man, The 27
Thomas, Terry 14, 15
Thorne, Ken 43, 73, 104, 109, 157
Thornton, Frank 8, 67
Three Musketeers, The vii, viii, 3, 76-90, 110, 112, 117, 131, 151, 162, 163, 166
Throne of Blood 121
Tippett, Michael 136n12
Tom Brown's Schooldays 106
Tom Jones 30, 107
Towering Inferno, The 92-3
Traffic 161
Tristan and Isolde 114, 124
Truffaut, Francois 20
Tushingham, Rita 2, 27, 69, 72

Under Fire 152
Unsworth, Geoffrey 116

Vaughn, Robert 161
Vertigo 60
Veterans 48
Vigo, Jean 3
Vincent, Gene 5
Visconti, Luchino 135

Wagner, Richard 113, 114
Wajda, Andrzej 118
Walker, Alexander 5, 33
Ward, Simon 82
War of the Worlds, The 157
Washbourne, Mona 69, 72
Waste Land, The 67
Watkin, David 33, 116, 125
Waugh, Evelyn 49
Weill, Kurt 73
Welch, Raquel 77
Weller, Peter 129
Welles, Orson 19
Weston, Jack 139, 143
West Side Story 43
What's New Pussycat? 30
Widdoes, Kathleen 59
Wilde, Cornel 13
Wilde, Oscar 135, 136n5
Williams, John 157
Williams, Patrick 134, 150
Williams, Raymond 18-19
Williams, Treat 141
Williamson, Nicol 117, 124
Wilson, Harold 10, 11, 19, 36
Wind and the Lion, The 124
Winters, Shelley 94
Wise, Robert 43
Wood, Charles 21, 28, 29, 33, 48, 49, 51, 52, 74n1, 139, 143, 147
Woolf, Virginia 62

Yates, Peter 5
Yellow Submarine, The 34
York, Michael 89